P9-APN-344

THE
CESSNA
150 AND 152

BILL CLARKE

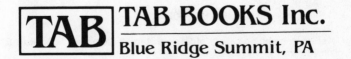

TAB BOOKS Inc.

Blue Ridge Summit, PA

FIRST EDITION

SECOND PRINTING

Copyright © 1987 by TAB BOOKS Inc.

Printed in the United States of America

Library of Congress Cataloging in Publication Data

Clarke, Bill (Charles W.)
    The Cessna 150 and 152.

    Includes index.
    1. Cessna 150 (Private planes) 2. Cessna 152
(Private planes) I. Title. II. Title: Cessna one
hundred fifty and one hundred fifty-two.
TL686.C4C55   1987   629.133'340422   87-1911
ISBN 0-8306-9022-0
ISBN 0-8306-0222-4 (pbk.)

TAB BOOKS Inc. offers software for
sale. For information and a catalog,
please contact TAB Software Department,
Blue Ridge Summit, PA 17294-0850.

Questions regarding the content of this book
should be addressed to:

    Reader Inquiry Branch
    TAB BOOKS Inc.
    Blue Ridge Summit, PA 17294-0214

Cover photographs courtesy of Cessna Aircraft Company, P.O. Box 1521, Wichita, Kansas.

Contents

Acknowledgments

This book was made possible by the kind assistance and contributions of:

Dean Humphrey, Lorretta Kelly, and Alice Helson of Cessna Aircraft Company.
Ken Johnson of AVCO Lycoming.
Dennis Jakoboski of Teledyne Continental.
A.O.P.A.
Federal Aviation Administration.
Smithsonian Institute.
Skip Carden of the Cessna 150/152 Club.
Joe Christy.

. . . and all those other wonderful "airplane" people who provided me with photographs, descriptions, advice, hardware, and friendship.

Introduction

The Cessna 150/152 airplanes are the most popular two-place airplanes ever produced.

This book was written to assist you—the pilot, the owner, the would-be owner, or the aviation buff—in gaining a complete understanding of these airplanes.

Here you will learn all about the various years and models and their differences, read about problems and how to fix them, and learn about modifications that can be made to improve performance and comfort.

If you're thinking of purchasing a used 150/152, you will discover where and how to locate a good one. Although the prospective buyer may have a basic idea of what an advertised airplane looks like, he should have a source to review for further information about the airplane, its equipment, and its value. This book is just such a source. A price guide, based on the current used airplane market, is to be found at the back of the book. A walk-through of all the purchase paperwork will be performed, with examples of the forms shown.

Read about how to care for your plane, and learn what preventive maintenance you may legally perform yourself. See what an annual is all about. An avionics section is included to aid you in making practical and economical decisions when you decide to upgrade your avionics.

Hangar-fly the 150/152 and see what the pilots of these planes have to say. Hear from the mechanics who service them, and read what the National Transportation Safety Board has to say about them compared to other small airplanes.

In summary, this book was written to provide the Cessna 150 and 152 owner/pilot with as much background material as possible in one handy-sized reference guide.

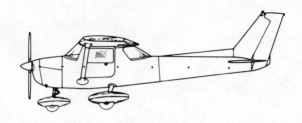

Chapter 1

Cessna Airplane
Company History

On a June day in 1911, Clyde Cessna started the engine of his home-made wood-and-fabric airplane and made his first successful flight. Thus, a 31 year-old farmer/mechanic from Rago, Kansas, became the first person to build and fly an airplane west of the Mississippi River and east of the Rocky Mountains. Clyde Cessna had laid the cornerstone of today's Cessna Aircraft Company, a world leader in general aviation production and sales (Fig. 1-1).

From that time until America's entry into World War I curtailed civilian flying, Clyde Cessna designed and built one airplane each year. Each year he improved and refined his basic design, then flew each on exhibition flights.

EARLY HISTORY

In the winter of 1916-17, Cessna accepted an invitation from the Jones Motor Car Company to build his newest airplane in their plant in Wichita, Kansas. Thus he pioneered the manufacture of powered aircraft in Wichita. Wichita is still home for the Cessna Aircraft Company.

On July 5, 1917, Cessna set a notable speed record of 124.62 mph on a cross-country flight from Blackwell, Oklahoma, to Wichita. This record was only the first of many racing and competition triumphs to be scored by Cessna airplanes.

In 1925, with a total of six successful airplane designs to his

1

Fig. 1-1. Clyde Cessna (right) and his nephew Dwane Wallace (left). Clyde started the Cessna Aircraft Company, and Dwane, who became president of Cessna in 1936, directed Cessna to leadership of the small plane industry. In 1985 Cessna became a subsidiary of General Dynamics. (courtesy Cessna Aircraft Company)

credit, Cessna joined Walter Beech and Lloyd Stearman in establishing the Travel Air Manufacturing Company at Wichita, and became its president. Cessna remained with Travel Air until 1927, when he sold his share to Beech. He then built his first production model airplane, the four-place full-cantilever high-winged "Comet" monoplane.

On December 31, 1927, the Cessna Aircraft Company officially came into being, and in 1928 Cessna placed the "A" series on the market. This was the year that a Cessna AW won the Class A Transcontinental Air Derby from New York to Los Angeles.

By 1929 the Cessna Aircraft Company had built a new factory southwest of Wichita on about 80 acres of land.

During the Depression years, Cessna built the CG-2 Glider. The CG indicated Cessna Glider, and the "2" indicated model number "2."

In 1931 two more trophies were won by the Cessna AW. These were for the Detroit News Trophy Race and the "World's Most Efficient Airplane" award. Always moving forward, Cessna built their first retractable landing gear airplane, the CR-2 Racer, in 1933. An updated version, the CR-3 Racer, set a world speed record for engines having less than 500 cubic inches of displacement at the American Air Races. The speed was 242.35 mph.

Continuing down the trophy trail, the Cessna Model C-34 won the Detroit News Trophy Race and "World's Most Efficient Airplane" award in 1935 and 1936.

1937 saw the introduction of the Airmaster series, starting with the C-37, then continuing with the C-146 and C-165 Airmasters in 1938 through 1940.

WORLD WAR II

In 1940 Cessna introduced the Model T-50, called the Bobcat, for World War II use. Over 5400 of these airplanes were produced. This was Cessna's first twin-engine airplane and the first low-wing design by the company. The T-50 is sometimes referred to as the Bamboo Bomber, and officially known as the UC-78. Other less-repeatable names have also been used to identify it, no doubt due to its tube-and-fabric design and unexceptional flying characteristics.

The T-50 was made famous to a nation of young television watchers as the *Songbird* flown by Kirby Grant in the TV series *Sky King* of the early 1950s.

During the war period, Cessna, like all the other aviation manufacturers, had grown. The Wichita-based company had constructed a new production plant in 1942 in nearby Hutchinson, Kansas.

3

POSTWAR

In the postwar period, starting in 1946, Cessna returned to commercial production with the Models 120 and 140 airplanes. These were the first Cessna airplanes produced utilizing all-metal construction methods. They were also the first Cessna airplanes with spring-steel landing gear. This spring landing gear later became a hallmark of the Cessna fixed-gear airplanes, and was not improved upon for nearly 25 years.

Just after introducing the two-place models to the postwar flying public, Cessna started production of the five-place Models 190 and 195. The 190 and 195 planes were Cessna's first truly all-metal airplanes.

Vying with the other postwar airplane manufacturers, Cessna introduced the Model 170, a four-place version of the 120/140 series airplanes. Introduced in 1948, the first 170s had metal fuselages and fabric-covered wings. Of course, they had "conventional" landing gear (tailwheels), as did most airplanes of that era.

In 1949, the 120/140 and 170 models were updated, and became all-metal airplanes. Gone were the rag-covered wings. This ended the fabric-covered airplane era for Cessna.

Cessna re-entered the military market in 1950 with the Bird Dog (L-19). This was the first production model Cessna airplane to incorporate high-lift wing flaps. In 1952 these flaps, then called "Para-Lift" flaps, were introduced on the Model 170B. Since that time, Cessna airplanes have always been known for their wonderful "barn door-sized" flaps.

In 1953 the Model 180 entered production, and has since become one of the most respected heavy-hauling single-engine airplanes ever built. Its most important hauling roles are in Alaska and Canada, where it can be found on wheels, skis, or floats.

Cessna also took another giant step forward in 1953 by producing its first jet airplane, the XT-37A. Later models of this airplane would provide flight training for U.S. Air Force pilots well into the 1980s, and continue in use for pilot proficiency flying in Air National Guard units for many years after that.

1953 was a very busy year for Cessna. They also built their first turboprop airplane (XL-19B) and set a world altitude record of 37,063 feet on July 16, 1953.

Cessna began production of the Model 310 in 1954. It was the first all-metal production twin-engine airplane by Cessna, and in appearance was miles ahead of the competition. The older Model

310s still look as modern as today.

In 1955, Cessna started production of the T-37A trainer. The first production models of the U.S. Marines' OE-2 were also built that year.

BIRTH OF THE MODERN CESSNAS

Modernization in 1956, resulted in introduction of the Model 172 and 182 airplanes. Both were tricycle landing-gear craft, displaying only minor differences from their predecessors, the 170s and 180s. New sales phrases heralded these tri-geared planes, and would be heard for many years: "Land-O-Matic," referring to the tricycle landing gear, and "driving the airplane into the air and back onto the ground," and "Para-Lift Flaps," referring to the exceptionally large flaps that have since become standard on all Cessna high-wing airplanes.

The year 1957 saw a sales lag of the conventional-geared Model 170, and its production was halted. The average flying family man wanted an easy-to-handle airplane, and the tri-geared 172 was the answer. This was not the case for the 180, as it served heavy hauling duties as a bushplane, thus having found its niche.

The popular Model 310 was given a U.S. Air Force designation, the U-3 (Utility 3), and in 1957 delivery began. The U-3s were used to transport VIPs, documents, and medical patients on short flights.

The T-37A was phased out in 1959 with the introduction of the T-37B jet trainer. This, however, was not the only news that Cessna made in the aviation market that year; 1959 was also the year Cessna re-entered the two-place airplane market with the Model 150. The 150 series machines were destined to become the most popular trainers ever built.

In 1960, all Cessna production airplanes adopted swept tails except the Models 150 and 180. The 150 would later get the swept tail. The 180 never would.

Also, 1960 saw Cessna's entry into the class of sleek, fast retractables with the Model 210. The 210 was unique in its field however, as it had a high wing, unlike the low wings of the competition. 1960 was also the year that Cessna purchased 49 percent interest in Reims Aviation, Reims, France. This is interesting to note, as Reims produces Cessna airplanes in France that are identical to the Wichita Cessnas. At the same time, Cessna also purchased

McCauley Industrial Corporation (makers of propellers) as a wholly-owned subsidiary.

The year 1961 saw the start of production of the Skyknight, Cessna's first supercharged twin-engine airplane. The Skyknight is an outgrowth of the Model 310, with similar sleek lines.

To better serve the users of the Model 180, Cessna introduced the Skywagon. An overgrown 180, the 185 is able to carry more than its own weight in cargo. Many Skywagons can be found in Alaska and Canada doing bush flying. Others will be seen in the outback of Australia and even in the African jungles.

In 1962 Cessna began updating some production models to Omni-Vision (wraparound windshields and rear windows). Models 210 and 182 were the first to be changed.

The famous L-19 was redesignated as the O-1, and production restarted in 1962. These craft saw extensive duty in Vietnam. 1962 also saw the introduction of the Model 205, a six-place tri-gear plane.

Omni-Vision was introduced on the 172 in 1963, and Cessna manufactured its 50,000th airplane, a Skyhawk (172).

In 1964, Cessna received a contract for 170 Model T-41A aircraft from the U.S. Air Force. The T-41A is a specially modified version of the Model 172, which became the Air Force's standard primary flight trainer.

Also in 1964, Cessna started production of the Model 411 executive twin airplane. The 411 was the first cabin-class airplane built by Cessna.

By 1965, Cessna production had reached the milestone of one airplane every 23 minutes during the eight-hour working day. This year also saw the delivery of the 10,000th Model 172 to a flying club in Elaine, Arkansas.

In 1966 a big step was taken by Cessna to broaden the base of the private aircraft market by launching a worldwide learn-to-fly campaign. This included an increase in the production of the 1966 Model 150 two-place trainer to 3000 units and reducing the price of the aircraft by more than 10 percent, thus making it more readily available to end users. Cessna also delivered its 60,000th airplane to an Oklahoma supermarket manager that year, and struck an agreement with the Argentine government allowing Cessna to manufacture certain models in Argentina. 1966 was also a milestone in France, as Cessna-owned Reims Aviation began production of the Model 150.

By 1967, the T-41A had proven its worth as an Air Force trainer and additional models of the T-41 were developed to satisfy the needs of the U.S. Army and the Air Force Academy. Cessna also delivered its 75,000th airplane in 1967.

That year also marked the first time since the 1930s that a U.S. manufacturer had build a combat-designated airplane. This new aircraft, designated the A-37 (A for attack), was a highly modified and heavily armored version of the T-37.

By 1968, deliveries had been made on the 10,000th Model 150 and the 10,000th Model 182/Skylane. This was also the year of T-37 jet trainer number 1000.

From 1969 until 1975 the production marks continued to rise, and in 1975 Cessna passed the 110,000th airplane mark in total production.

By 1978, the Cessna pilot training center program, started in 1966, had expanded into 33 countries worldwide. 1978 was also a record year for Cessna as the total yearly production reached a record of 9197 airplanes.

The year 1980 saw the "Silver Anniversary" of the Model 172 airplane. More than 31,000 had been delivered, but by this year there were clouds forming on the horizon of general aviation, and Cessna felt the brewing storm when it was forced to lay off 750 workers in anticipation of a reduced demand for single-engine airplanes.

These storm clouds continued, and in 1983 Cessna posted the first yearly loss in the company's 55-year history. In 1984 Cessna entered the "black hole" of zero production on some models. Sales lagged as the selling prices rose above what prospective purchasers were willing to pay.

The causes of the sharp price increases of Cessna airplanes, as well as those of other manufacturers, are several: increased labor costs, rising materials cost, soaring engine prices, and product liability costs. The first three items causing price increases can really be attributed to inflation, but the last cannot. Product liability is a new threat to general aviation manufacturing.

A prime example of a product liability claim is the infamous failure of the Cessna Model 172 seat tracks. Many such failures have resulted in crashes, extensive property damage, personal injuries, and deaths. The manufacturer—in this case, Cessna—was sued for having built a defective product in a product liability claim.

Cessna is by no means alone in defending itself from these legal actions. All general aviation aircraft manufacturers are facing similar battles, all involving alleged manufacturing or design defects.

It is currently claimed by Cessna and other manufacturers that the cost of protection, in the form of insurance, from product liability suits represents as much as 25 percent of the cost of a new airplane.

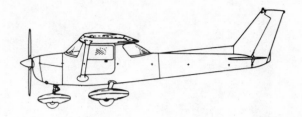

Chapter 2

History of the Cessna 150/152

In 1946 Cessna Aircraft Company returned to commercial airplane production by introducing a new two-place metal fuselage airplane. Introduced with these new planes, the Model 120 and 140 series, was the spring steel landing gear that was to become the strength and simplicity standard of the lightplane industry. These airplanes would later be the design base for the decade-later Model 150.

THE 120/140 AIRPLANES

The Cessna two-placers first appeared in 1946 as the Models 120 and 140. Both aircraft utilized the same basic airframe structure (Fig. 2-1).

The 120 was a metal fuselage craft with fabric-covered high wings. Naturally, it was a taildragger. The seating—as in all the Cessna two-placers—was side-by-side. Control wheels graced the instrument panel.

The Model 140 was a deluxe version of the 120. An electric system and flaps assisted the pilot, and a plusher cabin comforted the passenger.

Many model 120s have been updated to look like 140s by the addition of extra side windows and electric systems.

The 140A was a much improved version of the 140. It was also the final Cessna two-place airplane for almost a decade. The 140A was all-metal (no fabric-covered wings) and had the Continental C-90

Fig. 2-1. The Cessna 140 was the deluxe version of the 120/140 models. Early models had a metal fuselage, fabric-covered wings, and dual wing struts. (courtesy Cessna Aircraft Company)

engine. About 500 140As were built (Fig. 2-2).

It's interesting to note that the 140A airplane sold new for $3695 and now commands a price more than double that. Production ceased in 1950 after more than 7,000 120/140/140As had been manufactured.

Specifications
Model: 120, 140

Engine

Make :	Continental
Model :	C-85
hp :	85
TBO :	1800

Seats: two side-by-side
Speed

Max :	125 mph
Cruise:	105 mph
Stall :	49 mph (w/o flaps)
Stall :	45 mph (with flaps)

Fuel Capacity: 25 gal
Rate of Climb: 640 fpm
Transitions

Takeoff over 50′ obs :	1850	ft
Ground run :	650	ft
Landing over 50′ obs:	1530	ft
Ground roll :	460	ft

Weights

Gross :	1450 lbs
Empty:	800 lbs

Dimensions

Length:	20 ft	9 in	
Height :	6 ft	3 in	
Span :	32 ft	8 in	(120)
Span :	33 ft	3 in	(140)

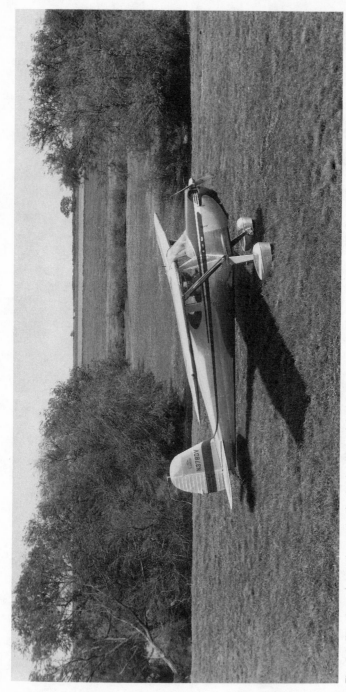

Fig. 2-2. The Cessna 140A was the last of the two-seat Cessnas for nearly a decade. It was all-metal, and had a single wing strut. (courtesy Cessna Aircraft Company)

Model: 140A

Engine

    Make : Continental
    Model : C-90
    hp   : 90
    TBO : 1800

Seats: two side-by-side
Speed

    Max   : 125 mph
    Cruise : 105 mph
    Stall : 45 mph

Fuel Capacity: 25 gal
Rate of Climb: 640 fpm
Transitions

    Takeoff over 50′ obs : 1850 ft
    Ground run   :   680 ft
    Landing over 50′ obs: 1530 ft
    Ground roll   :   460 ft

Weights

    Gross : 1500 lbs
    Empty: 850 lbs

Dimensions

    Length: 20 ft 9 in
    Height : 6 ft 3 in
    Span : 33 ft 3 in

Support

    Cessna is extremely supportive of all their products, and these classics are no exception. Parts are available for the 120/140 airplanes directly from Cessna, or through its many dealers. Many Model 150 parts fit the 120/140s. Additionally, there are many suppliers of parts who advertise in *Trade-A-Plane*.

    Some of these two-placers have been modified by the addition of the Continental O-200 engine, which is a complete bolt-in job, requiring no other modifications. Also, Cessna 150 seats have found new homes in some 120/140 planes.

There are several clubs that support these older Cessna products. These clubs provide a backbone of information for the owner with fly-ins, newsletters, etc. For more information, contact the appropriate club:

> International Cessna 120/140 Association
> Box 92
> Richardson, TX 75080
> Phone: (817) 497-4757
>
> West Coast 120/140 Club
> Box 5298
> San Mateo, CA 94402

THE 150

In late 1958, after a period of almost ten years, Cessna once again saw the need for a two-place trainer airplane. Since the 120/140 series had been such a success, Cessna felt that an updated version of these little airplanes would fill the bill for a new trainer.

The new airplane was given the tricycle landing gear that had proved so popular on the model 172, and a new engine, the Continental O-200 rated at 100 hp. This new all-metal airplane was called the 150 (Fig. 2-3).

In a news release, the Cessna Aircraft Company announced the complete performance and specifications for the new Model 150, and scheduled it for an October 1958 release. For historical interest, the Cessna news release that heralded the 150's arrival is reprinted here:

* * *

The new model is a two-place, high-wing, all-metal, single-engine airplane equipped with 'Land-O-Matic' landing gear. Cessna designed the new model to fill the increasing needs for a modern two-place trainer, charter, pleasure and inter-city airplane.

Powered with a four-cylinder Continental O-200-A engine, the 150 has a maximum speed of 124 mph at sea level and a maximum recommended cruising speed of 121 mph utilizing 70 percent power at 9,000 ft. Range at maximum cruise is 520 miles or 4.3 hours.

Fig. 2-3. The early Cessna 150 airplanes are called "fastbacks," due to the lack of rear windows. (courtesy Smithsonian Institute)

Maximum range at economy cruise or 43 percent power at 10,000 ft. is 630 miles or 6.6 hours with a true airspeed of 95 mph.

Exceptional performance features of the 150 are the rate of climb and service ceiling. Rate of climb is 740 feet per minute, while service ceiling is 15,300 ft. Gross weight of the 150 is 1,500 lbs. Empty weight is 962 lbs.

The Model 150 will be available in three different versions starting with the Standard at $6,995. Equipment on the Standard model will include all items listed under standard equipment. The Trainer is priced at $7,940 and will be equipped with a Narco Superhomer with nine crystals or a Sunair for export airplanes, microphone and cabin speaker, turn and bank indicator, rate of climb, outside air temperature gauges, dual controls, landing lights, sensitive altimeter, clock, sun visors, control lock and cigarette lighter. Cessna officials said the Trainer carries all the equipment necessary to accomplish a modern training mission for daytime and night flying.

The 'Inter-City' Commuter will sell for $8,545, which includes directional and horizon gyros with engine-driven vacuum system and a fin-mounted rotating beacon. Both the Trainer and Inter-City models have all standard equipment included in the Standard model. The Inter-City model also has all standard equipment included on the Trainer except dual controls.

A special patroller wing with an additional fuel capacity, for pipeline or special patrol duty where additional range is required, will be available as optional equipment in the near future. Other optional equipment items include shoulder harness kit, children's seat kit, winterization kit, tow bar, oil filter, fire extinguisher, stainless steel control cables, corrosion proofing, high intensity fluorescent paint, speed fairings, dual controls, and bullet-styled propeller spinner.

The Continental O-200-A engine is rated at 100 hp at 2750 rpm. Recommended overhaul time is set initially at 600 hours. Basic dry weight of the engine is 189.69 lbs. or 220 lbs. with accessories. Displacement is 200.91 cubic inches with a 7:1 compression ratio.

The engine is bolted to the engine mounts through resilient rubber cushions, providing complete separation between the engine and airframe, allowing vibration to dissipate before reaching the fuselage. This suspension system, combined with the newly designed Cessna mufflers, provides quiet and comfortable flight.

The propeller of the 150 is an all-metal Sensenich M69CK-52 with a ground clearance of 10 inches.

Oil capacity is five quarts. Operating oil weights are SAE 30 for temperatures below 40 degrees and SAE 50 for temperatures above 40 degrees. Fuel requirements are 80/87 octane.

Model 150 fuel tanks are of all-metal construction with total capacity of 26 gallons, of which 22-1/2 gallons are usable under all flight conditions, and 24.4 gallons are usable under level flight conditions. The anti-ice fuel vent is located in a protected area behind the strut on the left wing.

The airplane is equipped with large 'Para-Lift' flaps which have an area of 17.24 square feet or 2472 square inches. Flaps are manually operated by a lever between the two front seats in the cabin. The ailerons are large (2575 square inches) and give good positive control. Ailerons are effective throughout the entire stall. Control surfaces are mounted on friction-free compression-molded oilyte bearings.

The 150 landing gear is the same 'Land-O-Matic' design Cessna has used on the 172, 175, and 182. The chrome vanadium steel gear has been used on thousands of Cessna airplanes since it was first introduced. It is strong, durable, and constructed to withstand the shocks of rough field operation.

Tread width between the two main gears is 77 inches, which gives exceptionally good ground handling characteristics in crosswinds. The tread width allows good positive steering. New 'gear-toothed' Goodyear individually operated hydraulic toe brakes permit the pilot to turn the airplane in the radius of the wingspan. The new gear-toothed brakes have been incorporated on the main gears which offer positive braking action. Matched gears and teeth around the perimeter of the disc and the inside of the wheel castings have been used to replace keys and clips previously used to hold the discs in place.

Cessna has scored a first in the use of nylon tubeless tires on the 150. The tubeless tires are blowout resistant and will stand rugged shocks. Tire size (5:00 × 5) is the same for all three wheels.

The cabin area, which has excellent head and leg room, is tastefully decorated. Interiors are available in a choice of Cherokee Red or Amazon Blue. Headliners in both interiors will be ivory-colored and side panels are of ivory royalite.

The top and bottom of the seat back is adjustable both forward and aft. The top of the seat also folds forward to provide easy access to the baggage compartment, which has an 80 pound capacity. A utility shelf above the baggage area may be used for small articles that can be kept within easy reach of the pilot or passenger during a flight. A children's seat of sufficient size to accommodate two small youngsters will be available in kit form from the factory as optional equipment.

The windshield of the 150 is freeblown and free floating. It is designed with no center strip and provides unrestricted forward visibility. Ground visibility is exceptionally good from the airplane.

The shock-mounted instrument panel is clean, neat, and functional. Space has been maintained for installation of additional instruments, even with a full panel in the Inter-City Commuter. Arrangement of the instruments makes them clearly visible from either side. On the Inter-City Commuter, the radio is mounted directly in front of the pilot at the lower left of the panel for easy tuning. Engine controls and switches are grouped on the lower center of the panel.

The master switch, key ignition, and starter handle are located for ease of operation with the left hand while the right hand is free to operate the mixture control, primer and throttle. These switches and controls are all within easy reach of either hand, eliminating any cross-arm operation when starting.

A map case and glove compartment is located at the lower right side of the panel. Manually controlled ventilators are positioned on each side of the cabin above the windshield.

A positive control lock is standard equipment on the Trainer and Inter-City Commuter. The upper end of the lock passes through the control shaft and collar while the lower end fastens over the starter handle. The starter cannot be engaged until the control lock has been removed.

The tail group on the airplane incorporates compression-molded oilyte bearings for frictionless control movement. The massive dorsal fin provides good directional control as well as an added touch to styling.

The exterior of the Model 150 is available in a choice of three colors—Forest Green, Damask Red, Colonial Blue. Special high intensity fluorescent paint is also available at additional cost.

150 Equipment list:

Standard Model ($6,995):

- ☐ All-metal fixed-pitch propeller
- ☐ Starter
- ☐ Generator—20 amp
- ☐ Navigational lights
- ☐ Dome light
- ☐ Tachometer (recording)

- [ ] Altimeter (standard)
- [ ] Oil pressure
- [ ] Oil temperature
- [ ] Two electric fuel gauges
- [ ] Mixture control with safety lock
- [ ] Instrument panel lights
- [ ] Carburetor heater
- [ ] Gravity fuel system
- [ ] Shock-mounted instrument panel
- [ ] Stall warning indicator
- [ ] Airspeed indicator
- [ ] Compass
- [ ] Cabin heat control
- [ ] Parking brake
- [ ] Hydraulic individually toe-operated brakes (pilot side only)
- [ ] Steerable nosewheel
- [ ] 'Para-Lift' flaps
- [ ] Tiedown rings
- [ ] Engine mufflers, stainless steel
- [ ] Map compartment
- [ ] 12-volt electrical system
- [ ] Outside access step
- [ ] Key-operated ignition
- [ ] Generator indicator light
- [ ] Adjustable seat backs
- [ ] Individual ashtrays
- [ ] Carburetor air filter
- [ ] Two fresh-air vents
- [ ] Key-operated door lock
- [ ] Engine shielding
- [ ] Dual magnetos
- [ ] Landing light wiring and brackets
- [ ] Attachment for sun visors and shoulder harness
- [ ] Side-filling tubeless nylon tires
- [ ] Non-sag seat springs
- [ ] Propeller spinner

Trainer model ($7,940):

- [ ] All of the above standard equipment—plus:
- [ ] Narco Superhomer (9 crystals)
- [ ] Dual controls

- ☐ Dual brakes
- ☐ Turn and bank indicator
- ☐ Rate of climb
- ☐ Landing lights
- ☐ Outside air temperature gauge
- ☐ Control lock
- ☐ Sensitive altimeter
- ☐ Clock
- ☐ Cigarette lighter
- ☐ Sun visors
- ☐ Microphone and cabin speaker

The 'Inter-City' Commuter ($8,545):

- ☐ All of the above standard equipment on both Standard and Trainer Models—plus:
- ☐ Engine-driven vacuum system
- ☐ Horizon gyro
- ☐ Directional gyro
- ☐ Rotating fin-mounted beacon light

* * *

In 1970 Cessna introduced the Aerobat. Properly referred to as the Model A150, it is a structurally beefed-up adaptation of the 150 (Figs. 2-4, 2-5).

When introduced, Cessna called the Aerobat a "fun plane," stating that the A150 met the requirements for aerobatic maneuvers of 6Gs positive and 3Gs negative load and was certified for barrel rolls, aileron rolls, snap rolls, spins, chandelles, lazy eights, Immelmanns, vertical reversements, and Cuban eights. Additionally, the Aerobat was equipped with quick-release door mechanisms, seats with removable cushions to accommodate parachutes, quick-release lap belts and shoulder harnesses, skylights in the ceiling, and a G-meter.

The Aerobats have very distinctive paint jobs, as compared to standard 150s, and have matching, sharply decorated interiors.

THE 152

In April 1977, Cessna announced and began delivering, the Model 152. The 152 was the second—and last—two-seat trainer

Fig. 2-4. The Aerobat version of the 150/152 series is stressed for aerobatics and has a distinctive paint scheme. (courtesy Cessna Aircraft Company)

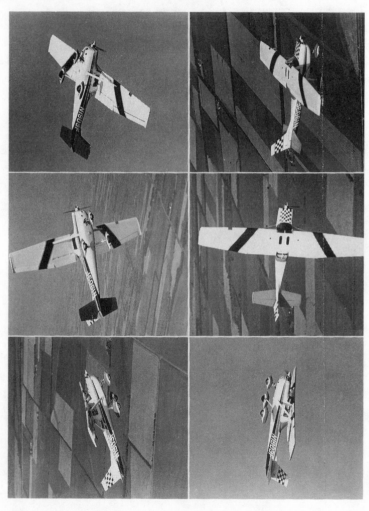

Fig. 2-5. An Aerobat doing what it does best. Pilots learning limited aerobatics will sharpen all their airplane-handling skills. (courtesy Cessna Aircraft Company)

of the series that had begun in 1946. The new plane, although very similar in appearance, was a complete revision of the Model 150 (Fig. 2-6).

The Model 152 was the last of the metal two-place Cessna airplanes. However, this was not known in 1977, when the following Cessna news release announced the new Model 152:

* * *

Cessna Aircraft Company has introduced a new training airplane, with deliveries of the 1978 Model 152 scheduled to begin in May.

Heading the list of new features engineered into the Model 152 is a 100 octane-burning Lycoming O-235-L2C engine rated at 110 horsepower.

Other all-new features include:

☐ An exclusive McCauley 'Gull wing' propeller, with redesigned spinner.
☐ An easily removable and replaceable one-piece cowling, held in place by quarter-turn, quick-release fasteners, for easy access to the engine.
☐ A 28-volt electrical system that provides more starting power and allows more avionics options.
☐ Redesigned fuel tanks that reduce unusable fuel to only 1.5 gallons.
☐ An oil cooler as standard equipment.

The new Lycoming 'Blue Streak' engine achieves its 110 horsepower at a low 2550 rpm. As a result, the derated powerplant reduces external and internal sound levels and puts the Model 152 five decibels below allowable FAA and ICAO maximums that will go into effect in 1980.

The 152 takes off in 725 feet, climbs at 715 feet per minute, and cruises at 107 knots (123 mph). Maximum range is 350 nautical miles at 75 percent power.

The maximum useful load of Cessna's new trainer is 589 pounds. With full fuel, the 152 has 433 pounds of payload for people, baggage, and/or accessories. Contributing to the impressive useful load is an unusable fuel quantity of only 1.5 gallons.

The Lycoming engine delivers improved specific fuel consumption and allows 2000 hours of operation between overhauls. The

Fig. 2-6. This 1978 model 152, actually introduced in 1977, replaced the 150. (courtesy Cessna Aircraft Company)

high compression ratio powerplant and slower-turning prop combine to provide significant fuel efficiency in flight training operations.

A dynafocal engine mount has been added to reduce vibration and engine noise and a new exhaust system with a single muffler reduces exhaust sound levels and contributes to engine efficiency. The new muffler uses a single exhaust on the right side of the lower cowl.

A new engine cooling system, paired with an oil cooler that is standard equipment, reduces engine operating temperatures in the hottest weather conditions.

The 28-volt electrical system produces more power for quicker cold starts and the frequent engine starts required in an active training environment. A heavy-duty voltage regulator and starter clutch are included in the system. The 152 will also accept 28-volt avionics and such items as bulbs, regulators, and other parts now standard across the Cessna line.

Engine starting characteristics of the new model will also be enhanced by a cylinder-direct primer system that will inject fuel directly into three cylinders, assuring even distribution and reliable cold weather starts.

The upper cowl on the 152 is a new design, with the engine baffling attached at the cowl instead of the engine for improved cooling and easier maintenance.

A one-piece upper cowl skin attached with quarter-turn, quick removal fasteners is easily removed to place all engine components and accessories within easy reach.

The nacelle nose cap is a one-piece unit designed to accept a single or dual landing light installation.

Cessna's new, 69-inch, fixed-pitch propeller teams with the derated engine to produce more efficient climb and cruise performance at a reduced rpm, resulting in quieter operation. The new prop design also eliminates the need for an attached spacer between the propeller and engine.

Electrically operated 'Para-Lift' flaps with 30-degree extension on the 152 provide better performance during a balked landing. During go-around, with full 30 degree flap extension, the airplane will climb at 450 feet per minute.

In the cabin, a new recessed window latch allows positive locking, tighter seal, and increased shoulder room.

Options on the airplane include a padded headset with attached microphone that can be operated by pressing a button on the control wheel. Rudder pedal extensions for shorter pilots are also optional.

A 152 Aerobat will also be available. It meets the requirements for aerobatic maneuvers of 6Gs positive and 3Gs negative load and is certified for barrel rolls, aileron rolls, snap rolls, spins, chandelles, lazy eights, Immelmanns, vertical reversements and Cuban eights.

The Model 152 will replace the Cessna's venerable Model 150 in the company's product line, ending a 19-year production run of almost 24,000 that began in 1958. More 150s have been sold than all other two-place training airplanes combined.

"We feel the 152 is the airplane that will replace the world's training fleets with modern, up-to-date equipment designed and engineered for the training environment of the 1980s," said Cessna Senior Vice President Bob Lair.

"Operators of the 150 told us they wanted a training airplane that would burn 100 octane fuel while producing lower sound levels inside and out, better fuel consumption, and more payload," Lair said. "These performance features are all found in the 152."

Suggested list prices of the 152 models, f.a.f. (fly away factory), Wichita, Kansas are: Model 152, $14,950; Model 152 II, $17,995; Model 152 with Nav Pac, $20,635; and Model 152 Aerobat, $19,500.

PRODUCTION FIGURES

The following charts list the years of production and number of units built for the Model 150 and 152 airplanes:

Model: 150

1958	122 (sold as 1959 models)
1959	648
1960	354
1961	344
1962	331
1963	472
1964	804
1965	1637
1966	3087
1967	2114
1968	2007

1969	1714
1970	832
1971	879
1972	1100
1973	1460
1974	1080
1975	1269
1976	1399
1977	429

Model: 152

1977	1522
1978	1918
1979	1268
1980	887
1981	634
1982	265
1983	167
1984	86
1985	n/a

Total 150 production in the U.S. was 22,082.
Total 152 production in the U.S. is 6,747.
Production by Reims:

150:	1,758
152:	573

These are the official figures as published by Cessna.

These may not be the world's record production figures, as held by the Cessna 172, for any type/model of airplane ever manufactured anywhere, but it is a lot of airplanes. With so many sold, and so very many current pilots trained in these airplanes, it is certainly easy to see why they are called "Little Wonders."

SERIAL NUMBERS

The following list gives the serial number ranges for all years and models of the 150/152 airplanes:

Year	Beginning	Ending

Model 150

Year	Beginning	Ending
1959	17001	17683
1960	17684	59018
1961*	59019	59350
1962	59351	59700
1963	59701	60087
1964	60088	60772
1965	60773	61532
1966	61533	64532
1967	64533	67198
1968	67199	69308
1969	69309	71128
1970	71129	72003
1971	72004	72628
1972	72629	73658
1973	73659	74850
1974	74851	75781
1975	75782	77005
1976	77006	78505
1977	78506	79405

Model A150 (Aerobat)

Year	Beginning	Ending
1970	0001	0226
1971	0227	0276
1972	0277	0342
1973	0343	0429
1974	0430	0523
1975	0524	0609
1976	0610	0684
1977	0685	0734

Model 152

Year	Beginning	Ending
1978	79406	82031
1979	82032	83591
1980	83592	84541
1981	84542	85161
1982	85162	85594

*Starting in 1961, Cessna serial numbers were prefixed with the model number (150, A150, 152, A152).

28

1983	85595	85833
1984	85834	85939
1985	85940	up

Model A152 (Aerobat)

1978	0735	0808
1979	0809	0878
1980	0879	0943
1981	0944	0983
1982	0984	1014
1983	1015	1025
1984	1026	1927
1985	1028	up

150/152 YEARLY CHANGES

Each year of production of the Model 150s—and the later 152s—saw changes to the airplane. Some of these changes were major, others merely cosmetic. The yearly changes are:

1959: The initial TBO of the Continental O-200 engine is raised from 600 to 1800 hours.

1960: A 35-amp generator becomes standard on the Commuter, and is optional on other models.

The patroller package with 35-gallon fuel tanks (maximum range of 980 miles) and plexiglass doors is offered as an option (Fig. 2-7).

1961: The main gear is moved two inches aft to eliminate the "light nose" problem experienced with the 150.

Cockpit glass (rear side windows) area is increased 15 percent.

Adjustable seats are offered as an option.

1962: A new propeller airfoil is introduced that increases the cruise speed by 2 knots.

Optional "family seat" becomes available (Fig. 2-8).

1963: Larger tires (6.00 × 6) are offered as an option.

Quick-drain fuel strainers are introduced.

1964: "Omni-Vision" is added to the Model 150 airplanes. This gives 360-degree vision (Fig. 2-9).

Gross weight is increased by 50 lbs to 1600 lbs.

Baggage load is increased from 80 lbs to 120 lbs.

1965: Improved seats, similar to those in the 172, are installed for pilot comfort.

Fig. 2-7. The Patroller doors give the pilot good vision below. This is for pipe-line and power-line observation. Included as part of the Patroller version are larger fuel tanks.

1966: The swept fin is added (Fig. 2-10).

Wider cabin doors, which are 23 percent larger, become standard.

New brakes and a standard change to the 6.00 × 6 tire is made.

Electric flaps replace the manually operated flaps of earlier versions.

A pneumatic reed stall warning system is installed.

The baggage compartment size is increased by 50 percent (Fig. 2-11).

1967: The fuselage is widened at the shoulder level to give three inches additional "spread."

A short-stroke nose gear is introduced to reduce drag.

A 60-amp gear driven alternator replaces the generator.

For the first time, the 150 is float certified (Fig. 2-12).

1968: A restyled center console gives slightly more leg room for the pilot and passenger.

A revised flap control system allows for hands-off operation.

1969: A key starter replaces the old pull-type.

A ground service plug becomes optional.

Improved rocker-type electrical switches replace the older style toggle switches.

1970: The Aerobat version is introduced.

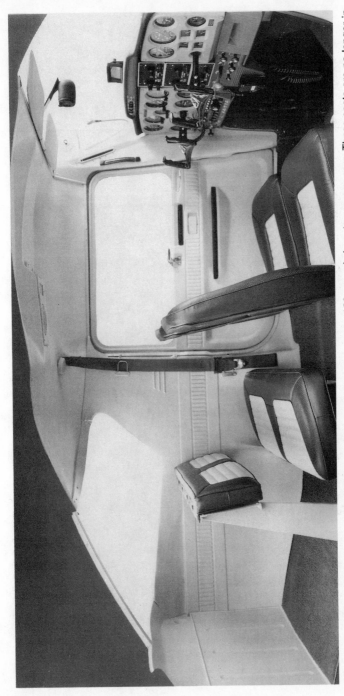

Fig. 2-8. Child seats installed in the baggage area allow you to carry up to 120 pounds in extra passengers. These seats are no longer in production, and are much sought after by 150 owners. (courtesy Cessna Aircraft Company)

Fig. 2-9. The second generation 150s have vertical tails, but were built after the introduction of Omni-Vision. (courtesy Cessna Aircraft Company)

Fig. 2-10. The 1967 Model 150 has a swept tail and Omni-Vision, as do all succeeding models. (courtesy Smithsonian Institute)

33

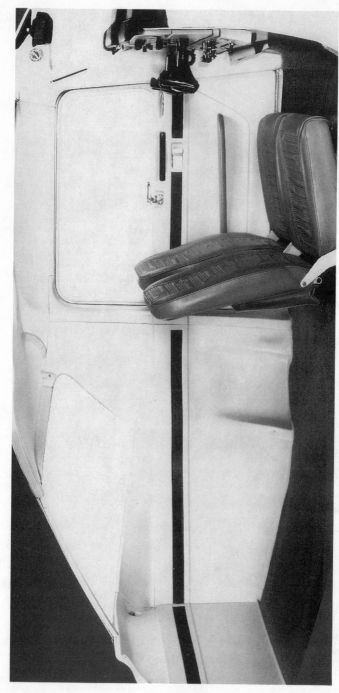

Fig. 2-11. Interior of a late model 150. Notice the large baggage space behind the seats. Unfortunately, it is very easy to overload this area. (courtesy Cessna Aircraft Company)

Fig. 2-12. There are not many Cessna 150s on floats—probably due to the cost of installation, and the poor performance returns. (courtesy Cessna Aircraft Company)

Conical cambered wingtips are added for better slow flight control (Figs. 2-13, 2-14).

1971: Tubular main gear legs replace the flat steel type (Figs. 2-15, 2-16). Also, the tread width is increased by 16 percent for better ground handling.

The landing lights are moved from the wing to the engine cowl.

1972: Improved fuel filler caps are installed to prevent water from entering the fuel tanks.

A more versatile seat and seat track are installed.

1973: The seats are lowered to give increased headroom in the cabin.

1974: The "Clark Y" airfoil propeller is installed on the Aerobat for improved (4 mph increase) cruise.

1975: The Commuter II is introduced with a special package of avionics.

The fin is increased in size by six inches.

Inertial reel shoulder harness/lap belts become an option.

1976: Circuit breakers replace the fuses.

Fully articulated seats are installed.

1977: Pre-selectable flap settings with detents are installed.

This is the last year of the 150.

In May, the 1978 Model 152 is introduced. (Fig. 2-17).

1978: No significant changes from the 152 first introduced in 1977.

1979: Dual impulse coupling is installed to increase the voltage to the magnetos and four-cylinder direct fuel priming make starting easier.

Seat padding is increased for comfort.

1980: An accelerator pump is installed to inject fuel directly into the throat of the carburetor, while a slower turning starter provides better starting performance.

Dual windshield defrosters become standard.

1981: A "hot microphone" intercom becomes standard on the Trainer and optional on other models.

Quick oil drain becomes available as an option.

1982: A third quick-drain fuel valve is installed for easier contamination checks.

1983: The Lycoming O-235-N2C rated at 108 hp is installed to reduce the 100 LL fuel problems.

1984: Landing and taxiing lights are moved back to the left wing, where they were on models prior to 1971 (Figs. 2-18, 2-19).

Fig. 2-13. Until 1969, this was the style of wingtip found on 150s.

Fig. 2-14. The improved conical cambered tips were used from 1970 to date. The conical tips provide for better slow-speed handling characteristics.

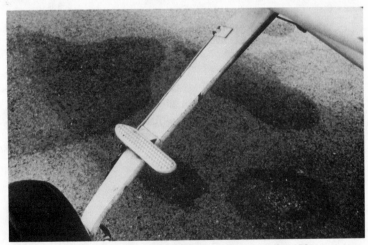

Fig. 2-15. Spring landing gear installed on 1970 and earlier 150s.

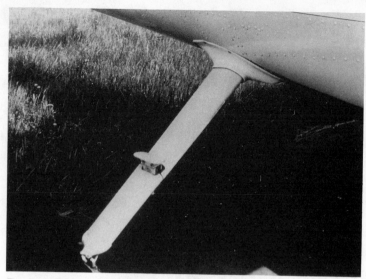

Fig. 2-16. Tubular landing gear found on later 150s and all 152s.

The list prices for 1984 are:

Model 152:	$29,700
Model 152II:	$36,400
Model 152 Trainer:	$38,750
Model 152 Aerobat:	$39,350

(As you can see, these prices were so high that they forced sales down to near zero. The average FBO could no longer afford the cost of a new Cessna two-seat airplane for training and rental. Hence, few were sold.)

1985: The end of the line arrives when Cessna announces, on May 31st, that they are shutting down all production of the Cessna 152. There are few purchasers for a two-place airplane that costs in excess of $40,000 (Figs. 2-20 through 2-24).

Fig. 2-17. 1977 was the end of the line for the 150, when Cessna introduced this new 152. (courtesy Cessna Aircraft Company)

39

Fig. 2-18. In the beginning, Cessna 150s had leading edge landing lights. This was changed in 1970, but returned in 1984.

Fig. 2-19. The improved cowl-mounted landing lights utilized during the '70s and early '80s.

40

Fig. 2-20. The final version of the Cessna 152, just prior to the end of 152 production. (courtesy Cessna Aircraft Company)

41

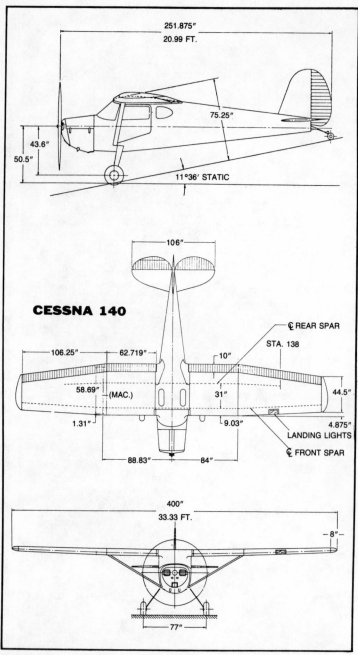

Fig. 2-21. This scale drawing of the Cessna 140A reveals resemblance to the model 150. (courtesy Cessna Aircraft Company)

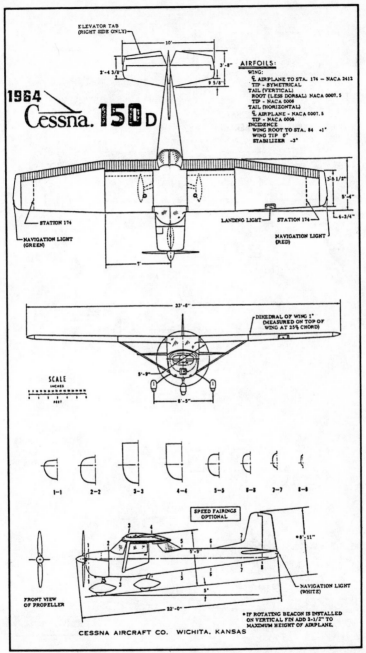

Fig. 2-22. Scale drawing of the first "Omni-Vision" 150. (courtesy Cessna Aircraft Company)

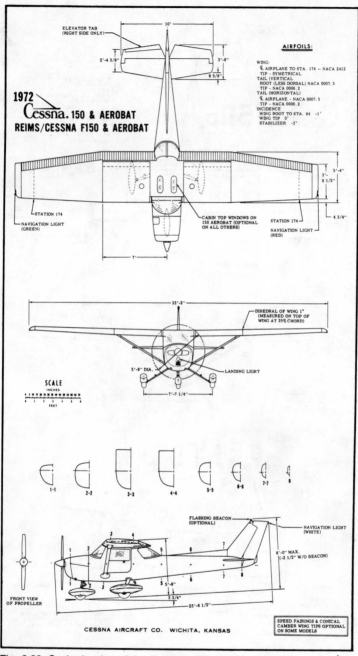

Fig. 2-23. Scale drawing of the "swept tail" 150. (courtesy Cessna Aircraft Company)

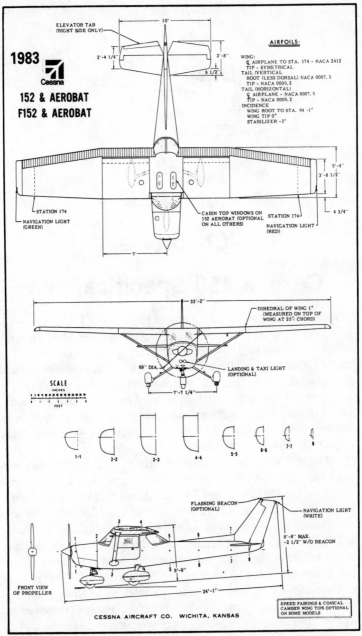

Fig. 2-24. Scale drawing of the 1983 Cessna 152. When compared to its ancestors, the 120/140 series and the 150, there is little difference in performance (courtesy Cessna Aircraft Company)

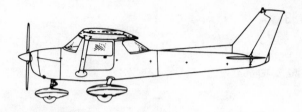

Chapter 3

Cessna 150 Specifications

When studying the specifications of the Cessna 150 airplanes, it is important to note that specific model differences between some years were very slight, while others vary greatly from preceding models. Certain model/year changes included drastic dimensional changes, significant changes in cruising range and/or speed, or only a Cessna rehash of the previous year's figures. Be that as it may, all yearly specifications are an important part of the history of these airplanes and are included for historical purposes—even those that reflect little yearly change.

The following specifications are those issued by Cessna Aircraft Company, and may be considered official. The specifications given are for the Commuter Models. Also available were Trainer and Standard Models. The differences between the Commuter and the Trainer Models are in speed and empty weight. The Commuter is 2 mph faster than the Trainer, and, due to the additional standard avionics in the Commuter, its empty weight exceeds that of the Trainer by 50 to 90 pounds. The Standard Model was so bare of instruments, options, etc., that its sales were almost nonexistent. The specifications difference reflects the same cruise speeds as the Trainer, but a reduced empty weight due to the lack of installed equipment.

1959

Year: 1959
Model: 150

Speed
Top Speed at Sea Level:	124	mph
Cruise (70 percent at 9000 ft):	121	mph

Range
Cruise (no allowance):	520	mi
	4.3	hrs
	121	mph
Maximum range at 10,000 ft:	630	mi
	6.3	hrs
	95	mph
Rate of Climb at Sea Level:	740	fpm
Service Ceiling:	15300	ft
Baggage:	80	lbs
Wing Loading: (lbs/sq ft)	9.4	
Power Loading: (lbs/hp)	15.0	

Fuel Capacity
Standard:	26	gal
Engine:	Continental O-200A	
TBO:	1800	hrs
Power:	100	hp
Wingspan:	33 ft 04	in
Wing Area: (sq ft)	160	
Length:	21 ft 00	in
Height:	6 ft 11	in
Gross Weight:	1500	lbs
Empty Weight:	962	lbs
Useful load:	538	lbs

1960

Year: 1960
Model: 150

Speed
Maximum at Sea Level:	124	mph
Cruise (70 percent at 9,000 ft):	121	mph

Range
Maximum (70 percent at 9,000 ft):	520	mi
	4.3	hrs

	121	mph
Maximum range at 10,000 ft:	630	mi
	6.6	hrs
	95	mph
Patroller version maximum:	980	mi
	10.3	hrs
Rate of Climb at Sea Level:	740	fpm
Service Ceiling:	15300	ft
Takeoff		
Ground run:	680	ft
Over 50-ft obstacle:	1205	ft
Landing		
Landing roll:	360	ft
Over 50-ft obstacle:	1055	ft
Fuel Capacity		
Standard:	26	gal
Patroller:	38	gal
Engine		
Make:	Continental O-200A	
TBO:	1800	hrs
Power:	100	hp
Oil capacity:	5	qts
Propeller:	Sensenich M69CK52	
Wingspan:	33 ft 04	in
Wing Area: (sq ft)	160	
Length:	21 ft 06	in
Height:	6 ft 11	in
Wing Loading: (lbs/sq ft)	9.4	
Power Loading: (lbs/hp)	15.0	
Weight		
Gross:	1500	lbs
Empty:	946	lbs
Baggage:	80	lbs

1961
Year: 1961
Model: 150A

Speed		
Maximum at Sea Level:	124	mph
Cruise (70 percent at 9,000 ft):	121	mph
Range		
Maximum (70 percent at 9,000 ft):	520	mi
	4.3	hrs
	121	mph

Maximum range at 10,000 ft:	630	mi
	6.6	hrs
	95	mph
Patroller version maximum:	980	mi
	10.3	hrs
Rate of Climb at Sea Level:	740	fpm
Service Ceiling:	15300	ft
Takeoff		
Ground run:	680	ft
Over 50-ft obstacle:	1205	ft
Landing		
Landing roll:	360	ft
Over 50-ft obstacle:	1055	ft
Fuel capacity		
Standard:	26	gal
Patroller:	38	gal
Engine		
Make:	Continental O-200A	
TBO:	1800	hrs
Power:	100	hp
Oil capacity:	5	qts
Propeller:	Sensenich M69CK52	
Wingspan:	33 ft 04	in
Wing Area: (sq ft)	160	
Length:	21 ft 06	in
Height:	6 ft 11	in
Wing Loading: (lbs/sq ft)	9.4	
Power Loading: (lbs/hp)	15.0	
Weight		
Gross:	1500	lbs
Empty:	950	lbs
Baggage:	80	lbs

1962

Year: 1962
Model: 150B

Speed		
Maximum at Sea Level:	127	mph
Cruise (75 percent at 7,500 ft):	125	mph
Range		
Maximum (75 percent at 7,500 ft):	500	mi
	4.0	hrs
	125	mph
Optimum range at 10,000 ft:	610	mi

	5.9	hrs
	104	mph
Patroller version maximum:	945	mi
	9.1	hrs
Rate of Climb at Sea Level:	760	fpm
Service Ceiling:	15600	ft
Takeoff		
Ground run:	680	ft
Over 50-ft obstacle:	1205	ft
Landing		
Landing roll:	360	ft
Over 50-ft obstacle:	1055	ft
Fuel capacity		
Standard:	26	gal
Patroller:	38	gal
Engine		
Make:	Continental O-200A	
TBO:	1800	hrs
Power:	100	hp
Oil capacity:	6	qts
Propeller: Metal, diameter:	69	in
Wingspan:	33 ft 04	in
Wing Area: (sq ft)	160	
Length:	21 ft 06	in
Height:	6 ft 11	in
Wing Loading: (lbs/sq ft)	9.4	
Power Loading: (lbs/hp)	15.0	
Weight		
Gross:	1500	lbs
Empty:	950	lbs
Baggage:	80	lbs

1963

Year: 1963
Model: 150C

Speed		
Maximum at Sea Level:	127	mph
Cruise (75 percent at 7,500 ft):	125	mph
Range		
Maximum (75 percent at 7,500 ft):	500	mi
	4.0	hrs
	125	mph
Optimum range at 10,000 ft:	610	mi
	5.9	hrs

	104	mph
Patroller version maximum:	945	mi
	9.1	hrs
Rate of Climb at Sea Level:	760	fpm
Service Ceiling:	15600	ft
Takeoff		
Ground run:	680	ft
Over 50-ft obstacle:	1205	ft
Landing		
Landing roll:	360	ft
Over 50-ft obstacle:	1055	ft
Fuel capacity		
Standard:	26	gal
Patroller:	38	gal
Engine		
Make:	Continental O-200A	
TBO:	1800	hrs
Power:	100	hp
Oil capacity:	6	qts
Propeller: Metal, diameter:	69	in
Wingspan:	33 ft 04	in
Wing Area: (sq ft)	160	
Length:	21 ft 06	in
Height:	6 ft 11	in
Wing Loading: (lbs/sq ft)	9.4	
Power Loading: (lbs/hp)	15.0	
Weight		
Gross:	1500	lbs
Empty:	950	lbs
Baggage:	80	lbs

1964

Year: 1964
Model: 150D

Speed		
Maximum at Sea Level:	125	mph
Cruise (75 percent at 7,500 ft):	122	mph
Range		
Maximum (75 percent at 7,500 ft):	490	mi
	4.0	hrs
	122	mph
Optimum range at 10,000 ft:	565	mi
	5.7	hrs
	99	mph

Patroller version maximum:	885	mi
	8.9	hrs
Rate of Climb at Sea Level:	670	fpm
Service Ceiling:	12650	ft
Takeoff		
Ground run:	735	ft
Over 50-ft obstacle:	1385	ft
Landing		
Landing roll:	445	ft
Over 50-ft obstacle:	1075	ft
Fuel capacity		
Standard:	26	gal
Patroller:	38	gal
Engine		
Make:	Continental O-200A	
TBO:	1800	hrs
Power:	100	hp
Oil capacity:	6	qts
Propeller: Metal, diameter:	69	in
Wingspan:	33 ft 06	in
Wing Area: (sq ft)	160	
Length:	21 ft 07	in
Height:	7 ft 10	in
Wing Loading: (lbs/sq ft)	10.0	
Power Loading: (lbs/hp)	16.0	
Weight		
Gross:	1600	lbs
Empty:	970	lbs
Baggage:	120	lbs

1965

Year: 1965
Model: 150E

Speed		
Maximum at Sea Level:	125	mph
Cruise (75 percent at 7,500 ft):	122	mph
Range		
Maximum (75 percent at 7,500 ft):	490	mi
	4.0	hrs
	122	mph
Optimum range at 10,000 ft:	565	mi
	5.7	hrs
	99	mph
Patroller version maximum:	885	mi

	8.9	hrs
Rate of Climb at Sea Level:	670	fpm
Service Ceiling:	12650	ft
Takeoff		
Ground run:	735	ft
Over 50-ft obstacle:	1385	ft
Landing		
Landing roll:	445	ft
Over 50-ft obstacle:	1075	ft
Fuel Capacity		
Standard:	26	gal
Patroller:	38	gal
Engine		
Make:	Continental O-200A	
TBO:	1800	hrs
Power:	100	hp
Oil Capacity:	6	gts
Propeller: Metal, diameter:	69	in
Wingspan:	33 ft 06	in
Wing Area: (sq ft)	160	
Length:	21 ft 07	in
Height:	7 ft 10	in
Wing Loading: (lbs/sq ft)	10.0	
Power Loading: (lbs/hp)	16.0	
Weight		
Gross:	1600	lbs
Empty:	1010	lbs
Baggage:	120	lbs

1966

Year: 1966
Model: 150F

Speed		
Maximum at Sea Level:	125	mph
Cruise (75 percent at 7,500 ft):	122	mph
Range		
Maximum (75 percent at 7,500 ft):	490	mi
	4.0	hrs
	122	mph
Optimum range at 10,000 ft:	565	mi
	5.7	hrs
	99	mph
Long range version maximum:	885	mi
	8.9	hrs
Rate of Climb at Sea Level:	670	fpm

Service Ceiling:	12650	ft
Takeoff		
Ground run:	735	ft
Over 50-ft obstacle:	1385	ft
Landing		
Landing roll:	445	ft
Over 50-ft obstacle:	1075	ft
Fuel Capacity		
Standard:	26	gal
Patroller:	38	gal
Engine		
Make:	Continental O-200A	
TBO:	1800	hrs
Power:	100	hp
Oil capacity:	6	qts
Propeller: metal, diameter	69	in
Wingspan:	32 ft 08	in
Wing Area: (sq ft)	157	
Length:	23 ft 09	in
Height:	8 ft 09	in
Wing Loading: (lbs/sq ft)	10.2	
Power Loading: (lbs/hp)	16.0	
Weight		
Gross:	1600	lbs
Empty:	1060	lbs
Baggage:	120	lbs

1967

Year: 1967
Model: 150G

Speed		
Maximum at Sea Level:	125	mph
Cruise (75 percent at 7,500 ft):	122	mph
Range		
Maximum (75 percent at 7,500 ft):	490	mi
	4.0	hrs
	122	mph
Optimum range at 10,000 ft:	565	mi
	5.7	hrs
	99	mph
Long-range version maximum:	880	mi
	8.9	hrs
Rate of Climb at Sea Level:	670	fpm
Service Ceiling:	12650	ft

Takeoff
  Ground run: 735 ft
  Over 50-ft obstacle: 1385 ft
Landing
  Landing roll: 445 ft
  Over 50-ft obstacle: 1075 ft
Fuel Capacity
  Standard: 26 gal
  Patroller: 38 gal
Engine
  Make: Continental O-200A
  TBO: 1800 hrs
  Power: 100 hp
  Oil capacity: 6 qts
  Propeller: Metal, diameter: 69 in
Wingspan: 32 ft 08 in
Wing Area: (sq ft)   157
Length: 23 ft 09 in
Height: 8 ft 07 in
Wing Loading: (lbs/sq ft)   10.2
Power Loading: (lbs/hp)   16.0
Weight
  Gross: 1600 lbs
  Empty: 1060 lbs
  Baggage: 120 lbs

Year: 1967
Model: 150G Floatplane

Speed
  Maximum at Sea Level: 103 mph
  Cruise (75 percent at 7,000 ft):   98 mph
Range
  Maximum (75 percent at 7,000 ft):   380 mi
                                         3.9 hrs
                                         98 mph
  Optimum range at 10,000 ft: 425 mi
                                         5.5 hrs
                                         78 mph
  Long-range version maximum: 670 mi
                                         8.6 hrs
Rate of Climb at Sea Level: 560 fpm
Service Ceiling: 10700 ft
Takeoff
  Water run: 1310 ft

Over 50-ft obstacle:	2075 ft
Landing	
Water run:	415 ft
Over 50-ft obstacle:	850 ft
Fuel Capacity	
Standard:	26 gal
Patroller:	38 gal
Engine	
Make:	Continental O-200A
TBO:	1800 hrs
Power:	100 hp
Oil capacity:	6 qts
Propeller: Metal, diameter:	75 in
Wingspan:	32 ft 08 in
Wing Area: (sq ft)	157
Length:	24 ft 01 in
Height:	9 ft 01 in
Wing Loading: (lbs/sq ft)	10.5
Power Loading: (lbs/hp)	16.5
Weight	
Gross:	1650 lbs
Empty:	1135 lbs
Baggage:	120 lbs

1968

Year: 1968
Model: 150H

Speed	
Maximum at Sea Level:	122 mph
Cruise (75 percent at 7,000 ft):	117 mph
Range	
Maximum (75 percent at 7,000 ft):	475 mi
	4.0 hrs
	117 mph
Optimum range at 10,000 ft:	565 mi
	6.1 hrs
	93 mph
Long-range version maximum:	880 mi
	9.4 hrs
Rate of Climb at Sea Level:	670 fpm
Service Ceiling:	12650 ft
Takeoff	
Ground run:	735 ft
Over 50-ft obstacle:	1385 ft

Landing
    Landing roll: 445 ft
    Over 50-ft obstacle: 1075 ft
Fuel Capacity
    Standard: 26 gal
    Patroller: 38 gal
Engine
    Make: Continental O-200A
    TBO: 1800 hrs
    Power: 100 hp
    Oil capacity: 6 qts
    Propeller: Metal, diameter: 69 in
Wingspan: 32 ft 08 in
Wing Area: (sq ft)   157
Length: 23 ft 09 in
Height: 8 ft 07 in
Wing Loading: (lbs/sq ft)   10.2
Power Loading: (lbs/hp)   16.0
Weight
    Gross: 1600 lbs
    Empty: 1060 lbs
    Baggage: 120 lbs

Year: 1968
Model: 150H Floatplane

Speed
    Maximum at Sea Level: 103 mph
    Cruise (75 percent at 7,000 ft):   98 mph
Range
    Maximum (75 percent at 7,000 ft):   380 mi
                                                        3.9 hrs
                                                         98 mph
    Optimum range at 10,000 ft: 425 mi
                                                        5.5 hrs
                                                         78 mph
    Long-range version maximum: 670 mi
                                                        8.6 hrs
Rate of Climb at Sea Level: 560 fpm
Service Ceiling: 10700 ft
Takeoff
    Water run: 1310 ft
    Over 50-ft obstacle: 2075 ft
Landing
    Water run: 415 ft
    Over 50-ft obstacle: 850 ft

Fuel Capacity
Standard:	26	gal
Patroller:	38	gal

Engine
Make:	Continental O-200A	
TBO:	1800	hrs
Power:	100	hp
Oil capacity:	6	qts
Propeller: Metal, diameter:	75	in

Wingspan:	32 ft 08	in
Wing Area: (sq ft)	157	
Length:	24 ft 01	in
Height:	9 ft 01	in
Wing Loading: (lbs/sq ft)	10.5	
Power Loading: (lbs/hp)	16.5	

Weight
Gross:	1650	lbs
Empty:	1135	lbs
Baggage:	120	lbs

1969

Year: 1969
Model: 150J

Speed
Maximum at Sea Level:	122	mph
Cruise (75 percent at 7,000 ft):	117	mph

Range
Maximum (75 percent at 7,000 ft):	475	mi
	4.0	hrs
	117	mph
Optimum range at 10,000 ft:	565	mi
	6.1	hrs
	93	mph
Long-range version maximum:	880	mi
	9.4	hrs

Rate of Climb at Sea Level:	670	fpm
Service Ceiling:	12650	ft

Takeoff
Ground run:	735	ft
Over 50-ft obstacle:	1385	ft

Landing
Landing roll:	445	ft
Over 50-ft obstacle:	1075	ft

Fuel Capacity
Standard: 26 gal
Patroller: 38 gal
Engine
Make: Continental O-200A
TBO: 1800 hrs
Power: 100 hp
Oil capacity: 6 qts
Propeller: Metal, diameter: 69 in
Wingspan: 32 ft 08 in
Wing Area: (sq ft)   157
Length: 23 ft 09 in
Height: 8 ft 07 in
Wing Loading: (lbs/sq ft)   10.2
Power Loading: (lbs/hp)   16.0
Weight
Gross: 1600 lbs
Empty: 1060 lbs
Baggage: 120 lbs

Year: 1969
Model: 150J Floatplane

Speed
Maximum at Sea Level: 103 mph
Cruise (75 percent at 7,000 ft):   98 mph
Range
Maximum (75 percent at 7,000 ft):   380 mi
                                                          3.9 hrs
                                                           98 mph
Optimum range at 10,000 ft: 425 mi
                                                          5.5 hrs
                                                           78 mph
Long-range version maximum: 670 mi
                                                          8.6 hrs
Rate of Climb at Sea Level: 560 fpm
Service Ceiling: 10700 ft
Takeoff
Water run: 1310 ft
Over 50-ft obstacle: 2075 ft
Landing
Water run: 415 ft
Over 50-ft obstacle: 850 ft
Fuel Capacity
Standard: 26 gal

Patroller:	38	gal

Engine
    Make: Continental O-200A

TBO:	1800	hrs
Power:	100	hp
Oil capacity:	6	qts
Propeller: Metal, diameter:	75	in
Wingspan:	32 ft 08	in
Wing Area: (sq ft)	157	
Length:	24 ft 01	in
Height:	9 ft 01	in
Wing Loading: (lbs/sq ft)	10.5	
Power Loading: (lbs/hp)	16.5	
Weight		
Gross:	1650	lbs
Empty:	1135	lbs
Baggage:	120	lbs

1970

Year: 1970
Model: 150K

Speed		
Maximum at Sea Level:	122	mph
Cruise (75 percent at 7,000 ft):	117	mph
Range		
Cruise (75 percent at 7,000 ft):	475	mi
with 26 gallons fuel	4.1	hrs
	117	mph
Cruise (75 percent at 7,000 ft):	725	mi
with 38 gallons fuel	6.2	hrs
	117	mph
Optimum range at 10,000 ft:	565	mi
with 26 gallons fuel	6.1	hrs
	93	mph
Optimum range at 10,000 ft:	880	mi
with 38 gallons fuel	9.4	hrs
	93	mph
Rate of Climb at Sea Level:	670	fpm
Service Ceiling:	12650	ft
Takeoff		
Ground run:	735	ft
Over 50-ft obstacle:	1385	ft
Landing		
Landing roll:	445	ft

Over 50-ft obstacle:	1075 ft
Stall Speed	
Flaps up, power off:	55 mph
Flaps down, power off:	48 mph
Fuel Capacity	
Standard:	26 gal
Optional:	38 gal
Engine	
Make:	Continental O-200A
TBO:	1800 hrs
Power:	100 hp
Oil capacity:	6 qts
Propeller: Metal, diameter:	69 in
Wingspan:	33 ft 02 in
Wing Area: (sq ft)	159.5
Length:	23 ft 09 in
Height:	8 ft 07 in
Wing Loading: (lbs/sq ft)	10.2
Power Loading: (lbs/hp)	16.0
Weight	
Gross:	1600 lbs
Empty:	1060 lbs
Baggage:	120 lbs

Year: 1970
Model: 150K Aerobat

Speed	
Maximum at Sea Level:	120 mph
Cruise (75 percent at 7,000 ft):	115 mph
Range	
Cruise (75 percent at 7,000 ft):	470 mi
with 26 gallons fuel	4.1 hrs
	115 mph
Cruise (75 percent at 7,000 ft):	715 mi
with 38 gallons fuel	6.2 hrs
	115 mph
Optimum range at 10,000 ft:	555 mi
with 26 gallons fuel	6.1 hrs
	91 mph
Optimum range at 10,000 ft:	885 mi
with 38 gallons fuel	9.4 hrs
	91 mph
Rate of Climb at Sea Level:	670 fpm
Service Ceiling:	12650 ft

Takeoff
    Ground run: 735 ft
    Over 50-ft obstacle: 1385 ft
Landing
    Landing roll: 445 ft
    Over 50-ft obstacle: 1075 ft
Stall Speed
    Flaps up, power off: 55 mph
    Flaps down, power off: 48 mph
Fuel Capacity
    Standard: 26 gal
    Optional: 38 gal
Engine
    Make: Continental O-200A
    TBO: 1800 hrs
    Power: 100 hp
    Oil capacity: 6 qts
    Propeller: Metal, diameter: 69 in
Wingspan: 33 ft 02 in
Wing Area: (sq ft)   157
Length: 23 ft 07 in
Height: 8 ft 07 in
Wing Loading: (lbs/sq ft)   10.2
Power Loading: (lbs/hp)   16.0
Weight
    Gross: 1600 lbs
    Empty: 1020 lbs
    Baggage: 120 lbs

Year: 1970
Model: 150K Floatplane

Speed
    Maximum at Sea Level: 103 mph
    Cruise (75 percent at 7,000 ft):   98 mph
Range
    Cruise (75 percent at 7,000 ft):   380 mi
        with 26 gallons fuel   3.9 hrs
                                                            98 mph

    Cruise (75 percent at 7,000 ft):   590 mi
        with 38 gallons fuel   6.0 hrs
                                                            98 mph

    Optimum range at 10,000 ft: 425 mi
        with 26 gallons fuel   5.5 hrs
                                                            78 mph

Optimum range at 10,000 ft:	670	mi
with 38 gallons fuel	8.6	hrs
	78	mph
Rate of Climb at Sea Level:	560	fpm
Service Ceiling:	10700	ft
Takeoff		
Water run:	1310	ft
Over 50-ft obstacle:	2075	ft
Landing		
Water run:	415	ft
Over 50-ft obstacle:	850	ft
Stall Speed		
Flaps up, power off:	54	mph
Flaps down, power off:	48	mph
Fuel Capacity		
Standard:	26	gal
Optional:	38	gal
Engine		
Make:	Continental O-200A	
TBO:	1800	hrs
Power:	100	hp
Oil capacity:	6	qts
Propeller: Metal, diameter:	75	in
Wingspan:	33 ft 02	in
Wing Area: (sq ft)	157	
Length:	24 ft 01	in
Height:	9 ft 01	in
Wing Loading: (lbs/sq ft)	10.5	
Power Loading: (lbs/hp)	16.5	
Weight		
Gross:	1650	lbs
Empty:	1135	lbs
Baggage:	120	lbs

1971

Year: 1971
Model: 150L

Speed		
Maximum at Sea Level:	122	mph
Cruise (75 percent at 7,000 ft):	117	mph
Range		
Cruise (75 percent at 7,000 ft):	475	mi
with 26 gallons fuel	4.1	hrs
	117	mph

Cruise (75 percent at 7,000 ft):	725	mi
with 38 gallons fuel	6.2	hrs
	117	mph
Optimum range at 10,000 ft:	565	mi
with 26 gallons fuel	6.1	hrs
	93	mph
Optimum range at 10,000 ft:	880	mi
with 38 gallons fuel	9.4	hrs
	93	mph
Rate of Climb at Sea Level:	670	fpm
Service Ceiling:	12650	ft
Takeoff		
Ground run:	735	ft
Over 50-ft obstacle:	1385	ft
Landing		
Landing roll:	445	ft
Over 50-ft obstacle:	1075	ft
Stall Speed		
Flaps up, power off:	55	mph
Flaps down, power off:	48	mph
Fuel Capacity		
Standard:	26	gal
Optional:	38	gal
Engine		
Make:	Continental O-200A	
TBO:	1800	hrs
Power:	100	hp
Oil capacity:	6	qts
Propeller: Metal, diameter:	69	in
Wingspan:	32 ft 08	in
Wing Area: (sq ft)	159.5	
Length:	23 ft 09	in
Height:	8 ft 07	in
Wing Loading: (lbs/sq ft)	10.2	
Power Loading: (lbs/hp)	16.0	
Weight		
Gross:	1600	lbs
Empty:	1070	lbs
Baggage:	120	lbs

Year: 1971
Model: 150L Aerobat

Speed		
Maximum at Sea Level:	120	mph

Cruise (75 percent at 7,000 ft):	115	mph
Range		
Cruise (75 percent at 7,000 ft):	470	mi
with 26 gallons fuel	4.1	hrs
	115	mph
Cruise (75 percent at 7,000 ft):	715	mi
with 38 gallons fuel	6.2	hrs
	115	mph
Optimum range at 10,000 ft:	555	mi
with 26 gallons fuel	6.1	hrs
	91	mph
Optimum range at 10,000 ft:	885	mi
with 38 gallons fuel	9.4	hrs
	91	mph
Rate of Climb at Sea Level:	670	fpm
Service Ceiling:	12650	ft
Takeoff		
Ground run:	735	ft
Over 50-ft obstacle:	1385	ft
Landing		
Landing roll:	445	ft
Over 50-ft obstacle:	1075	ft
Stall Speed		
Flaps up, power off:	55	mph
Flaps down, power off:	48	mph
Fuel Capacity		
Standard:	26	gal
Optional:	38	gal
Engine		
Make:	Continental O-200A	
TBO:	1800	hrs
Power:	100	hp
Oil capacity:	6	qts
Propeller: Metal, diameter:	69	in
Wingspan:	32 ft 08	in
Wing Area: (sq ft)	157	
Length:	23 ft 09	in
Height:	8 ft 07	in
Wing Loading: (lbs/sq ft)	10.2	
Power Loading: (lbs/hp)	16.0	
Weight		
Gross:	1600	lbs
Empty:	1030	lbs
Baggage:	120	lbs

1972

Year: 1972
Model: 150L

Speed
    Maximum at Sea Level: 122 mph
    Cruise (75 percent at 7,000 ft): 117 mph
Range
    Cruise (75 percent at 7,000 ft): 475 mi
      with 26 gallons fuel 4.1 hrs
       117 mph

    Cruise (75 percent at 7,000 ft): 725 mi
      with 38 gallons fuel 6.2 hrs
       117 mph

    Optimum range at 10,000 ft: 565 mi
      with 26 gallons fuel 6.1 hrs
       93 mph

    Optimum range at 10,000 ft: 880 mi
      with 38 gallons fuel 9.4 hrs
       93 mph

Rate of Climb at Sea Level: 670 fpm
Service Ceiling: 12650 ft
Takeoff
    Ground run: 735 ft
    Over 50-ft obstacle: 1385 ft
Landing
    Landing roll: 445 ft
    Over 50-ft obstacle: 1075 ft
Stall Speed
    Flaps up, power off: 55 mph
    Flaps down, power off: 48 mph
Fuel Capacity
    Standard: 26 gal
    Optional: 38 gal
Engine
    Make: Continental O-200A
    TBO: 1800 hrs
    Power: 100 hp
    Oil capacity: 6 qts
    Propeller: Metal, diameter: 69 in
Wingspan
    Trainer: 32 ft 08 in
    Commuter: 33 ft 01 in
Wing Area: (sq ft) 157
Length: 23 ft 09 in

Height:	8 ft 00	in
Wing Loading: (lbs/sq ft)	10.2	
Power Loading: (lbs/hp)	16.0	
Weight		
Gross:	1600	lbs
Empty:	1065	lbs
Baggage:	120	lbs

Year: 1972
Model: 150L Aerobat

Speed		
Maximum at Sea Level:	120	mph
Cruise (75 percent at 7,000 ft):	115	mph
Range		
Cruise (75 percent at 7,000 ft):	470	mi
with 26 gallons fuel	4.1	hrs
	115	mph
Cruise (75 percent at 7,000 ft):	715	mi
with 38 gallons fuel	6.2	hrs
	115	mph
Optimum range at 10,000 ft:	555	mi
with 26 gallons fuel	6.1	hrs
	91	mph
Optimum range at 10,000 ft:	855	mi
with 38 gallons fuel	9.4	hrs
	91	mph
Rate of Climb at Sea Level:	670	fpm
Service Ceiling:	12650	ft
Takeoff		
Ground run:	735	ft
Over 50-ft obstacle:	1385	ft
Landing		
Landing roll:	445	ft
Over 50-ft obstacle:	1075	ft
Stall Speed		
Flaps up, power off:	55	mph
Flaps down, power off:	48	mph
Fuel Capacity		
Standard:	26	gal
Optional:	38	gal
Engine		
Make:	Continental O-200A	
TBO:	1800	hrs
Power:	100	hp
Oil capacity:	6	qts

Propeller: Metal, diameter:	69	in
Wingspan:	32 ft 08	in
Wing Area: (sq ft)	157	
Length:	23 ft 09	in
Height:	8 ft 00	in
Wing Loading: (lbs/sq ft)	10.2	
Power Loading: (lbs/hp)	16.0	
Weight		
Gross:	1600	lbs
Empty:	1035	lbs
Baggage:	120	lbs

1973

Year: 1973
Model: 150L

Speed		
Maximum at Sea Level:	122	mph
Cruise (75 percent at 7,000 ft):	117	mph
Range		
Cruise (75 percent at 7,000 ft):	475	mi
with 26 gallons fuel	4.1	hrs
	117	mph
Cruise (75 percent at 7,000 ft):	725	mi
with 38 gallons fuel	6.2	hrs
	117	mph
Optimum range at 10,000 ft:	565	mi
with 26 gallons fuel	6.1	hrs
	93	mph
Optimum range at 10,000 ft:	880	mi
with 38 gallons fuel	9.4	hrs
	93	mph
Rate of Climb at Sea Level:	670	fpm
Service Ceiling:	12650	ft
Takeoff		
Ground run:	735	ft
Over 50-ft obstacle:	1385	ft
Landing		
Landing roll:	445	ft
Over 50-ft obstacle:	1075	ft
Stall Speed		
Flaps up, power off:	55	mph
Flaps down, power off:	48	mph
Fuel Capacity		
Standard:	26	gal

Optional:	38	gal
Engine		
Make:	Continental O-200A	
TBO:	1800	hrs
Power:	100	hp
Oil capacity:	6	qts
Propeller: Metal, diameter:	69	in
Wingspan		
Trainer:	32 ft 08	in
Commuter:	33 ft 02	in
Wing Area (sq ft)		
Trainer:	157	
Commuter:	159.5	
Length:	23 ft 09	in
Height:	8 ft 00	in
Wing Loading (lbs/sq ft)		
Trainer:	10.2	
Commuter:	10.0	
Power Loading: (lbs/hp)	16.0	
Weight		
Gross:	1600	lbs
Empty:	1060	lbs
Baggage:	120	lbs

Year: 1973
Model: 150L Aerobat

Speed		
Maximum at Sea Level:	120	mph
Cruise (75 percent at 7,000 ft):	115	mph
Range		
Cruise (75 percent at 7,000 ft):	470	mi
with 26 gallons fuel	4.1	hrs
	115	mph
Cruise (75 percent at 7,000 ft):	715	mi
with 38 gallons fuel	6.2	hrs
	115	mph
Optimum range at 10,000 ft:	555	mi
with 26 gallons fuel	6.1	hrs
	91	mph
Optimum range at 10,000 ft:	855	mi
with 38 gallons fuel	9.4	hrs
	91	mph
Rate of Climb at Sea Level:	670	fpm
Service Ceiling:	12650	ft

Takeoff
    Ground run: 735 ft
    Over 50-ft obstacle: 1385 ft
Landing
    Landing roll: 445 ft
    Over 50-ft obstacle: 1075 ft
Stall speed
    Flaps up, power off: 55 mph
    Flaps down, power off: 48 mph
Fuel Capacity
    Standard: 26 gal
    Optional: 38 gal
Engine
    Make: Continental O-200A
    TBO: 1800 hrs
    Power: 100 hp
    Oil capacity: 6 qts
    Propeller: Metal, diameter: 69 in
Wingspan: 32 ft 08 in
Wing Area: (sq ft)   157
Length: 23 ft 09 in
Height: 8 ft 00 in
Wing Loading: (lbs/sq ft)   10.2
Power Loading: (lbs/hp)   16.0
Weight
    Gross: 1600 lbs
    Empty: 1040 lbs
    Baggage: 120 lbs

1974

Year: 1974
Model: 150L

Speed
    Maximum at Sea Level: 122 mph
    Cruise (75 percent at 7,000 ft):   117 mph
Range
    Cruise (75 percent at 7,000 ft):   475 mi
        with 26 gallons fuel   4.1 hrs
                                                        117 mph
    Cruise (75 percent at 7,000 ft):   725 mi
        with 38 gallons fuel   6.2 hrs
                                                        117 mph
    Optimum range at 10,000 ft: 565 mi
        with 26 gallons fuel   6.1 hrs

70

	93	mph
Optimum range at 10,000 ft:	880	mi
with 38 gallons fuel	9.4	hrs
	93	mph
Rate of Climb at Sea Level:	670	fpm
Service Ceiling:	12650	ft
Takeoff		
Ground run:	735	ft
Over 50-ft obstacle:	1385	ft
Landing		
Landing roll:	445	ft
Over 50-ft obstacle:	1075	ft
Stall Speed		
Flaps up, power off:	55	mph
Flaps down, power off:	48	mph
Fuel Capacity		
Standard:	26	gal
Optional:	38	gal
Engine		
Make:	Continental O-200A	
TBO:	1800	hrs
Power:	100	hp
Oil capacity:	6	qts
Propeller: Metal, diameter:	69	in
Wingspan		
Trainer:	32 ft 08	in
Commuter:	33 ft 02	in
Wing Area (sq ft)		
Trainer:	157	
Commuter:	159.5	
Length:	23 ft 09	in
Height:	8 ft 00	in
Wing Loading (lbs/sq ft)		
Trainer:	10.2	
Commuter:	10.0	
Power Loading: (lbs/hp)	16.0	
Weight		
Gross:	1600	lbs
Empty:	1060	lbs
Baggage:	120	lbs

Year: 1974
Model: 150L Aerobat

Speed
    Maximum at Sea Level: 124 mph

Cruise (75 percent at 7,000 ft):	119	mph
Range		
Cruise (75 percent at 7,000 ft):	485	mi
with 26 gallons fuel	4.1	hrs
	119	mph
Cruise (75 percent at 7,000 ft):	735	mi
with 38 gallons fuel	6.2	hrs
	119	mph
Optimum range at 10,000 ft:	580	mi
with 26 gallons fuel	6.1	hrs
	96	mph
Optimum range at 10,000 ft:	900	mi
with 38 gallons fuel	9.4	hrs
	96	mph
Rate of Climb at Sea Level:	670	fpm
Service Ceiling:	14000	ft
Takeoff		
Ground run:	735	ft
Over 50-ft obstacle:	1385	ft
Landing		
Landing roll:	445	ft
Over 50-ft obstacle:	1075	ft
Stall Speed		
Flaps up, power off:	55	mph
Flaps down, power off:	48	mph
Fuel Capacity		
Standard:	26	gal
Optional:	38	gal
Engine		
Make:	Continental O-200A	
TBO:	1800	hrs
Power:	100	hp
Oil capacity:	6	qts
Propeller: Metal, diameter:	69	in
Wingspan:	32 ft 08	in
Wing Area: (sq ft)	157	
Length:	23 ft 09	in
Height:	8 ft 00	in
Wing Loading: (lbs/sq ft)	10.2	
Power Loading: (lbs/hp)	16.0	
Weight		
Gross:	1600	lbs
Empty:	1040	lbs
Baggage:	120	lbs

1975

Year: 1975
Model: 150M

Speed
Maximum at Sea Level: 125 mph
Cruise (75 percent at 7,000 ft):   122 mph
Range
Cruise (75 percent at 7,000 ft):   500 mi
    with 26 gallons fuel   4.1 hrs
                                                           122 mph

Cruise (75 percent at 7,000 ft):   755 mi
    with 38 gallons fuel   6.2 hrs
                                                           122 mph

Optimum range at 10,000 ft: 660 mi
    with 26 gallons fuel   6.9 hrs
                                                            95 mph

Optimum range at 10,000 ft: 1025 mi
    with 38 gallons fuel   10.8 hrs
                                                            95 mph

Rate of Climb at Sea Level: 670 fpm
Service Ceiling: 14000 ft
Takeoff
    Ground run: 735 ft
    Over 50-ft obstacle: 1385 ft
Landing
    Landing roll: 445 ft
    Over 50-ft obstacle: 1075 ft
Stall Speed
    Flaps up, power off: 55 mph
    Flaps down, power off: 48 mph
Fuel Capacity
    Standard: 26 gal
    Optional: 38 gal
Engine
    Make: Continental O-200A
    TBO: 1800 hrs
    Power: 100 hp
    Oil capacity: 6 qts
    Propeller: Metal, diameter: 69 in
Wingspan: 33 ft 02 in
Wing Area (sq ft):   159.5
Length: 23 ft 11 in
Height: 8 ft 06 in
Wing Loading (lbs/sq ft):   10.0

Power Loading: (lbs/hp)	16.0	
Weight		
Gross:	1600	lbs
Empty		
Commuter:	1065	lbs
Commuter II:	1085	lbs
Baggage:	120	lbs

Year: 1975
Model: 150M Aerobat

Speed		
Maximum at Sea Level:	124	mph
Cruise (75 percent at 7,000 ft):	121	mph
Range		
Cruise (75 percent at 7,000 ft):	495	mi
with 26 gallons fuel	4.1	hrs
	121	mph
Cruise (75 percent at 7,000 ft):	750	mi
with 38 gallons fuel	6.2	hrs
	121	mph
Optimum range at 10,000 ft:	650	mi
with 26 gallons fuel	6.9	hrs
	94	mph
Optimum range at 10,000 ft:	1010	mi
with 38 gallons fuel	10.8	hrs
	94	mph
Rate of Climb at Sea Level:	670	fpm
Service Ceiling:	14000	ft
Takeoff		
Ground run:	735	ft
Over 50-ft obstacle:	1385	ft
Landing		
Landing roll:	445	ft
Over 50-ft obstacle:	1075	ft
Stall Speed		
Flaps up, power off:	55	mph
Flaps down, power off:	48	mph
Fuel Capacity		
Standard:	26	gal
Optional:	38	gal
Engine		
Make:	Continental O-200A	
TBO:	1800	hrs
Power:	100	hp

Oil capacity:	6	qts
Propeller: Metal, diameter:	69	in
Wingspan:	32 ft 08	in
Wing Area: (sq ft)	157	
Length:	23 ft 11	in
Height:	8 ft 06	in
Wing Loading: (lbs/sq ft)	10.2	
Power Loading: (lbs/hp)	16.0	
Weight		
Gross:	1600	lbs
Empty:	1040	lbs
Baggage:	120	lbs

1976

Year: 1976
Model: 150M

Speed		
Maximum at Sea Level:	125	mph
Cruise (75 percent at 7,000 ft):	122	mph
Range		
Cruise (75 percent at 7,000 ft):	500	mi
with 26 gallons fuel	4.1	hrs
	122	mph
Cruise (75 percent at 7,000 ft):	755	mi
with 38 gallons fuel	6.2	hrs
	122	mph
Optimum range at 10,000 ft:	660	mi
with 26 gallons fuel	6.9	hrs
	95	mph
Optimum range at 10,000 ft:	1025	mi
with 38 gallons fuel	10.8	hrs
	95	mph
Rate of Climb at Sea Level:	670	fpm
Service Ceiling:	14000	ft
Takeoff		
Ground run:	735	ft
Over 50-ft obstacle:	1385	ft
Landing		
Landing roll:	445	ft
Over 50-ft obstacle:	1075	ft
Stall Speed		
Flaps up, power off:	55	mph
Flaps down, power off:	48	mph
Fuel Capacity		

| Standard: | 26 gal |
| Optional: | 38 gal |

Engine
Make:	Continental O-200A
TBO:	1800 hrs
Power:	100 hp
Oil capacity:	6 qts
Propeller: Metal, diameter:	69 in

Wingspan:	33 ft 02 in
Wing Area (sq ft):	159.5
Length:	23 ft 11 in
Height:	8 ft 06 in
Wing Loading (lbs/sq ft):	10.0
Power Loading: (lbs/hp)	16.0

Weight
Gross:	1600 lbs
Empty	
Commuter:	1065 lbs
Commuter II:	1085 lbs
Baggage:	120 lbs

Year: 1976
Model: 150M Aerobat

Speed
| Maximum at Sea Level: | 124 mph |
| Cruise (75 percent at 7,000 ft): | 121 mph |

Range
Cruise (75 percent at 7,000 ft):	495 mi
with 26 gallons fuel	4.1 hrs
	121 mph
Cruise (75 percent at 7,000 ft):	750 mi
with 38 gallons fuel	6.2 hrs
	121 mph
Optimum range at 10,000 ft:	650 mi
with 26 gallons fuel	6.9 hrs
	94 mph
Optimum range at 10,000 ft:	1010 mi
with 38 gallons fuel	10.8 hrs
	94 mph

| Rate of Climb at Sea Level: | 670 fpm |
| Service Ceiling: | 14000 ft |

Takeoff
| Ground run: | 735 ft |
| Over 50-ft obstacle: | 1385 ft |

Landing
    Landing roll: 445 ft
    Over 50-ft obstacle: 1075 ft
Stall Speed
    Flaps up, power off: 55 mph
    Flaps down, power off: 48 mph
Fuel Capacity
    Standard: 26 gal
    Optional: 38 gal
Engine
    Make: Continental O-200A
    TBO: 1800 hrs
    Power: 100 hp
    Oil capacity: 6 qts
    Propeller: Metal, diameter: 69 in
Wingspan: 32 ft 08 in
Wing Area: (sq ft)   157
Length: 23 ft 11 in
Height: 8 ft 06 in
Wing Loading: (lbs/sq ft)   10.2
Power Loading: (lbs/hp)   16.0
Weight
    Gross: 1600 lbs
    Empty: 1040 lbs
    Baggage: 120 lbs

1977

Year: 1977
Model: 150M

Speed
    Maximum at Sea Level: 109 kts
    Cruise (75 percent at 7,000 ft): 106 kts
Range
    Cruise (75 percent at 7,000 ft): 340 nm
      with 22.5 gals usable: 3.3 hrs
    Cruise (75 percent at 7,000 ft): 580 nm
      with 35 gals usable: 5.5 hrs
    Maximum range at 10,000 ft: 420 nm
      with 22.5 gals usable: 4.9 hrs
    Maximum range at 10,000 ft: 735 nm
      with 35 gals usable: 8.5 hrs
Rate of Climb at Sea Level: 670 fpm
Service Ceiling: 14000 ft
Takeoff

Ground run:	735	ft
Over 50-ft obstacle:	1385	ft
Landing		
Landing roll:	445	ft
Over 50-ft obstacle:	1075	ft
Stall Speed		
Flaps up, power off:	48	kts
Flaps down, power off:	42	kts
Fuel Capacity		
Standard:	26	gal
Long-range:	38	gal
Engine		
Make:	Continental O-200A	
TBO:	1800	hrs
Power:	100	hp
Oil capacity:	6	qts
Propeller: Metal, diameter:	69	in
Wingspan:	33 ft 02	in
Wing Area: (sq ft)	159.5	
Length:	23 ft 11	in
Height:	8 ft 06	in
Wing Loading: (lbs/sq ft)	10.0	
Power Loading: (lbs/hp)	16.0	
Weight		
Gross:	1600	lbs
Empty		
Commuter:	1111	lbs
Commuter II:	1129	lbs
Baggage:	120	lbs

Year: 1977
Model: 150M Aerobat

Speed		
Maximum at Sea Level:	108	kts
Cruise (75 percent at 7,000 ft):	105	kts
Range		
Cruise (75 percent at 7,000 ft):	335	nm
with 22.5 gals usable:	3.3	hrs
Cruise (75 percent at 7,000 ft):	570	nm
with 35 gals usable:	5.5	hrs
Maximum range at 10,000 ft:	415	nm
with 22.5 gals usable:	4.9	hrs
Maximum range at 10,000 ft:	725	nm
with 35 gals usable:	8.5	hrs

Rate of Climb at Sea Level:	670	fpm
Service Ceiling:	14000	ft
Takeoff		
Ground run:	735	ft
Over 50-ft obstacle:	1385	ft
Landing		
Landing roll:	445	ft
Over 50-ft obstacle:	1075	ft
Stall Speed		
Flaps up, power off:	48	kts
Flaps down, power off:	42	kts
Fuel Capacity		
Standard:	26	gal
Long-range:	38	gal
Engine		
Make:	Continental O-200A	
TBO:	1800	hrs
Power:	100	hp
Oil capacity:	6	qts
Propeller: Metal, diameter	69	in
Wingspan:	32 ft 08	in
Wing Area (sq ft):	157	
Length:	23 ft 11	in
Height:	8 ft 06	in
Wing Loading (lbs/sq ft):	10.2	
Power Loading: (lbs/hp)	16.0	
Weight		
Gross:	1600	lbs
Empty:	1093	lbs
Baggage:	120	lbs

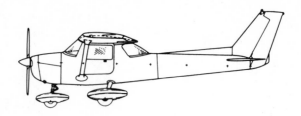

Chapter 4

Cessna 152 Specifications

In 1978, Cessna introduced the new Model 152. As with the Model 150 airplanes, some of the specification changes from one year to the next are minimal; however, for historical purposes, all are included.

The wing area and wingspan specifications shown are for an airplane equipped with the optional modified conical wing tips. For an airplane equipped with standard wingtips, the wing area is 157 square feet and the wingspan is 32 feet 8.5 inches.

The speed performance specifications are for an airplane equipped with the optional speed fairings, which increase the speed by approximately 2 knots. There is a corresponding difference in range. All other performance figures remain unchanged when speed fairings are installed.

Empty weight differences occur between the 152 and 152 II Models, with the latter being the heaviest by about 40 pounds, all in additional avionics equipment. The specifications given are for the 152.

1978
Year: 1978
Model: 152

Speed
    Maximum at Sea Level: 110 kts

Cruise (75 percent at 8,000 ft):	107	kts

Range

Cruise (75 percent at 8,000 ft):	350	nm
with 24.5 gals usable:	3.4	hrs
Cruise (75 percent at 8,000 ft):	580	nm
with 37.5 gals usable:	5.5	hrs
Maximum range at 10,000 ft:	415	nm
with 24.5 gals usable:	5.2	hrs
Maximum range at 10,000 ft:	690	nm
with 37.5 gals usable:	8.7	hrs

Rate of Climb at Sea Level:	715	fpm
Service Ceiling:	14700	ft

Takeoff

Ground run:	725	ft
Over 50-ft obstacle:	1340	ft

Landing

Landing roll:	475	ft
Over 50-ft obstacle:	1200	ft

Stall Speed

Flaps up, power off:	48	kts
Flaps down, power off:	43	kts

Fuel Capacity

Standard:	26	gal
Long-range:	39	gal

Engine

Make:	AVCO Lycoming O-235-L2C	
TBO:	2000	hrs
Power:	110	hp
Oil capacity:	6	qts
Propeller: Metal, diameter:	69	in

Wingspan:	33 ft 02	in
Wing Area (sq ft):	159.5	
Length:	24 ft 01	in
Height:	8 ft 06	in
Wing Loading (lbs/sq ft):	10.5	
Power Loading: (lbs/hp)	15.2	

Weight

Gross:	1670	lbs
Empty:	1081	lbs
Baggage:	120	lbs

Year: 1978
Model: 152 Aerobat

Speed

Maximum at Sea Level:	109	kts

Cruise (75 percent at 8,000 ft):	106	kts
Range		
Cruise (75 percent at 8,000 ft):	345	nm
with 24.5 gals usable:	3.4	hrs
Cruise (75 percent at 8,000 ft):	575	nm
with 37.5 gals usable:	5.5	hrs
Maximum range at 10,000 ft:	410	nm
with 24.5 gals usable:	5.2	hrs
Maximum range at 10,000 ft:	685	nm
with 37.5 gals usable:	8.7	hrs
Rate of Climb at Sea Level:	715	fpm
Service Ceiling:	14700	ft
Takeoff		
Ground run:	725	ft
Over 50-ft obstacle:	1340	ft
Landing		
Landing roll:	475	ft
Over 50-ft obstacle:	1200	ft
Stall Speed		
Flaps up, power off:	48	kts
Flaps down, power off:	43	kts
Fuel Capacity		
Standard:	26	gal
Long-range:	39	gal
Engine		
Make:	AVCO Lycoming O-235-L2C	
TBO:	2000	hrs
Power:	110	hp
Oil capacity:	6	qts
Propeller: Metal, diameter:	69	in
Wingspan:	33 ft 02	in
Wing Area (sq ft):	159.5	
Length:	24 ft 01	in
Height:	8 ft 06	in
Wing Loading (lbs/sq ft):	10.5	
Power Loading: (lbs/hp)	15.2	
Weight		
Gross:	1670	lbs
Empty:	1125	lbs
Baggage:	120	lbs

1979

Year: 1979
Model: 152

Speed
- Maximum at Sea Level: 110 kts
- Cruise (75 percent at 8,000 ft): 107 kts

Range
- Cruise (75 percent at 8,000 ft): 350 nm
- with 24.5 gals usable: 3.4 hrs
- Cruise (75 percent at 8,000 ft): 580 nm
- with 37.5 gals usable: 5.5 hrs
- Maximum range at 10,000 ft: 415 nm
- with 24.5 gals usable: 5.2 hrs
- Maximum range at 10,000 ft: 690 nm
- with 37.5 gals usable: 8.7 hrs

Rate of Climb at Sea Level: 715 fpm

Service Ceiling: 14700 ft

Takeoff
- Ground run: 725 ft
- Over 50-ft obstacle: 1340 ft

Landing
- Landing roll: 475 ft
- Over 50-ft obstacle: 1200 ft

Stall Speed
- Flaps up, power off: 48 kts
- Flaps down, power off: 43 kts

Fuel Capacity
- Standard: 26 gal
- Long-range: 39 gal

Engine
- Make: AVCO Lycoming O-235-L2C
- TBO: 2000 hrs
- Power: 110 hp
- Oil capacity: 6 qts
- Propeller: Metal, diameter: 69 in

Wingspan: 33 ft 02 in

Wing Area (sq ft): 159.5

Length: 24 ft 01 in

Height: 8 ft 06 in

Wing Loading (lbs/sq ft): 10.5

Power Loading: (lbs/hp) 15.2

Weight
- Gross: 1670 lbs
- Empty: 1101 lbs
- Baggage: 120 lbs

Year: 1979
Model: 152 Aerobat

Speed

Maximum at Sea Level:	109	kts
Cruise (75 percent at 8,000 ft):	106	kts

Range

Cruise (75 percent at 8,000 ft):	345	nm
with 24.5 gals usable:	3.4	hrs
Cruise (75 percent at 8,000 ft):	575	nm
with 37.5 gals usable:	5.5	hrs
Maximum range at 10,000 ft:	410	nm
with 24.5 gals usable:	5.2	hrs
Maximum range at 10,000 ft:	685	nm
with 37.5 gals usable:	8.7	hrs

Rate of Climb at Sea Level:	715	fpm
Service Ceiling:	14700	ft

Takeoff

Ground run:	725	ft
Over 50-ft obstacle:	1340	ft

Landing

Landing roll:	475	ft
Over 50-ft obstacle:	1200	ft

Stall Speed

Flaps up, power off:	48	kts
Flaps down, power off:	43	kts

Fuel Capacity

Standard:	26	gal
Long-range:	39	gal

Engine

Make:	AVCO Lycoming O-235-L2C	
TBO:	2000	hrs
Power:	110	hp
Oil capacity:	6	qts
Propeller: Metal, diameter:	69	in

Wingspan:	33 ft	02	in
Wing Area (sq ft):	159.5		
Length:	24 ft	01	in
Height:	8 ft	06	in
Wing Loading (lbs/sq ft):	10.5		
Power Loading: (lbs/hp)	15.2		

Weight

Gross:	1670	lbs
Empty:	1132	lbs
Baggage:	120	lbs

1980

Year: 1980
Model: 152

Speed
    Maximum at Sea Level: 110 kts
    Cruise (75 percent at 8,000 ft):   107 kts
Range
    Cruise (75 percent at 8,000 ft):   320 nm
        with 24.5 gals usable: 3.1 hrs
    Cruise (75 percent at 8,000 ft):   545 nm
        with 37.5 gals usable: 5.2 hrs
    Maximum range at 10,000 ft: 415 nm
        with 24.5 gals usable: 5.2 hrs
    Maximum range at 10,000 ft: 690 nm
        with 37.5 gals usable: 8.7 hrs
Rate of Climb at Sea Level: 715 fpm
Service Ceiling: 14700 ft
Takeoff
    Ground run: 725 ft
    Over 50-ft obstacle: 1340 ft
Landing
    Landing roll: 475 ft
    Over 50-ft obstacle: 1200 ft
Stall Speed
    Flaps up, power off: 48 kts
    Flaps down, power off: 43 kts
Fuel Capacity
    Standard: 26 gal
    Long-range: 39 gal
Engine
    Make: AVCO Lycoming O-235-L2C
    TBO: 2000 hrs
    Power: 110 hp
    Oil capacity: 6 qts
    Propeller: Metal, diameter: 69 in
Wingspan: 33 ft   02 in
Wing Area (sq ft):   159.5
Length: 24 ft   01 in
Height: 8 ft   06 in
Wing Loading (lbs/sq ft):   10.5
Power Loading: (lbs/hp)   15.2
Weight
    Gross: 1670 lbs
    Empty: 1109 lbs
    Baggage: 120 lbs

Year: 1980
Model: 152 Aerobat

Speed
    Maximum at Sea Level: 109 kts
    Cruise (75 percent at 8,000 ft):   106 kts

Range
    Cruise (75 percent at 8,000 ft):   315 nm
        with 24.5 gals usable: 3.1 hrs
    Cruise (75 percent at 8,000 ft):   540 nm
        with 37.5 gals usable: 5.2 hrs
    Maximum range at 10,000 ft: 410 nm
        with 24.5 gals usable: 5.2 hrs
    Maximum range at 10,000 ft: 680 nm
        with 37.5 gals usable: 8.7 hrs

Rate of Climb at Sea Level: 715 fpm
Service Ceiling: 14700 ft

Takeoff
    Ground run: 725 ft
    Over 50-ft obstacle: 1340 ft

Landing
    Landing roll: 475 ft
    Over 50-ft obstacle: 1200 ft

Stall Speed
    Flaps up, power off: 48 kts
    Flaps down, power off: 43 kts

Fuel Capacity
    Standard: 26 gal
    Long-range: 39 gal

Engine
    Make: AVCO Lycoming O-235-L2C
    TBO: 2000 hrs
    Power: 110 hp
    Oil capacity: 6 qts
    Propeller: Metal, diameter: 69 in

Wingspan: 33 ft 02 in
Wing Area (sq ft):   159.5
Length: 24 ft 01 in
Height: 8 ft 06 in
Wing Loading (lbs/sq ft):   10.5
Power Loading: (lbs/hp)   15.2

Weight
    Gross: 1670 lbs
    Empty: 1135 lbs
    Baggage: 120 lbs

1981

Year: 1981
Model: 152

Speed
    Maximum at Sea Level: 110 kts
    Cruise (75 percent at 8,000 ft):   107 kts

Range
    Cruise (75 percent at 8,000 ft):   320 nm
        with 24.5 gals usable: 3.1 hrs
    Cruise (75 percent at 8,000 ft):   545 nm
        with 37.5 gals usable: 5.2 hrs
    Maximum range at 10,000 ft: 415 nm
        with 24.5 gals usable: 5.2 hrs
    Maximum range at 10,000 ft: 690 nm
        with 37.5 gals usable: 8.7 hrs

Rate of Climb at Sea Level: 715 fpm
Service Ceiling: 14700 ft

Takeoff
    Ground run: 725 ft
    Over 50-ft obstacle: 1340 ft

Landing
    Landing roll: 475 ft
    Over 50-ft obstacle: 1200 ft

Stall Speed
    Flaps up, power off: 48 kts
    Flaps down, power off: 43 kts

Fuel Capacity
    Standard: 26 gal
    Long-range: 39 gal

Engine
    Make: AVCO Lycoming O-235-L2C
    TBO: 2000 hrs
    Power: 110 hp
    Oil capacity: 7 qts
    Propeller: Metal, diameter: 69 in

Wingspan: 33 ft 02 in
Wing Area (sq ft):   159.5
Length: 24 ft 01 in
Height: 8 ft 06 in
Wing Loading (lbs/sq ft):   10.5
Power Loading: (lbs/hp)   15.2

Weight
    Gross: 1670 lbs
    Empty: 1104 lbs
    Baggage: 120 lbs

Year: 1981
Model: 152 Aerobat

Speed
    Maximum at Sea Level: 109 kts
    Cruise (75 percent at 8,000 ft): 106 kts
Range
    Cruise (75 percent at 8,000 ft): 315 nm
        with 24.5 gals usable: 3.1 hrs
    Cruise (75 percent at 8,000 ft): 540 nm
        with 37.5 gals usable: 5.2 hrs
    Maximum range at 10,000 ft: 410 nm
        with 24.5 gals usable: 5.2 hrs
    Maximum range at 10,000 ft: 680 nm
        with 37.5 gals usable: 8.7 hrs
Rate of Climb at Sea Level: 715 fpm
Service Ceiling: 14700 ft
Takeoff
    Ground run: 725 ft
    Over 50-ft obstacle: 1340 ft
Landing
    Landing roll: 475 ft
    Over 50-ft obstacle: 1200 ft
Stall Speed
    Flaps up, power off: 48 kts
    Flaps down, power off: 43 kts
Fuel Capacity
    Standard: 26 gal
    Long-range: 39 gal
Engine
    Make: AVCO Lycoming O-235-L2C
    TBO: 2000 hrs
    Power: 110 hp
    Oil capacity: 7 qts
    Propeller: Metal, diameter: 69 in
Wingspan: 33 ft 02 in
Wing Area (sq ft): 159.5
Length: 24 ft 01 in
Height: 8 ft 06 in
Wing Loading (lbs/sq ft): 10.5
Power Loading: (lbs/hp) 15.2
Weight
    Gross: 1670 lbs
    Empty: 1129 lbs
    Baggage: 120 lbs

1982

Year: 1982
Model: 152

Speed
      Maximum at Sea Level: 110 kts
      Cruise (75 percent at 8,000 ft):   107 kts

Speed		
Maximum at Sea Level:	110	kts
Cruise (75 percent at 8,000 ft):	107	kts
Range		
Cruise (75 percent at 8,000 ft):	320	nm
with 24.5 gals usable:	3.1	hrs
Cruise (75 percent at 8,000 ft):	545	nm
with 37.5 gals usable:	5.2	hrs
Maximum range at 10,000 ft:	415	nm
with 24.5 gals usable:	5.2	hrs
Maximum range at 10,000 ft:	690	nm
with 37.5 gals usable:	8.7	hrs
Rate of Climb at Sea Level:	715	fpm
Service Ceiling:	14700	ft
Takeoff		
Ground run:	725	ft
Over 50-ft obstacle:	1340	ft
Landing		
Landing roll:	475	ft
Over 50-ft obstacle:	1200	ft
Stall Speed		
Flaps up, power off:	48	kts
Flaps down, power off:	43	kts
Fuel Capacity		
Standard:	26	gal
Long-range:	39	gal
Engine		
Make:	AVCO Lycoming O-235-L2C	
TBO:	2000	hrs
Power:	110	hp
Oil capacity:	7	qts
Propeller: Metal, diameter:	69	in
Wingspan:	33 ft 02	in
Wing Area (sq ft):	159.5	
Length:	24 ft 01	in
Height:	8 ft 06	in
Wing Loading (lbs/sq ft):	10.5	
Power Loading: (lbs/hp)	15.2	
Weight		
Gross:	1670	lbs
Empty:	1112	lbs
Baggage:	120	lbs

Year: 1982
Model: 152 Aerobat

Speed
Maximum at Sea Level:	109 kts
Cruise (75 percent at 8,000 ft):	106 kts

Range
Cruise (75 percent at 8,000 ft):	315 nm
with 24.5 gals usable:	3.1 hrs
Cruise (75 percent at 8,000 ft):	540 nm
with 37.5 gals usable:	5.2 hrs
Maximum range at 10,000 ft:	410 nm
with 24.5 gals usable:	5.2 hrs
Maximum range at 10,000 ft:	680 nm
with 37.5 gals usable:	8.7 hrs

Rate of Climb at Sea Level:	715 fpm
Service Ceiling:	14700 ft

Takeoff
Ground run:	725 ft
Over 50-ft obstacle:	1340 ft

Landing
Landing roll:	475 ft
Over 50-ft obstacle:	1200 ft

Stall Speed
Flaps up, power off:	48 kts
Flaps down, power off:	43 kts

Fuel Capacity
Standard:	26 gal
Long-range:	39 gal

Engine
Make:	AVCO Lycoming O-235-L2C
TBO:	2000 hrs
Power:	110 hp
Oil capacity:	7 qts
Propeller: Metal, diameter:	69 in

Wingspan:	33 ft 02 in
Wing Area (sq ft):	159.5
Length:	24 ft 01 in
Height:	8 ft 06 in
Wing Loading (lbs/sq ft):	10.5
Power Loading: (lbs/hp)	15.2

Weight
Gross:	1670 lbs
Empty:	1133 lbs
Baggage:	120 lbs

1983

Year: 1983
Model: 152

Speed
Maximum at Sea Level: 109 kts
Cruise (75 percent at 8,000 ft): 106 kts
Range
Cruise (75 percent at 8,000 ft): 315 nm
with 24.5 gals usable: 3.0 hrs
Cruise (75 percent at 8,000 ft): 540 nm
with 37.5 gals usable: 5.2 hrs
Maximum range at 10,000 ft: 370 nm
with 24.5 gals usable: 4.1 hrs
Maximum range at 10,000 ft: 625 nm
with 37.5 gals usable: 6.9 hrs
Rate of Climb at Sea Level: 715 fpm
Service Ceiling: 14700 ft
Takeoff
Ground run: 725 ft
Over 50-ft obstacle: 1340 ft
Landing
Landing roll: 475 ft
Over 50-ft obstacle: 1200 ft
Stall Speed
Flaps up, power off: 48 kts
Flaps down, power off: 43 kts
Fuel Capacity
Standard: 26 gal
Long-range: 39 gal
Engine
Make: AVCO Lycoming O-235-N2C
TBO: 2000 hrs
Power: 108 hp
Oil capacity: 7 qts
Propeller: Metal, diameter: 69 in
Wingspan: 33 ft 02 in
Wing Area (sq ft): 159.5
Length: 24 ft 01 in
Height: 8 ft 06 in
Wing Loading (lbs/sq ft): 10.5
Power Loading: (lbs/hp) 15.2
Weight
Gross: 1670 lbs
Empty: 1104 lbs
Baggage: 120 lbs

Year: 1983
Model: 152 Aerobat

Speed
Maximum at Sea Level: 108 kts
Cruise (75 percent at 8,000 ft): 105 kts
Range
Cruise (75 percent at 8,000 ft): 310 nm
with 24.5 gals usable: 3.0 hrs
Cruise (75 percent at 8,000 ft): 530 nm
with 37.5 gals usable: 5.2 hrs
Maximum range at 10,000 ft: 365 nm
with 24.5 gals usable: 4.1 hrs
Maximum range at 10,000 ft: 615 nm
with 37.5 gals usable: 6.9 hrs
Rate of Climb at Sea Level: 715 fpm
Service Ceiling: 14700 ft
Takeoff
Ground run: 725 ft
Over 50-ft obstacle: 1340 ft
Landing
Landing roll: 475 ft
Over 50-ft obstacle: 1200 ft
Stall Speed
Flaps up, power off: 48 kts
Flaps down, power off: 43 kts
Fuel Capacity
Standard: 26 gal
Long-range: 39 gal
Engine
Make: AVCO Lycoming O-235-N2C
TBO: 2000 hrs
Power: 108 hp
Oil capacity: 7 qts
Propeller: Metal, diameter: 69 in
Wingspan: 33 ft 02 in
Wing Area (sq ft): 159.5
Length: 24 ft 01 in
Height: 8 ft 06 in
Wing Loading (lbs/sq ft): 10.5
Power Loading: (lbs/hp) 15.2
Weight
Gross: 1670 lbs
Empty: 1131 lbs
Baggage: 120 lbs

1984

Year: 1984
Model: 152

Speed
    Maximum at Sea Level: 109 kts
    Cruise (75 percent at 8,000 ft):   106 kts

Range
    Cruise (75 percent at 8,000 ft):   315 nm
        with 24.5 gals usable: 3.0 hrs
    Cruise (75 percent at 8,000 ft):   540 nm
        with 37.5 gals usable: 5.2 hrs
    Maximum range at 10,000 ft: 370 nm
        with 24.5 gals usable: 4.1 hrs
    Maximum range at 10,000 ft: 625 nm
        with 37.5 gals usable: 6.9 hrs

Rate of Climb at Sea Level: 715 fpm
Service Ceiling: 14700 ft

Takeoff
    Ground run: 725 ft
    Over 50-ft obstacle: 1340 ft

Landing
    Landing roll: 475 ft
    Over 50-ft obstacle: 1200 ft

Stall Speed
    Flaps up, power off: 48 kts
    Flaps down, power off: 43 kts

Fuel Capacity
    Standard: 26 gal
    Long-range: 39 gal

Engine
    Make: AVCO Lycoming O-235-N2C
    TBO: 2000 hrs
    Power: 108 hp
    Oil capacity: 7 qts
    Propeller: Metal, diameter: 69 in

Wingspan: 33 ft 02 in
Wing Area (sq ft):   159.5
Length: 24 ft 01 in
Height: 8 ft 06 in
Wing Loading (lbs/sq ft):   10.5
Power Loading: (lbs/hp)   15.2

Weight
    Gross: 1670 lbs
    Empty: 1104 lbs
    Baggage: 120 lbs

Year: 1984
Model: 152 Aerobat

Speed
    Maximum at Sea Level: 108 kts
    Cruise (75 percent at 8,000 ft):   105 kts
Range
    Cruise (75 percent at 8,000 ft):   310 nm
      with 24.5 gals usable: 3.0 hrs
    Cruise (75 percent at 8,000 ft):   530 nm
      with 37.5 gals usable: 5.2 hrs
    Maximum range at 10,000 ft: 365 nm
      with 24.5 gals usable: 4.1 hrs
    Maximum range at 10,000 ft: 615 nm
      with 37.5 gals usable: 6.9 hrs
Rate of Climb at Sea Level: 715 fpm
Service Ceiling: 14700 ft
Takeoff
    Ground run: 725 ft
    Over 50-ft obstacle: 1340 ft
Landing
    Landing roll: 475 ft
    Over 50-ft obstacle: 1200 ft
Stall Speed
    Flaps up, power off: 48 kts
    Flaps down, power off: 43 kts
Fuel Capacity
    Standard: 26 gal
    Long-range: 39 gal
Engine
    Make: AVCO Lycoming O-235-N2C
    TBO: 2000 hrs
    Power: 108 hp
    Oil capacity: 7 qts
   Propeller: Metal, diameter: 69 in
Wingspan: 33 ft 02 in
Wing Area (sq ft):   159.5
Length: 24 ft 01 in
Height: 8 ft 06 in
Wing Loading (lbs/sq ft):   10.5
Power Loading: (lbs/hp)   15.2
Weight
    Gross: 1670 lbs
    Empty: 1131 lbs
    Baggage: 120 lbs

1985

Year: 1985
Model: 152

Speed
    Maximum at Sea Level: 109 kts
    Cruise (75 percent at 8,000 ft):   106 kts
Range
    Cruise (75 percent at 8,000 ft):   315 nm
        with 24.5 gals usable: 3.0 hrs
    Cruise (75 percent at 8,000 ft):   540 nm
        with 37.5 gals usable: 5.2 hrs
    Maximum range at 10,000 ft: 370 nm
        with 24.5 gals usable: 4.1 hrs
    Maximum range at 10,000 ft: 625 nm
        with 37.5 gals usable: 6.9 hrs
Rate of Climb at Sea Level: 715 fpm
Service Ceiling: 14700 ft
Takeoff
    Ground run: 725 ft
    Over 50-ft obstacle: 1340 ft
Landing
    Landing roll: 475 ft
    Over 50-ft obstacle: 1200 ft
Stall Speed
    Flaps up, power off: 48 kts
    Flaps down, power off: 43 kts
Fuel Capacity
    Standard: 26 gal
    Long-range: 39 gal
Engine
    Make: AVCO Lycoming O-235-N2C
    TBO: 2000 hrs
    Power: 108 hp
    Oil capacity: 7 qts
    Propeller: Metal, diameter: 69 in
Wingspan: 33 ft 02 in
Wing Area (sq ft):   159.5
Length: 24 ft 01 in
Height: 8 ft 06 in
Wing Loading (lbs/sq ft):   10.5
Power Loading: (lbs/hp)   15.2
Weight
    Gross: 1670 lbs
    Empty: 1104 lbs
    Baggage: 120 lbs

Chapter 5

Cessna 150/152 Engines

There have been only two basic engines utilized in the Cessna 150 series airplanes. These are the Continental O-200 engines found in all Model 150s, and the Lycoming O-235 engines found in the 152s (Figs. 5-1, 5-2).

CONTINENTAL ENGINES

The Continental engines used in the 150s are now out of production. This does not mean they are not good engines, just that they are no longer made. The Continental O-200 engines were designed to operate on 80/87 octane fuel. This fuel, for a number of reasons, is no longer available; hence, there is no longer a market for engines using it. However, this should be a consideration when making a purchase, as "no longer in production" will mean dwindling parts, supplies, and higher costs for repairs.

In actuality, the O-200 engines are very similar to the O-300s found in the early Cessna Model 172s, just two less cylinders. Many small parts are interchangeable between the O-200 and O-300 engines.

Specifications: Continental O-200-A

Horsepower: 100 at 2750 rpm
Number of Cylinders: 4 Horizontally Opposed
Displacement: 200.91 cu. in.

Fig. 5-1. The Continental O-200 engine powers all Cessna 150 airplanes. (courtesy Teledyne Continental)

Bore:	4.0625 in.
Stroke:	3.875 in.
Compression Ratio:	7.0:1
Magnetos:	Slick 4001
Right:	Fires 28 degrees BTC upper
Left:	Fires 28 degrees BTC lower

Fig. 5-2. The AVCO Lycoming O-235 engine powers the Cessna 152s. Pictured here is the L2C version found on pre-'84 models. (courtesy AVCO Lycoming)

Firing Order:	1-3-2-4
Spark Plugs:	SH15
Gap:	.018 to .022 in.
Torque:	330 lbs-in.
Carburetor:	Marvel-Schebler MA-3-SPA
Alternator:	14 volts at 60 amps
Starter:	Automatic engagement
Tachometer:	Mechanical
Oil Capacity:	6 qts. (7 qts with external oil filter)
Oil Pressure	
Minimum at idle:	10 psi.
Normal:	30-60 psi.
Oil Temperature, Red Line:	225 Degrees F
Propeller Rotation:	Clockwise (view from rear)
Dry Weight:	200 lbs.

LYCOMING ENGINES

The basic Lycoming engine found in the 152 is the O-235. Cessna used two versions. The first is the O-235-L2C, which was first introduced in 1977 (1978 model) and remaining through 1982.

Although the O-235-L2C was designed to operate on 100LL avgas, the new Lycoming suffered from lead fouling problems, although to a lesser extent than did the Continental O-200 engines.

In 1983, the O-235-L2C was replaced with the O-235-N2C. The N2C has "lead gathering pockets" inside the combustion chamber. The new N2C version does, at this time, appear to be working well.

Spark plug life is a good indicator of reduced lead fouling. The plug life appears to be about three times greater than that of the L2C. This would also mean fewer valve problems too.

Specifications: Lycoming O-235-L2C & N2C

Horsepower:	(L2C)	110 at 2250 rpm
	(N2C)	108 at 2250 rpm
Number of Cylinders:		4 Horizontally Opposed
Displacement:		233.3 cu. in.
Bore:		4.375 in.
Stroke:		3.875 in.
Compression Ratio:		
(L2C)		8.5:1
(N2C)		8.1:1

Magnetos: Bendix S4LN-20 or S4LN-204 (right)

	S4LN-21 (left)
Slick	4250 (right)
	4281 or 4252 (left)

Firing Order: 1-3-2-4
Carburetor: Marvel-Schebler MA-3 or MA-3PA
Alternator: 28 volts after 1977
Starter: Automatic engagement
Tachometer Mechanical
Oil Capacity: 6 qts.
Propeller Rotation: Clockwise (view from rear)
Dry Weight: 252 lbs.

ENGINE TALK

Engines are the lifeblood of powered flight, and the more you know about them, the better. Here are a few definitions to help you understand and discuss airplane engines:

TBO: The "time between overhaul" recommended by the manufacturer as the maximum engine life. It has no legal bearing on airplanes not used in commercial service; it's only an indicator. Many well-cared-for engines last hundreds of hours beyond TBO—but not all.

*Remanufacture:** The complete disassembly, as-needed repair, alteration/updates, and inspection of an airplane engine. This includes bringing all engine specifications back to factory new limits. A factory remanufactured engine comes with new logs and zero time. FARs state that only the engine manufacturer, or a factory-approved agency (there are none), may "zero" an engine. The factory remanufactured engine is the next thing to a new engine.

Overhaul: The disassembly, inspection, cleaning, repair, and reassembly of an airplane engine. The work may be done to new limits or to service limits.

Top overhaul: The rebuilding of the head assemblies, but not of the entire engine. In other words, the case of the engine is not split, only the cylinders are pulled. Top overhaul is utilized to bring oil burning and/or low compression engines within specifications. It is a method of stretching the life of an otherwise sound engine. A top overhaul can include such work as valve replacement/grinding, cylinder replacement/repair, piston and ring replacement, etc.

---

*There is considerable confusion about the terms *remanufactured* and *rebuilt.* FAR 91.175 refers to factory rebuilt engines, and defines them as *remanufactured* (above). The key word is "factory."

It is not necessarily an indicator of a poor engine. The need for a "top" may have been brought on by such things as pilot abuse, lack of care, lack of use of the engine, or plain abuse (i.e., hard climbs and fast let-downs). An interesting note: The term top overhaul does not indicate the extent of the rebuild job (i.e., number of cylinders rebuilt or the completeness of the job).

New limits: The dimensions/specifications used when constructing a new engine. Parts meeting new limits will normally reach TBO with no further attention, save for routine maintenance.

Service limits: The dimensions/specifications below which use is forbidden. Many used engine parts will fit into this category; however, they are unlikely to last the full TBO, as they are already partially worn.

Magnaflux/Magnaglow: Terms associated with methods of detecting invisible defects in ferrous metals (i.e., cracks). Parts normally Magnafluxed/Magnaglowed are crankshafts, camshafts, piston pins, rocker arms, etc. Such inspections are routinely done during remanufacture and overhaul.

Nitriding: A method of hardening cylinder barrels and crankshafts. The purpose is to create a hard surface that resists wear, thereby extending the useful life of the part.

Chrome Plating: Used to bring the internal dimensions of the cylinders back to specifications. It produces a hard, machinable, and long-lasting surface. There is one major drawback of chrome plating: longer break-in times. However, an advantage of the chrome plating is its resistance to destructive oxidation (rust) within combustion chambers.

USED ENGINES

Many airplane ads proudly state the hours on the engine (i.e., 716 SMOH). Basically, this means that there have been 716 hours of operation since the engine was overhauled. Not stated is *how* it was used, or how *completely* it was overhauled. There are few standards.

The time on an engine, since new or overhaul, is an important factor when placing a value on an airplane. The recommended TBO, less the hours currently on the engine, is the time remaining. The difference between these times is the expected remaining life of the engine.

Three basic terms are normally used when referring to time on an airplane engine:

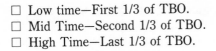

- ☐ Low time—First 1/3 of TBO.
- ☐ Mid Time—Second 1/3 of TBO.
- ☐ High Time—Last 1/3 of TBO.

Naturally, other variables come into play when referring to TBO: Are the hours on the engine since new, remanufacture, or overhaul? What type of flying has the engine seen? Was it flown on a regular basis? Lastly, what kind of maintenance did the engine get? The engine logbook will indicate whether the engine is operating on time since new, remanufacture, or overhaul. The logs should also be of some help in determining questions about engine maintenance.

Naturally, preventive maintenance should have been accomplished and logged throughout the engine's life (i.e., oil changes, plug changes, etc.). In accordance with FARs, all maintenance must be logged.

Airplanes that have not been flown on a regular basis—and maintained in a like fashion—will never reach full TBO. Manufacturers refer to regular usage as 20 to 40 hours monthly. However, there are few privately owned airplanes meeting the upper limits of this requirement. Let's face it, most of us don't have the time or money required for such constant use. This 20-to-40 hours monthly equates to 240 to 480 hours yearly. That's a lot of flying.

When an engine isn't run, acids and moisture in the oil will oxidize (rust) engine components. In addition, the lack of lubricant movement will cause the seals to dry out. Left long enough, the engine will seize and no longer be operable.

Just as hard on engines as no use is abuse. Hard climbs and fast descents, causing abnormal heating and cooling conditions, are extremely destructive to air-cooled engines. Training aircraft often exhibit this trait due to their type of usage (i.e., take off and landing practice).

The Overhauled Engine

Beware of the engine that has just a few hours on it since an overhaul. Perhaps something is not right with the overhaul, or it was a very cheap job, just to make the plane more salable..

When it comes to overhauls, I always recommend the large shops that specialize in aircraft engine rebuilding. I'm not saying that the local FBO can't do a good job; I just feel that the large organizations specializing in this work have more experience and equipment to work with. In addition, they have reputations to live up to, and most will back you in the event of difficulties.

Engines are expensive to rebuild/overhaul. Here are some typical costs for a complete overhaul (based on current 1987 pricing).

Engine	Cost
O-200	$3400—4500
O-235	$3500—4500

These prices include installation.

Cylinder Color Codes

When looking at the engine of an airplane you can sometimes see a little of the past work done on it. You will notice that some of the cylinders (jugs) may be painted or banded. The colors of the paint or band tell you about the physical properties of the individual cylinder.

Orange indicates a chrome-plated cylinder barrel.
Blue indicates a nitrided cylinder barrel.
Green indicates internal cylinder dimension is .010 oversize.
Yellow indicates .020 oversize.

AVIATION FUELS AND THEIR PROBLEMS

Airplane owners have recently been voicing many questions and concerns about the limited availability of 80/87 grade fuel, and the use of higher leaded fuel in engines rated for grade 80/87 fuel.

A quick look around the country indicates that fuel suppliers are not making 80/87 grade aviation fuel available. The suppliers claim there is too little profit in 80/87 manufacture and supply. They also state that the new 100LL avgas is a replacement for the 80/87. It all boils down to supply and demand: The customer will use the *supply* that the supplier *demands* him to! The trend is toward a complete phaseout of 80/87 aviation grade fuel.

Color Coding of Avgas

Avgas is color-coded to preclude introducing the incorrect fuel into your aircraft when refueling.

Red: 80 Octane containing .50ml lead/gal.
Blue: 100 Octane containing 2ml lead/gal.
Green: 100 Octane containing 3ml lead/gal.

It's interesting to note that the "Blue 100," also referred to as 100 LL (LL for low lead), contains four times the amount of lead as did the 80/87 octane fuel. This "low lead" fuel will gradually become the only fuel available for small piston airplane engines. It must be used as a replacement fuel whenever 80/87 is not available.

The continuous use of the 100LL fuel as a replacement for 80/87 *will* result in increased engine deposits both in the combustion chamber and in the engine oil, and subsequent increased spark plug maintenance and more frequent oil changes. The frequency of spark plug maintenance and oil drain periods can be controlled to some extent by the type of operation.

Reducing 100LL Problems

The following instructions are directed towards the operators of Continental O-200 engines; however, adherence by the operators of Lycoming O-235 engines can bring reduced engine maintenance benefits also.

Operation at full rich mixture requires more frequent maintenance; therefore, it is very important to learn—and use—proper leaning techniques.

To keep engine deposits at a minimum when using the higher leaded 100 LL avgas blue, it is essential that the following four conditions of operation and maintenance be met:

☐ Proper fuel management.
☐ Proper shutdown technique.
☐ Frequent oil changes.
☐ Additional spark plug maintenance.

Proper Fuel Management

The use of economy cruise engine leaning will keep deposits to a minimum, and, as a side benefit, reduce the direct operating (fuel) costs.

General Leaning Rules

1. Never lean the mixture from full rich during takeoff, climb, or high-performance cruise operation. (Exception: during takeoff from high elevation airports or during climb at higher altitudes, leaning may be required to eliminate roughness or the reduction of

power that may occur at full rich mixtures. In such instances the mixture should be adjusted only enough to obtain smooth engine operation.) Careful observation of temperature instruments should be practiced.

2. Always return the mixture to full rich before increasing power settings.

3. During the approach and landing sequence, the mixture should be placed in the full rich position. (Exception: unless landing at high elevation fields where leaning may be necessary.)

4. Recommended methods for setting maximum power or best economy mixture.

RPM/Airspeed Method. The engine tachometer and/or the airspeed indicator may be used to approximate the maximum power and best economy mixture ranges.

Set the controls for the desired cruise power as shown in the owner's manual, then gradually lean the mixture from full rich until either the tachometer or the airspeed indicator reach their highest readings. At peak indication, the engine is operating at maximum power.

Where best economy operation is desired, the mixture is first leaned from full rich to maximum power, then slowly continued until engine power is rapidly diminishing as noted by a decrease in airspeed. When this reduction occurs, enrich the mixture sufficiently to regain most of the lost airspeed or engine rpm. Some slight engine power and airspeed must be sacrificed to gain best economy mixture setting.

An alternate method of leaning at altitude is to lean the mixture until engine operation becomes slightly rough, then move the mixture control towards rich until the engine is again evenly firing.

Remember: Proper leaning will not only result in less engine deposits and reduced maintenance cost, but will provide more economical operation and fuel saving.

Proper Shutdown Technique. The deposit formation rate can be greatly reduced by controlling ground operations to minimize the separation of non-volatile components of the higher leaded aviation fuels. The formation rate is accelerated by low fuel mixture temperatures caused by the rich fuel/air mixtures associated with idling and taxiing operations.

To reduce the effects of this high deposit formation situation it is important that engine idling speeds should be set in the 600 to 650 rpm range with the idle mixture adjusted properly to provide smooth idling operation. Additionally, engine speed should be increased to 1200 rpm for one minute prior to shutdown. This will increase the combustion chamber temperature and allow the deposits to dissipate. After one minute, slow the engine down and lean until operation ceases.

Frequent Oil Changes. Many of the engine deposits formed by the use of the higher leaded 100LL fuel are in suspension within the engine oil, yet are not removed by a full flow filter. When large amounts of these contaminants in the oil reach a high temperature area of the engine they can be "baked out." This baking out, and the subsequent deposits left in such areas as the exhaust valve guides, can cause sticking valves. Left unattended, sticking valves can cause extensive engine damage. Extensive may be alternately spelled E-X-P-E-N-S-I-V-E!

When using the higher leaded fuels (100LL), the recommended oil drain period of 50 hours should not be extended, and if occurrences of valve sticking is noted, all valve guides should be reamed and a reduction made in the oil drain periods. It is not uncommon for oil changes to be made on a 25-hour basis.

Additional Spark Plug Maintenance. Spark plugs should be rotated from the top cylinder position to the bottom position on a 50-hour basis, and should be cleaned, inspected, and regapped on a 100-hour basis. Depending on the lead content of the fuel and the type of operation, more frequent cleaning of the spark plugs may be necessary.

If excessive spark plug lead fouling occurs, the selection of a hotter plug may be necessary. However, depending on the type of lead deposit formed, a colder plug may better resolve the problem. Where the majority of operation is at low power, such as patrol, a hotter plug would be advantageous. If the majority of operation is at high cruise power, a colder plug is recommended. If in doubt as to the plug temperature range that is proper for your particular circumstance, I recommend you pay a visit to your friendly mechanic and get his advice.

A Word from the FAA

In April 1977, the use of Tricresyl Phosphate (TCP) was approved for use in Lycoming and Continental engines that do not incorporate turbosuperchargers. TCP is a fuel additive that is used to prevent lead fouling. It is available from:

Alcor, Inc.
10130 Jones-Maltsberger Rd.
Box 32516
San Antonio, TX 73284
and from most FBOs.

AUTO FUELS

As a result of the scarcity of 80/87 avgas, there has been considerable controversy and discussion about the use of "auto" fuels (sometimes referred to as *mogas*) in certified aircraft engines. This would be in lieu of the 100LL products.

The use of auto fuels has many pros and cons. This debate has been going on for several years, and will probably continue until piston airplane engines are no longer used.

I feel it is up to the individual pilot to make his own choice about the use of non-aviation fuels in his airplane. To aid in this decision-making, consider the following:

1. Unleaded auto fuel is certainly less expensive than 100LL.

2. Auto fuel does appear to operate well in the older engines that require 80 octane fuel.

3. If you have a private gas tank/pump, it might be advantageous to utilize auto fuel. It'll be far easier to locate an auto fuel supplier willing to keep your tank filled than it will be to find an avgas supplier willing to make small deliveries. This could be the deciding factor at a small private strip.

4. There is a decided lack of consistency among the various brands of auto fuels (gasolines) and their additives. In particular, many low-lead auto fuels have alcohol in them. Alcohol is destructive to some parts of the typical aircraft fuel system.

5. The engine manufacturers claim the use of auto fuels will void warranty service. This is not really important unless you have a new or factory remanufactured engine.

6. Many FBOs are reluctant to make auto fuels available for reasons such as product liability and less profit.

However, just to fuel the fire even further, here is a partial reprint of Advisory Circular #AC 150/5190-"A, dated 4 Apr 72 (be familiar with this, as you will see it again, and you may someday need to quote from it to stand up for your rights!):

d. Restrictions on self-service.

Any unreasonable restriction imposed on the owners and operators of aircraft regarding the servicing of their own aircraft and equipment may be considered as a violation of agency policy. The owner of an aircraft should be permitted to fuel, wash, repair, paint, and otherwise take care of his own aircraft, provided there is no attempt to perform such services for others. Restrictions which have the effect of diverting activity of this type to a commercial enterprise amount to an exclusive right contrary to law."

If you desire further information about the legal use of auto fuels in your airplane, contact the EAA (Experimental Aircraft Association), which has an ongoing program of testing airplanes and obtaining STCs (Supplemental Type Certificates) for the use of auto fuel.

> EAA-STC
> Wittman Airfield
> Oshkosh, WI 54903

Mogas STCs are available from the EAA for the Cessna 150 at a minimal fee. The STCs allow the use of unleaded regular automobile gasoline manufactured to the ASTM Specification D-439 (American Society for Testing Materials, 1916 Race St., Phila., PA 19103).

Not all states comply with the ASTM specifications. The following is a list of states requiring compliance with this standard for automobile gasolines:

Arizona	Maryland
Arkansas	Montana
Alabama	Nebraska
California	Nevada
Colorado	New Mexico
Connecticut	New York
Florida	N. Carolina
Georgia	S. Carolina
Hawaii	N. Dakota
Idaho	S. Dakota
Iowa	Oklahoma
Indiana	Rhode Island
Kansas	Texas
Louisiana	Tennessee
Maine	Utah

Massachusetts   Virginia
Minnesota   Wisconsin
Mississippi   Wyoming

Petersen Aviation, Inc., also can provide auto fuel STCs for the Cessna 150. The Petersen STCs differ from the EAA STCs in that Petersen allows the use of leaded auto fuels. This provides an additional savings in hourly operation. For further information, contact:

Petersen Aviation, Inc.
Rt 1 Box 18
Minden, NE 68959
Phone: (308)832-2200

WARNING
A note of advice: Prior to purchasing the auto fuel STC, check with your insurance carrier and get their approval . . . *in writing.* Some aviation insurance companies are not keen on the use of mogas, and if you don't comply with their wishes, they could deny a claim.

CAUTION
Never use fuel containing alcohol!

ENGINE MONITORING
There are various gauges and instruments available for monitoring what is going on inside the engine.

Most, such as the tachometer, oil temperature, and oil pressure gauges are all familiar and found on the typical instrument panel. However there are others that will aid the pilot in closely monitoring the operation of his engine:

EGT: The *exhaust gas temperature* gauge measures the temperature of the exhaust gases as they enter the exhaust manifold. This instrument is extremely valuable for monitoring leaning procedures.

CHT: The *cylinder head temperature* gauge indicates the temperature of the cylinder heads. Problems such as inadequate engine cooling can be detected by its use.

Carburetor ice detector: The carburetor ice detector is designed to actually detect ice, not just low carburetor throat temperature. As ice is a product of both temperature and humidity, mere temperature indication is not satisfactory, as it does not relate the whole picture. The detector utilizes an optical probe in the carburetor

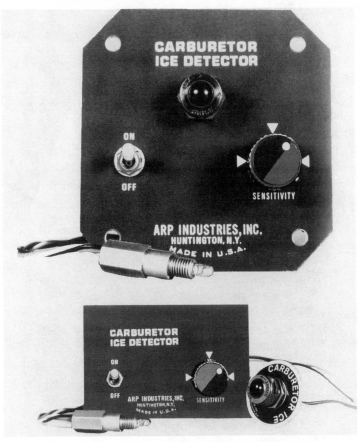

Fig. 5-3. This ice detector could save your life by informing you of ice forming inside the carburetor (courtesy of ARP Industries, Inc., 36 Bay Drive E., Huntington, NY 11743).

throat and is so sensitive that it can detect "frost" up to five minutes before ice begins to form, allowing the pilot plenty of time to take corrective action (Fig. 5-3).

EXTENDED WARRANTY

A recent entry into the aviation field is a commercially available extended warranty plan for engines; new, used, or overhauled.

The theory is not new, as automobile dealers have been selling similar coverage for many years to the purchasers of new and used automobiles. The warranty, actually called a service agreement, covers the major parts of the aircraft engine and protects you from spending large sums of money in repairs.

Compared to repair costs, the fee paid for this service agreement is nominal. For further information, contact:

> First Continental Engine Warranty, Inc.
> P.O. Box 16098
> Jackson, MS 39236
> Phone: (800)233-1099
>   MS: (601)352-4207

The following parts are covered by the service agreement:

- ☐ Pistons
- ☐ Piston Rings
- ☐ Connecting Rods
- ☐ Rod Bolts
- ☐ Rod Bearings
- ☐ Crankshaft
- ☐ Bearings
- ☐ Camshaft
- ☐ Timing Gear
- ☐ Valves
- ☐ Valve Guides
- ☐ Valve Springs
- ☐ Valve Spring Keepers
- ☐ Valve Spring Retainers
- ☐ Rocker Arms
- ☐ Rocker Arm Shafts
- ☐ Push Rods
- ☐ Lifters
- ☐ Oil Pump
- ☐ Counter Weight Assemblies
- ☐ Gear Case.

The engine case and cylinders are also covered if the mechanical failure was caused by any of the above listed internal engine parts.

PROPELLERS

Many pilots may not give much thought to the metal propeller. They should. Even though a high margin of safety is built into the design of metal propeller blades, failures do occur.

Most propeller blade failures occur because of fatigue cracks that started as dents, cuts, scars, scratches, nicks, or leading edge pits. Only in rare instances have failures been caused by material defects or surface discontinuities existing before the blades were placed in service.

Improperly performed repairs can also lead to failure. Fatigue failures of blades have occurred at the place where previous damage has been repaired. This may be due to the failure having actually started prior to the repair, and the repair merely amplifying the problem. Too much flexing of the blade—such as in blade-straightening or blade-pitching operations—can overstress the metal, causing it to fail.

Metal propeller blade failure may also occur in areas seldom inspected, such as under leading edge abrasion boots and under propeller blade decals. It is advisable to inspect these hidden areas when the propeller is serviced/repaired.

Another cause of metal propeller blade failure (though less frequent) is flutter. This flutter, a vibration, causes the ends of the blade to twist back and forth at a high frequency around an axis perpendicular to the crankshaft. At certain engine speeds, this vibration can become critical and, if the propeller is allowed to operate in this range, propeller blade failure may occur. At the very least, metal fatigue will result. It is for this reason that tachometer accuracy is so very important. Periodic tachometer accuracy checks should be made using reliable testing instruments. Then, by referencing your tachometer, you may avoid propeller speeds that can be damaging. These speeds are indicated as red arcs on the tachometer, and listed in the operations manual.

There are many stresses on a propeller. The propeller is at the end of the energy chain, and is responsible for efficiently converting engine power into thrust. During normal operation, four separate stresses are imposed on a propeller:

- ☐ Thrust.
- ☐ Torques.
- ☐ Centrifugal force.
- ☐ Aerodynamic force.

The stresses that normally occur in the propeller blades may be viewed as parallel lines of force that run within the blade approximately parallel to the surface. Additional stresses can be imposed by vibration caused by fluttering or uneven tracking of the blades.

When a defect occurs (scratch, nick, dent) these lines of force will be squeezed together, concentrating the stress. The increase in stress can be sufficient to cause a crack to start, which results in a greater stress concentration. This greater stress concentration causes the crack to enlarge until the inevitable blade failure.

Most blade failures occur within a few inches of the blade tip. However, failures can occur in other portions of the blade when dents, cuts, scratches, or nicks are ignored. *No* damage should be overlooked or allowed to go without repair.

When performing preflight inspection of the propeller, inspect not only the leading edge but the entire blade for erosion, scratches, nicks, and cracks. Regardless of how small any surface irregularities may appear, consider each as a stress point subject to fatigue failure.

The following tips will help you care for your propeller, and provide for its long life:

Keep the blades clean, as complete inspections cannot be made if they're covered with dirt, oil, or other foreign matter.

Avoid engine runup areas containing loose sand, stones, gravel, or broken asphalt. These particles can result in nicks to the propeller if sucked into it during run-up.

Propeller blades are not designed to be used as handles for moving an airplane.

During the normal 100-hour or annual inspection, the engine tachometer should be checked for accuracy to preclude operation in any restricted rpm range.

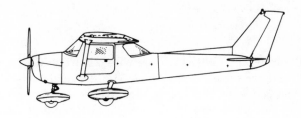

Chapter 6

ADs and Other Problems

Unfortunately, airplanes are not perfect in design or manufacture, and will from time to time require inspection/repairs/service as a result of unforeseen problems. These problems generally affect a large group/number of a particular make/model.

The required procedures are set forth in ADs (Airworthiness Directives). ADs are described in FAR Part 39, and *must* be complied with. The AD may be a simple one-time inspection, a periodic inspection (i.e., every 50 hours of operation), or a major modification to the airframe/engine.

Some ADs are relatively inexpensive to comply with, as they are basically inspections; others can be very expensive, involving extensive engine or airframe modifications/repairs. ADs are not normally handled like automobile "recalls," with the manufacturer being responsible for the costs involved. Sometimes the manufacturers will offer the parts/labor free of charge, but don't count on it. Even though ADs correct deficient design or poor quality control of parts or workmanship, AD compliance is usually paid for by the owner! There is no large consumer voice involving aircraft manufacturer responsibility.

Notice of an AD will be placed on the Federal Register and sent by mail to registered owners of the aircraft concerned. In an emergency, the information will be sent by telegram to registered owners. Either way, its purpose is to assure the integrity of your flying machine, and your safety.

The records of AD compliance become a part of the aircraft's logbooks. When looking at an airplane with purchase in mind, check for AD compliance.

AD LIST

Basically, the 150/152 airplanes are relatively AD-free; however, there are some. The following AD list should not be considered last end word; it is only an abbreviated guide to assist the owner/would-be owner/pilot in checking for AD compliance. Not all ADs listed affect all 150/152 airplanes.

For a complete check of ADs on an airplane, see your mechanic, or contact the AOPA (Aircraft Owners and Pilots Association):

AOPA
421 Aviation Way
Frederick, MD 21701

The latter will provide a list of ADs for a particular aircraft (by serial number) for a small fee. This type of search is highly accurate, and well worth the money spent.

Model 150

62-22-1: Reinstall the vacuum pump on all O-200A engines.

67-3-1: Modify the cabin heat unit on SN 15017001 through 15061328.

67-31-4: Modify the glove compartment on G and H models.

68-17-4: Test and rework as needed stall warning system on all models.

71-22-2: Inspect and replace as needed the nose gear fork after 1000 hours of operation.

72-3-3: Each 100 hours of operation, inspect the flap screw jack.

73-23-7: Replace the wing attachment fittings.

74-24-13: Replace altimeter if part no. 5932 or 5934.

74-26-9: Inspect Bendix magnetos for solid steel drive shaft bushing. Replace as necessary.

75-15-8: Rework the Beryl oil filter.

76-1-1: Placard speeds in the Aerobat if Flint long-range fuel tanks are installed.

77-2-9: Replace the flap actuator ball nut assembly on some models.

77-13-3: Reset the magnetic timing on the O-200 engine.

78-25-7: Replace the vertical fin brackets on some Aerobats.

79-8-3: Remove and/or modify the cigarette lighter wiring harness.

79-10-14: Install a vented fuel cap, and placard same.

79-13-8: Replace the Airborne dry air pump, if installed after 5-15-79.

79-18-5: Replace LiS02 ELT batteries.

80-6-3: Install a new flap cable clamp.

80-6-5: Test the magnetic impulse coupling.

80-11-4: Inspection of the eight nut plates on the vertical aft fin for cracks in the body or base of nut plates.

81-7-6: Inspect and replace if needed the AC fuel pump on O-200 engines.

81-15-3: Replace Brackett engine air filter.

81-16-5: Inspect and replace as needed the Slick magneto coil for cracks.

82-13-1: Periodic inspection and/or replace the gripper bushing block and check pistons/valves on engines with S-1200 series Bendix magnetos.

82-20-1: Inspect the Bendix impulse couplers prior to 300 hours usage on the magnetos.

83-17-83: Rebalance the ailerons on some Robertson STOL conversions.

83-22-6: Inspection of the aileron hinges.

84-26-2: Replace paper air filter elements each 500 hours.

Model 152

78-25-7: Replace the vertical fin brackets on some Aerobats.

79-2-6: Inspect or replace the heater muffler.

79-13-8: Replace the Airborne dry air pump, if installed after 5-15-79.

79-18-5: Replace LiS02 ELT batteries.

80-1-6: Modify the flap actuator assembly.

80-6-3: Install a new flap cable clamp.

80-6-5: Test the magnetic impulse coupling.

80-11-4: Inspection of the eight nut plates on the vertical aft fin for cracks in the body or base of nut plates.

80-25-2: Check and record valve tappet clearances on some engines (see AD for serial numbers).

80-25-7: Check the Stewart-Warner oil cooler for oil leaks. Replace if needed.

81-5-1: Check the fuel gauge markings.

81-16-5: Inspect and replace as needed the Slick magneto coil for cracks.

81-18-4: Replace the oil pump impeller and shaft on Lycoming O-235 engines.

83-22-6: Inspection of the aileron hinges.

84-26-2: Replace paper air filter elements each 500 hours.

DANGEROUS SEATS

"WARNING," says the 1968 Cessna service manual for 150 series airplanes, "It is extremely important that the pilot's seat stops are installed, since acceleration and deceleration could possibly permit the seat to become disengaged from the seat rails and create a hazardous situation, especially during takeoff and landing."

This is *very* serious. How would you feel if you had just started your climbout and suddenly were pitched over backwards, seat and all? From this new position it would be impossible to regain control of the aircraft.

For several years, letters to editors and various articles have been appearing in the various general aviation magazines pointing out the seat problem found in the Cessna single-engine airplanes. Basically, the pilot's seat is mounted to two aluminum tracks (rails), sliding back and forth for adjustment. A pin holds the seat position on the track. The following is quoted from *Airworthiness Alerts*, a monthly publication of the FAA Aviation Standards National Field Office, Oklahoma City, OK:

Cessna Single-Engine Models

Numerous reports indicate that difficulties continue to be encountered with seat attachments, structure, locking mechanisms, tracks, and stops. When required inspections are made, it is suggested the following items be examined:

1. Check the seat assembly for structural integrity.

2. Inspect the roller brackets for separation and wear.

3. Examine the locking mechanism (actuating arm, linkage, locking pin) for wear and evidence of impending failure.

4. Inspect the floor-mounted seat rails for condition and security, locking pin holes for wear, and rail stops for security.

5. Determine that the floor structure in the vicinity of

the rails is not cracked or distorted.

Defective or worn parts are a potential hazard which should be given prompt attention. Accomplish repair and/or replacement of damaged components in accordance with the manufacturer's service publications.

NOTE: This article was previously published in Alerts No. 32, dated March 1981. The same type problems are still being reported.

The NTSB (National Transportation Safety Board) has identified these problems as the probable cause in several fatal accidents.

I strongly recommend that you keep this seat problem in mind at preflight time, and always check the seat after locking it in place.

EXPENSIVE STARTERS

In later 150 models, the starter switch was incorporated as a part of the ignition switch. On the earlier models the starter was activated by pulling a T handle mounted on the instrument panel. The latter has never been a problem except for infrequent cable breaks. However, when this happens, the pilot can either hand-prop the engine (which is dangerous to those unschooled in this method) or open the cowl, reach in, and depress the starter switch. If you elect to do the manual depress, be sure the engine throttle is set at its lowest setting, the parking brake is set, and the wheels chocked (better yet, have some knowledgable person sitting in the cabin to monitor the airplane).

If the key start fails, you will have to hand-prop the airplane. When it fails, you can count on spending several hundred dollars in repairs to the starter clutch unit. This has been a prevailing problem with all key start 150 airplanes.

The rate of mechanical failure of the older pull system is very low, and repairs considerably more economical.

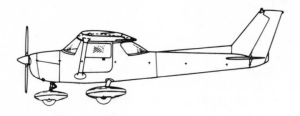

Chapter 7

Buying a Used Airplane

Once the decision has been made to purchase an airplane, a game plan must be set up to make the purchase in an orderly manner—perhaps a checklist arrangement. After all, pilots are familiar with checklists.

The checklist is made of three parts: The search, the inspection, and the paperwork.

THE SEARCH

Locating a good used 150 or 152 should not be difficult. The hard part is in finding it *where* you want it, and at a price that is agreeable. The search for a good used Cessna 150/152 does not usually have to be wide and exhaustive, as simply by sheer numbers, there are so many. This is good for the buyer, as it assures an adequate selection from which to choose.

As there are many model years and price ranges to select from, the purchaser is encouraged to set a range of expectations. This could be based on features desired, options available, a particular favorite model—or, most likely, the cash available for such a purchase.

The search starts locally, as this makes it easy to see what is available on the market. In fact, the search usually starts at the home field. If you know the FBO and feel comfortable with him, then perhaps this is a good way to do your searching. Tell him what you're looking for. It could be that the FBO is considering selling one of his trainers. If not, he will know of airplanes for sale—or nearly for sale—that have yet to be advertised. After all, he is an insider to the business.

If there is nothing of interest at your airport, then broaden the search. Check the bulletin boards at other nearby airports. While you're checking the bulletin boards, ask around. Then walk around and look for airplanes with "For Sale" signs in the windows.

While walking around the tiedown area, pay particular attention to airplanes that appear to be little used. Sometimes the owner of a seldom-flown airplane will suddenly sell his plane if approached by a purchaser equipped with the proper interest (and money). You could even put an "Airplane Wanted" ad on the bulletin boards.

Reading the Ads

Most ads for airplanes for sale will make use of various more-or-less standard abbreviations. These abbreviations describe the individual airplane, and tell how it is equipped. Also in the ad will be a telephone number, but seldom a location of where the airplane is located. The clue here is the area code. A typical ad would appear as:

> 65 C150,4106TT,265 SMOH,June ANN,FGP,
> NAV/COM,ELT,NDH. $5750 firm.
> 800-555-1212

Translated, this ad reads: For sale, a 1965 Cessna 150 airplane with 4106 total hours on the airframe, and an engine with 265 hours since a major overhaul. The next annual inspection is due in June. It is equipped with a full gyro instrument panel, has a navigation and communication radio, an Emergency Locator Transmitter, and, best of all, the airplane has no damage history. The price is $5750, and the seller claims he will not bargain. (Most do, however.) Last is the telephone number.

As you can see, there sure was a lot of information inside those three little lines.

To assist you in reading these ads, see Appendix A for a complete listing of the popular advertising abbreviations and Appendix B for a listing of Area Codes and their locations.

Local newspapers sometimes have airplanes listed in their classified ads, and these should be checked. However, in this day of specialization, several publications have become leaders in airplane advertising.

Trade-A-Plane is the king of all aviation advertising. The "yellow sheet," as it's sometimes called, is published three times monthly. The paper contains commercial advertising of just about everything and anything aviation-related. *Trade-A-Plane* is required reading for all aviation buffs, even if not actively searching for an airplane. *Trade-A-Plane* is available from:

> *Trade-A-Plane*
> Crossville
> Tenn 38555

Aircraft Owners Multi-Listing is a computer-generated listing of airplanes for sale. The listings are custom-made for each patron and can be as narrow or broad as the customer wants. Usually the listings are based on make, model, year, and price. For further information, contact:

> *Aircraft Owners MLS, Inc.*
> 200 North Andrews Ave.
> Fort Lauderdale, FL 33301,
> Phone: (305) 462-2524

or

> 1430 Arroyo Way
> Walnut Creek, CA 94596
> Phone: (800)327-9630

Other listings of used airplanes can be found in the various flight-oriented magazines (i.e., *AOPA Pilot, Flying, Plane & Pilot, Private Pilot,* etc.).

Searching for a good used airplane can be expensive and very time-consuming. You'll read ads, make telephone calls (always long distance) and even have to travel great distances to see the airplanes that are advertised.

Often I've seen what really looked interesting in an ad (words always look good), called the telephone number, listened to the seller's spiel about his wonderful airplane, then spent my time and my money to travel halfway across the country to look at the airplane.

All too often the airplane that was represented as a "10" turned out to be a gasping "2" or "3." Perhaps in the eyes of the owner the airplane was a 10, but not in mine. I would never purchase an airplane unseen, but it is done every day—and very successfully by many people. The choice—and risk—is up to the purchaser.

Some of these "sight unseen" sales are handled by merely reading the ad and conversing with the seller; others involve postal exchanges of photographs and copies of the logbooks. Now, through the use of state-of-the-art electronics and home video systems, it is possible to see a plane long distance.

Air Show, an aircraft marketing firm, has recently introduced a complete sales system designed to aid the long distance buyer. Air Show lists aircraft for sale in their paper and lists a toll free "800" telephone number to call for further information.

Air Show has a 15-minute VHS-formatted videotape documentary about each airplane they list for sale. If, after the telephone inquiry, the airplane interests you, a copy of the tape can be purchased. Then, in the privacy and convenience of your own home, inspection of the prospective aircraft can be made.

These video recordings follow a general walk-around inspection format, and are, for the most part, filmed outside, and not under "studio" conditions. The net result is a very informative video representation of the aircraft being examined. For more information about this new service, contact:

Air Show Journal
45 West Broadway
Suite 205
Eugene, OR 97401
Phone: (800)247-9005
in OR: (503)344-7813

Used Trainers

Most—but not all—150/152 airplanes have been used as trainers at one time or another in their lives. After all, this is what they were designed for. Keep this in mind when shopping.

A trainer was probably kept by an FBO, and was subject to hard use—and often lots of abuse. In later years this abuse can show up in the form of unusual flying characteristics commonly known as "out of rigging." This can be caused by past stress on the airframe, or improperly corrected damage to the airframe. In almost all cases the nosewheel will shimmy from the thousands of landings at the hands of neophytes. The doors and seats have been operated thousands of times and the controls will be sloppy. In short, everything will have extensive wear.

On the brighter side, the FBO, using such airplanes on a commercial basis, had to maintain them in a stiffer manner than the individual owner. Instead of annual inspections, the FBO had 100-hour inspections. Being used as a trainer, the plane was subjected to more careful preflight inspections than any other type of airplane. The eagle-eyed student will usually not overlook even very minor problems that the rest of us may.

With its continuous use, the trainer's engine is probably in better shape than one that has only been flown 20 hours in the past year. Engines thrive on constant use and lubrication. By the same token, training is hard on engines if not performed properly. In particular, I am referring to hard climbs that overheat an engine and the fast, low-power let-downs that supercool the cylinders. Either of these scenerios will lead to early engine failure, and subsequent high maintenance expenses.

Don't let an airplane that was a trainer be eliminated from your list of possibilities, though; just be careful. There is nothing on either a 150 or 152 that cannot be repaired just like new. But such repairs will cost money.

It is certainly a tribute to these fine little airplanes that they can take the abuse and punishment of training, yet continue many thousands of hours with little or no serious structural problems. They are tough planes.

THE INSPECTION

The object of the pre-purchase inspection of a used airplane is to preclude the purchase of a "dog." No one wants to buy someone else's troubles. The pre-purchase inspection must be completed in an orderly manner. Take your time during this inspection; a few extra minutes spent inspecting could well save you thousands of dollars later.

The very first item of inspection is a question directed to the current owner: "Why are you selling it?" Of course, if the seller has something to hide, you may not get a correct answer. Fortunately, most people will answer honestly. Often the owner is moving up to a larger airplane, and if so he will start to tell you all about his new prospective purchase. Let him talk; you can learn a lot about the owner by listening to him.

You can gain insight into his flying habits and how he treated the plane you are considering purchasing. Perhaps he has other commitments (i.e., spouse says sell, or perhaps he can no longer afford the plane). Financial or family pressures can work to your advantage; however, there is a warning here also. If the seller is having financial difficulties, consider the quality of maintenance that was performed on the airplane.

Ask the seller if he knows of any problems or defects with the airplane. Most sellers will give you their honest answer, but there could be things he doesn't know about.

Remember: *Buyer beware*: it is *your* money and *your* safety.

Definitions

Airworthy: The airplane must conform to the original type certificate, or those STCs (Supplemental Type Certificates) issued for this particular airplane (by serial number). In addition the airplane must be in safe operating condition, relative to wear and deterioration.

Annual Inspection: All small airplanes must be inspected annually by an FAA-certified Airframe and Powerplant mechanic who holds an IA (Inspection Authorization), by an FAA certified repair station, or by the airplane's manufacturer. This is a complete inspection of the airframe, powerplant, and all subassemblies.

100-Hour Inspection: Is of the same scope as the annual, and is required on all commercially operated small airplanes (i.e., rental, training, etc.), and must be accomplished after every 100 hours of operation. This inspection may be performed by an FAA-certified Airframe and Powerplant mechanic without an IA rating. An annual inspection will fulfill the 100-hour requirement, but the reverse is not true.

Preflight Inspection: A thorough inspection, by the pilot, of an aircraft prior to flight. The purpose is to spot obvious discrepancies by inspection of the exterior, interior, and engine of the airplane.

Preventive Maintenance: FAR Part 43 lists a number of maintenance operations that are considered preventive in nature and may be performed by a certificated pilot on an airplane he/she owns, provided the airplane is not flown in commercial service. (These operations are described in Chapter 8 of this book.)

Repairs and Alterations: There are two classes of repairs and/or alterations: *Major* and *Minor*.

Major repairs and alterations must be approved for a return to service by an FAA-certified Airframe and Powerplant mechanic holding an IA authorization, a repair station, or by the FAA.

Minor repairs and alterations may be returned to service by an FAA-certified Airframe and Powerplant mechanic.

Airworthiness Directives: Often called ADs, are defined in FAR Part 39, and must be complied with. As described in Chapter 6, they are a required maintenance/repair step.

Files of Ads and their requirements are kept by mechanics and the FAA offices. A compliance check of ADs is a part of the annual inspection.

Service Difficulty Reports: Referred to as SDRs, are prepared by the FAA from Malfunction or Defect Reports (MDRs) that are initiated by owners, pilots, and mechanics. SDRs are not the word of law that ADs are; however, they should be adhered to for your own safety.

The Visual Inspection

The visual inspection of a used airplane is a very thorough preflight, with a few extras included. It's divided into four simple, yet logical, steps.

1. The cabin: Open the door and look inside, notice the general condition of the interior. Does it appear clean, or has it just been scrubbed after a long period of inattention? Look in the corners, just as you would if you were buying a used car. Does the air smell musty and damp? Is the headliner in one tight piece, and the upholstery unfrayed? What condition are the door panels in? The care given the interior of an airplane can be a good indication of what care was given to the remainder of the airplane. If you have purchased used cars in the past, and have been successful, you are qualified for this phase of the inspection.

Look at the instrument panel. Does it have what you want/need? Are the instruments in good condition, or are there knobs missing and glass faces broken? Is the equipment all original, or have there been updates made? If updates have been made, are they neat in appearance and workable? I say workable, because updating— particularly in avionics—is often done haphazardly, with results that are neither attractive nor workable.

Look out the windows. Are they clear, unyellowed, and uncrazed? Side windows are not expensive to replace, and you can do it yourself. Windshields are another story, and another price.

Check the operation of the doors. They should close and lock with little effort. No outside light should be seen around edges of the doors.

Check the seats for freedom of movement and adjustability. *Check the seat tracks and the adjustment locks for damage. The seat tracks and locks have long been a recognized problem with Cessna airplanes.*

2. Airframe: Do a walk-around and look for the following:

Is the paint in good condition, or is some of it laying on the ground under the airplane? Paint jobs are expensive, yet necessary for the protection of the metal surfaces from corrosive elements. Paint jobs should also please the eye of the beholder. A good paint job may cost in excess of $2500.

Dents, wrinkles, or tears of the metal skin may indicate prior damage—or just careless handling. Each discrepancy must be examined very carefully by an experienced mechanic. Total consideration of all the dings and dents should tell if the airplane has had an easy or a rough life.

Corrosion or rust on skin surfaces or control systems should be cause for alarm. Corrosion is to aluminum what rust is to iron. It's destructive. Any corrosion or rust should be brought to the attention of a mechanic for his judgement. Corrosion that appears as only minor skin damage may continue, unseen, into the interior structure. Damage such as this creates dangerous structural problems that can be very costly to repair. Having a little corrosion in the wing structure is similar to having a little lung cancer. The word "little" is irrelevant.

Check for fuel leaks around the wings, in particular where the wings attach to the fuselage. If leakage evidence is seen, have a mechanic check its source.

The landing gear should be checked for evidence of being sprung. Check the tires for signs of unusual wear that might indicate other structural damage. Also look at the nosewheel oleo strut for signs of fluid leakage and proper extension.

Move all the control surfaces, and check each for damage. They should be free and smooth in movement. When the controls are centered, the surfaces should also be centered. If they are not centered, a problem in the control rigging exists.

3. Engine: Open or remove the cowling to inspect the engine. If you cannot see the engine, you cannot inspect it! Search for signs of oil leakage. Do this by looking at the engine, the inside of the cowl, and on the firewall. If the leaks are bad enough, there will be oil dripping to the ground or onto the nosewheel. Naturally, the seller has probably cleaned all the old oil drips away; however, oil leaves stains. Look for these stains.

Check all the fuel and vacuum hoses/lines for signs of deterioration or chafing. Also check the connections for tightness and/or signs of leakage.

Check control linkages and cables for obvious damage and ease of movement. Be sure none of the cables are frayed.

Check the battery box and battery for corrosion.

Check the propeller for damage, such as nicks, cracks, or gouges. Even very small defects can cause stress areas on the prop (see Chapter 5). Any visible damage to a propeller must be checked by a mechanic. Also check it for movement that would indicate propeller looseness at the hub.

Check the exhaust pipes for rigidity, then reach inside them by rubbing your finger along the inside wall. If your finger comes back perfectly clean, you can be assured that someone has cleaned the inside of the pipe—possibly to remove the oily deposits that form there when an engine is burning a lot of oil. If your fingers come out of the pipe covered with a black oily goo, have your mechanic determine the cause. It could only be a carburetor in need of adjustment. It could also be caused by a large amount of oil blow-by, the latter indicating an engine in need of large expenditures for overhaul. A light grey dusty coating indicates proper operation.

Check for exhaust stains on the belly of the plane to the rear of the exhaust pipe. This area has probably been washed, but look anyway. If you find black oily goo, then, as above, see your mechanic.

4. Logbooks: If you are satisfied with what you've seen up to this point, then go back to the cabin, have a seat, and check that all required paperwork is with the airplane. This includes:

☐ Airworthiness Certificate
☐ Aircraft Registration Certificate
☐ FCC Station License
☐ Flight manual or operating limitations
☐ Logbooks (airframe, engine and propeller)
☐ Current equipment list
☐ Weight & balance chart

These items are required by the FARs to be in the plane (except for the logs, which must be available).

Pull out the logbooks and start reading them. Sitting there will also allow you to look once again around the cockpit.

Be sure you're looking at the proper logs for this particular aircraft, and that they are the original logs. Sometimes logbooks get "lost" and are replaced with new ones. This can happen because of carelessness or theft. This is why many owners do not keep their logs in the plane, and may only provide copies for a sales inspection. Replacement logs may be lacking very important information, or could be outright frauds. Fraud is not unheard of in the used airplane business. Be on your guard if the original logs are not available.

Start with the airframe log by looking in the back for the AD compliance section (see Chapter 6 for a list of the ADs). Check that the list is up-to-date, and that any required periodic inspections have been made. Now go back to the most recent entry; it probably is an annual or 100-hour inspection. The annual inspection will be a statement that reads:

> March 21, 1985   Total Time: 3126 hrs.
> I certify that this aircraft has been
> inspected in accordance with an annual
> inspection and was determined to be in
> airworthy condition.
>
> signed here
> IA # 0000000

From this point back to the first entry in the logbook you'll be looking for similar entries, always keeping track of the total time, for continuity purposes and to indicate the regularity of usage (i.e., number of hours flown between inspections). Also, you will be looking for indications of major repairs and modifications. This will be signaled by the phrase, "Form 337 filed." A copy of this form should be with the logs, and will tell what work was done. The work may also be described in the logbook.

Form 337, Major Repair and Alteration, is filed with the FAA, and copies are a part of the official record of each airplane. They are retrievable from the FAA, for a fee.

The engine log will be quite similar in nature to the airframe log, and will contain information from the annual/100-hour inspections. Total engine time will be given, and possibly an indication of time since any overhaul work, although you may have to do some math here. It's quite possible that this log—and engine—will not be the original for the aircraft. As long as the facts are well-documented in both logs, there is no cause for alarm. After all, this would be the case if the original engine was replaced with a factory rebuilt one, or even a used engine from another plane.

Pay particular attention to the numbers that indicate the results of a differential compression check. These numbers are the best single indicator of the overall health of an engine.

Each number is given as a fraction, with the bottom number always being 80. The 80 indicates the air pressure that was utilized for the check. 80 psi (pounds per square inch) is the industry standard. The top number is the air pressure that the combustion chamber was able to maintain while being tested. 80 would be perfect, but it isn't attainable, it will always be less. The reason for the lower number is the air pressure loss that results from loose, worn, or broken rings; scored or cracked cylinder walls; or burned, stuck, or poorly seated valves. There are methods mechanics use to determine which of the above is the cause and, of course, repair the damage.

Normal readings would be no less than 70/80, and should be uniform (within 2 or 3 lbs) for all cylinders. A discrepancy between cylinders could indicate the need of a top overhaul of one or more cylinders. The FAA says that a loss in excess of 25 percent is cause for further investigation. That would be a reading of 60/80. (Such a low reading as this indicates a very tired engine in need of considerable work and expenditures.)

Read the information from the last oil change; it may contain a statement about debris found on the oil screen or in the oil filter. However, oil changes are often performed by owners, and may or may not be recorded in the log, even though the FARs requires all maintenance to be logged. If the oil changes are recorded, how regular were they? I prefer every 25 hours, but 50 is the norm. Is there a record of oil analysis available? If so, ask for it.

If the engine has been top overhauled or majored, there will be a description of the work performed, a date, and the total time on the engine when the work was accomplished.

Check to see if the ADs have been complied with, and the appropriate entries made in the log (see Chapter 6 for a listing of the ADs).

The Test Flight

The test flight is a flight to determine if the airplane "feels" right to you. The flight should last at least 30 minutes, but two hours would not be too much.

For insurance purposes, I recommend that either the owner or a competent flight instructor accompany you on the test flight. This will also eliminate problems of currency, ratings, etc., with the FAA, and it will foster better relations with the owner.

After starting the engine, pay particular attention to the gauges. Do they jump to life, or are the sluggish? Watch the oil pressure gauge in particular. Did the oil pressure rise within a few seconds of start? Check the other gauges. Are they indicating as should be expected? Check them during your ground run-up, then again during the takeoff and climbout. Do the numbers match those called for in the operations manual? In order to pay more attention to the gauges it might be advisable to have the other pilot make the takeoff.

After you're airborne, check the gyro instruments. Be sure they are stable.

Check the ventilation and heating system for proper operation.

Do a few turns, stalls, and some level flight. Does the airplane perform as expected? Can it be trimmed for hands-off flight?

Check all the avionics for proper operation (NAV/COMM, MBR, ADF, LORAN, ILS, etc.). A complete check may require a short cross-country flight to an instrument-equipped airport. That's all right; it will give you time to see if you like the plane.

Return to the airport and make a couple of landings. Check for proper brake operation and for nosewheel shimmy.

After returning to the parking ramp, open the engine compartment and look again for oil leaks. Also, check along the belly for indications of oil leakage and blow-by. A short flight should be enough to "dirty" things up again, if they had been dirty to begin with.

If, after the test flight, you decide not to purchase the airplane, it would be ethical to at least offer to pay for the fuel used.

Mechanic's Inspection

If you are still satisified with the airplane and desire to pursue the matter further, then have it inspected by an A&P or AI. This inspection will cost you a few dollars; however, it could save you thousands. The average for a pre-purchase inspection is three to four hours labor, at shop rates. That can be as low as $75, even here in Virginia.

The mechanic will accomplish a search of ADs, a complete check of the logs, and an overall check of the plane. A compression check and a borescope examination must be made to determine the internal condition of the engine. A borescope examination means looking into a cylinder and viewing the top of the piston, the valves, and the cylinder walls. This is done by use of a device called a borescope.

Always use your own mechanic for the pre-purchase inspection. By this I mean someone *you* are paying to watch out for *your* interests, not someone who may have an interest in the sale of the plane (i.e., employee of the seller).

Have the plane checked even if an annual was just done, unless you know and trust the AI who did the inspection. You may be able to make a deal with the owner over the cost of the mechanic's inspection, particularly if an annual is due.

It's not uncommon to see airplanes listed for sale with the phrase "annual at date of sale." I am always leary of this, because I don't know who did the annual, or how complete the annual was. All annuals are not created equal! An annual at the date of sale is coming with the airplane, done by the seller, as part of the sale. Who is looking out for *your* interests?

In each of my books about purchasing used airplanes, I always give the following advice:

If an airplane seller refuses you anything that has been mentioned in this chapter, then thank him for his time, walk away, and look elsewhere. Do not let a seller control the situation. Your money, your safety, and possibly your very life are at stake. Airplanes are not hot sellers, and there is rarely a line forming to make a purchase. *You* are the buyer; *you* have the final word.

In retrospect, after a few sales pitches I've recently heard, I would make the "thanking" part optional.

THE PAPERWORK

You have decided this airplane is it, and just cannot do without it. All inspections have been made, and you are satisfied the airplane will suit your needs. Is the price agreeable?

Used Airplane Prices

Used airplane prices can fluctuate to the extreme, and are dependent on more than the physical airframe and its contents. The actual selling price is the amount mutually agreed on by the seller and buyer. This agreed-upon sum is arrived at by bargaining.

Bargaining, or the trading or price offers and counter-offers, is the norm in aircraft trade. The concept of bargaining is to find the point where the owner's selling price equals the buyer's purchase price.

The selling price is the least amount the owner will take for his airplane, and the purchasing price is the most the buyer will pay.

An old friend who has bought and sold airplanes for a living sums it up thus: "The selling price is that asked for the one-owner, super-clean, low-time, family pride of an airplane. The purchasing price is that offered for the same box of rocks!"

To sum it up: How bad does the seller want to sell, and how bad does the buyer want to buy?

Now you're ready to sit down and complete the paperwork that will lead to ownership.

Title Search

The first step in the purchasing of an airplane is to assure the craft has a clear title. This is done by a title search.

A title search is accomplished by checking the aircraft's individual records at the Mike Monroney Aeronautical Center in Oklahoma City, Oklahoma. These records include title information, chain of ownership, Major Repair/Alteration (Form 337) information, and other data pertinent to a particular airplane. The FAA files this information by N-number.

The object of a title search is to ascertain that there are no liens or other hidden encumberances, against the ownership of the airplane. This search may be done by you, your attorney, or other representative selected by you.

Since most prospective purchasers would find it inconvenient to travel to Oklahoma City to do the search themselves, it is advisable to contract with a third party specializing in this service to do the searching. One such organization is the AOPA (Airplane Owners and Pilots Association), which has an Oklahoma City office just for this purpose. For further information, contact:

AOPA
421 Aviation Way
Frederick, MD 21701
Phone: (301)695-2000

There are other organizations that provide similar services. They advertise in *Trade-A-Plane*.

In addition to title searches, AOPA offers inexpensive title insurance, which protects the owner against unrecorded liens, FAA recording mistakes, or other clouds on the title.

Documents

The following documents must be given to you with your airplane:

1. Bill of Sale
2. Airworthiness Certificate
3. Logbooks
   a. Airframe
   b. Engine/propeller
4. Equipment List (including weight and balance data)
5. Flight Manual

Forms to be Completed

AC Form 8050-2, Bill of Sale, is the standard means of recording transfer of ownership (Figs. 7-1, 7-2).

AC Form 8050-1, Aircraft Registration, is filed with the Bill of Sale, or its equivalent (Fig. 7-3). If you are purchasing the airplane under a Contract of Conditional Sale, then that contract must accompany the registration application in lieu of the AC Form 8050-2. The pink copy of the registration is retained by you, and will remain in the airplane until the new registration is issued by the FAA.

AC 8050-41, Release of Lien, must be filed by the seller if a lien is recorded (Fig. 7-4).

AC 8050-64, Assignment of Special Registration Number, is for "vanity" registration numbers. All U.S. aircraft registration numbers consist of the prefix N, and are followed by:

☐ One to five numbers,
☐ One to four numbers and a letter suffix, or
☐ One to three numbers and a two letter suffix.

This is similar to obtaining personalized license plates for your automobile.

FCC (Federal Communications Commission) Form 404, Application for Aircraft Radio Station License, must be completed if you have any radio equipment on board (Fig. 7-5). The tear-off section will remain in your airplane as temporary authorization until the

UNITED STATES OF AMERICA

DEPARTMENT OF TRANSPORTATION — FEDERAL AVIATION ADMINISTRATION

AIRCRAFT BILL OF SALE INFORMATION

PRIVACY ACT OF 1974 (PL 93-579) requires that users of this form be informed of the authority which allows the solicitation of the information and whether disclosure of such information is mandatory or voluntary; the principal purpose for which the information is intended to be used; the routine uses which may be made of the information gathered; and the effects, if any, of not providing all or any part of the requested information.

The Federal Aviation Act of 1958 requires the registration of each United States civil aircraft as a prerequisite to its operation. The applicant for registration must submit proof of ownership that meets the requirements prescribed in Part 47 of the Federal Aviation Regulations.

This form identifies the aircraft being purchased, and provides space for purchaser and seller identification and signature. This is intended only to be a suggested bill of sale form which meets the recording requirements of the Federal Aviation Act, and the regulations issued thereunder. In addition to these requirements, the form of bill of sale should be drafted in accordance with the pertinent provisions of local statutes and other applicable federal statutes.

The following routine uses are made of the information gathered:

(1) To support investigative efforts of investigation and law enforcement agencies of Federal, state, and foreign governments.

(2) To serve as a repository of legal documents used by individuals and title search companies to determine the legal ownership of an aircraft.

(3) To provide aircraft owners and operators information about potential mechanical defects or unsafe conditions of their aircraft in the form of airworthiness directives.

(4) To provide supporting information in court cases concerning liability of individual in law suits.

(5) To serve as a data source for management information for production of summary descriptive statistics and analytical studies in support of agency functions for which the records are collected and maintained.

(6) To respond to general requests from the aviation community or the public for statistical information under the Freedom of Information Act or to locate specific individuals or specific aircraft for accident investigation, violation, or other safety related requirements.

(7) To provide data for the automated aircraft registration master file.

(8) To provide documents for microfiche backup record.

(9) To provide data for development of the aircraft registration statistical system.

(10) To prepare an aircraft register in magnetic tape and publication form required by ICAO agreement containing information on aircraft owners by name, address, N-Number, and type aircraft, used for internal FAA safety program purposes and also available to the public (individuals, aviation organizations, direct mail advertisers, state and local governments, etc.) upon payment of user charges reimbursing the Federal Government for its costs.

Fig. 7-1. Privacy Act statement found on all FAA forms.

new license is sent to you (Fig. 7-6).

Most forms sent to the FAA or FCC will result in the issuance of a document to you. Be patient; it all takes time.

ASSISTANCE

Although not complicated, there are many forms to be completed when purchasing an airplane, and you may wish to seek assistance in filling them out. You can check with your FBO, or call upon another party, such as the AOPA.

The AOPA, for a small fee, will provide closing services via telephone, and prepare/file the necessary forms to complete the transaction. This is particularly nice if the parties involved in the transaction are spread all over the country, as would be the case if you are purchasing an airplane "sight unseen."

Another source of assistance in completing the necessary paperwork is your bank. This is particularly true if the bank has a vested interest in your airplane (i.e., they hold the note!).

Fig. 7-2. 8050-2, Aircraft Bill of Sale.

UNITED STATES OF AMERICA DEPARTMENT OF TRANSPORTATION
FEDERAL AVIATION ADMINISTRATION-MIKE MONRONEY AERONAUTICAL CENTER
AIRCRAFT REGISTRATION APPLICATION

CERT. ISSUE DATE

UNITED STATES
REGISTRATION NUMBER **N**

AIRCRAFT MANUFACTURER & MODEL

AIRCRAFT SERIAL No.

FOR FAA USE ONLY

TYPE OF REGISTRATION (Check one box)

☐ 1. Individual ☐ 2. Partnership ☐ 3. Corporation ☐ 4. Co-owner ☐ 5. Gov't. ☐ 8. Foreign-owned Corporation

NAME OF APPLICANT (Person(s) shown on evidence of ownership. If individual, give last name, first name, and middle initial.)

TELEPHONE NUMBER: (   )   −

ADDRESS (Permanent mailing address for first applicant listed.)

Number and street: _____

Rural Route: _____

P.O. Box: _____

CITY	STATE	ZIP CODE

☐   **CHECK HERE IF YOU ARE ONLY REPORTING A CHANGE OF ADDRESS**

ATTENTION! Read the following statement before signing this application.

A false or dishonest answer to any question in this application may be grounds for punishment by fine and / or imprisonment (U.S. Code, Title 18, Sec. 1001).

CERTIFICATION

I/WE CERTIFY:

(1) That the above aircraft is owned by the undersigned applicant, who is a citizen (including corporations) of the United States.

(For voting trust, give name of trustee: _____), or:

CHECK ONE AS APPROPRIATE:

a. ☐ A resident alien, with alien registration (Form 1-151 or Form 1-551) No. _____

b. ☐ A foreign-owned corporation organized and doing business under the laws of (state or possession) _____ , and said aircraft is based and primarily used in the United States. Records of flight hours are available for inspection at _____

(2) That the aircraft is not registered under the laws of any foreign country; and
(3) That legal evidence of ownership is attached or has been filed with the Federal Aviation Administration.

NOTE: If executed for co-ownership all applicants must sign. Use reverse side if necessary.

TYPE OR PRINT NAME BELOW SIGNATURE

	SIGNATURE	TITLE	DATE
EACH PART OF THIS APPLICATION MUST BE SIGNED IN INK.	SIGNATURE	TITLE	DATE
	SIGNATURE	TITLE	DATE

NOTE: Pending receipt of the Certificate of Aircraft Registration, the aircraft may be operated for a period not in excess of 90 days, during which time the PINK copy of this application must be carried in the aircraft.

AC FORM 8050-1 (1-83) (0052-00-628-9005)

Fig. 7-3. 8050-1, Aircraft Registration.

THIS FORM SERVES TWO PURPOSES

PART I acknowledges the recording of a security conveyance covering the collateral shown.
PART II is a suggested form of release which may be used to release the collateral from the terms of the conveyance.

PART I – CONVEYANCE RECORDATION NOTICE

NAME (last name first) OF DEBTOR

NAME and ADDRESS OF SECURED PARTY/ASSIGNEE

NAME OF SECURED PARTY'S ASSIGNOR (if assigned)

Do Not Write In This Block
FOR FAA USE ONLY

FAA REGISTRA-TION NUMBER	AIRCRAFT SERIAL NUMBER	AIRCRAFT MFd. (BUILDER) and MODEL

ENGINE MFR. and MODEL

ENGINE SERIAL NUMBER(S)

PROPELLER MFR. and MODEL

PROPELLER SERIAL NUMBER(S)

THE SECURITY CONVEYANCE DATED_____COVERING THE ABOVE COLLATERAL WAS RECORDED BY THE FAA AIRCRAFT REG-
ISTRY ON _____ AS CONVEYANCE NUMBER_____

FAA CONVEYANCE EXAMINER

PART II – RELEASE – (This suggested release form may be executed by the secured party and returned to the FAA Aircraft Registry when terms of the conveyance have been satisfied. See below for additional information.)

THE UNDERSIGNED HEREBY CERTIFIES AND ACKNOWLEDGES THAT HE IS THE TRUE AND LAWFUL HOLDER OF THE NOTE OR OTHER EVIDENCE OF INDEBTEDNESS SECURED BY THE CONVEYANCE REFERRED TO HEREIN ON THE ABOVE-DESCRIBED COLLATERAL AND THAT THE SAME COLLATERAL IS HEREBY RELEASED FROM THE TERMS OF THE CONVEYANCE. ANY TITLE RETAINED IN THE COLLATERAL BY THE CONVEYANCE IS HEREBY SOLD, GRANTED, TRANS-FERRED, AND ASSIGNED TO THE PARTY WHO EXECUTED THE CONVEYANCE, OR TO THE ASSIGNEE OF SAID PARTY IF THE CONVEYANCE SHALL HAVE BEEN ASSIGNED: PROVIDED, THAT NO EXPRESS WARRANTY IS GIVEN NOR IMPLIED BY REASON OF EXECUTION OR DELIVERY OF THIS RELEASE.

This form is only intended to be a suggested form of release, which meets the recording requirements of the Federal Aviation Act of 1958, and the regulations issued thereunder. In addition to these requirements, the form used by the security holder should be drafted in accordance with the pertinent provisions of local statutes and other applicable federal statutes. This form may be reproduced. There is no fee for recording a release. Send to FAA Aircraft Registry, P. O. Box 25504, Oklahoma City, Oklahoma 73125.

ACKNOWLEDGEMENT (If Required By Applicable Local Law):

DATE OF RELEASE: ....

....
(Name of security holder)

SIGNATURE (in ink) ....

TITLE ....

(A person signing for a corporation must be a corporate officer or hold a managerial position and must show his title. A person signing for another should see Parts 47 and 49 of the Federal Aviation Regulations (14 CFR).

Fig. 7-4. 8050-41, Release of Lien.

Insurance

No one can afford to take risks. Insure your airplane from the moment you sign on the dotted line.

Basically, there are two types of insurance you will be looking at: *Liability insurance* protects you, or your heirs, in instances of claims against you, or your estate, resulting from your operation of an airplane (i.e., bodily injury or property damage, death). In this the age of litigation, you can be sure you will be sued if any-one is injured or killed while riding in your airplane, or struck by it on the ground.

Hull insurance protects your investment from loss caused by the elements of nature, fire, theft, vandalism, or accident. There

136

Federal Communications Commission
Gettysburg, PA 17325

Approved by OMB
3060-0040
Expires 3/31/86

APPLICATION FOR AIRCRAFT RADIO STATION LICENSE

- Read instructions above before completing application.
- Sign and date application.
- Use typewriter or print clearly in ink.
- Place First Class Postage on the reverse side of the card and mail.

1. FAA Registration or FCC Control Number.
(If FAA Registration is not required for your aircraft, explain in item 8.)

N

2. Is application for a fleet license? ☐ No ☐ Yes
If yes, give the number of aircraft in fleet, including planned expansion ....

4. Applicant/Licensee Name (See Instructions)

5. Mailing Address (Number and Street, P.O. Box or Route No., City, State, ZIP Code)

3. Type of applicant (check one)

☐ I—Individual ☐ C—Corporation

☐ P—Partnership ☐ D—Individual with Business Name

☐ A—Association ☐ G—Governmental entity

6. Frequencies Requested (check appropriate box(es) in 6.A and/or 6.B.)

6A. DO NOT CHECK BOTH BOXES

☐ A—Private Aircraft ☐ C—Air Carrier

6B. ADDITIONAL INFORMATION IS REQUIRED IF YOU CHECK HERE (See Instructions)

☐ T—Flight Test HF ☐ V—Flight Test VHF ☐ O—Other (Specify)

7. Application is for:

☐ New Station ☐ Renewal

☐ Modification

8. Answer space for any required statements

10. Signature   Date

9. READ CAREFULLY BEFORE SIGNING: 1. Applicant waives any claim to the use of any particular frequency regardless of prior use by license or otherwise. 2. Applicant will have unlimited access to the radio equipment and will control access to exclude unauthorized persons. 3. Neither applicant nor any member thereof is a foreign government or representative thereof. 4. Applicant certifies that all statements made in this application and attachments are true, complete, correct and made in good faith. 5. Applicant certifies that the signature is that of the individual, or partner, or officer or duly authorized employee of a corporation, or officer who is a member of an unincorporated association, or appropriate elected or appointed official on behalf of a governmental entity.

WILLFUL FALSE STATEMENTS MADE ON THIS FORM ARE PUNISHABLE BY FINE AND/OR IMPRISONMENT U.S. CODE TITLE 18, SECTION 1001.

FCC 404
October 1984

Fig. 7-5. FCC 404, Aircraft Radio Station License.

137

Federal Communications Commission
Gettysburg, PA 17325

TEMPORARY AIRCRAFT RADIO STATION OPERATING AUTHORITY

Approved by OMB
3060-0040
Expires 3/31/86

Use this form if you want a temporary operating authority while your regular application, FCC Form 404, is being processed by the FCC. This authority authorizes the use of transmitters operating on the appropriate frequencies listed in Part 87 of the Commission's Rules.

ALL APPLICANTS MUST CERTIFY:
1. I am not a representative of a foreign government.
2. I have applied for an Aircraft Radio Station License by mailing a completed FCC Form 404 to the Federal Communications Commission, P.O. Box 1030, Gettysburg, PA 17325.
3. I have not been denied a license or had my license revoked by the FCC.

- DO NOT use this form if you already have a valid aircraft station license.
- DO NOT use this form when renewing your aircraft license.
- DO NOT use this form if you are applying for a fleet license.
- DO NOT use this form if you do not have an FAA Registration Number.

4. I am not the subject of any adverse legal action concerning the operation of a radio station.
5. I will ensure that the Aircraft Radio Station will be operated by an individual holding the proper class of license or permit required by the Commission's Rules.

WILLFUL FALSE STATEMENTS VOID THIS PERMIT AND ARE PUNISHABLE BY FINE AND/OR IMPRISONMENT.

Name of Applicant (Print or Type)	Signature of Applicant
FAA Registration Number (Use as Temporary Call Sign)	Date FCC Form 404 Mailed

Your authority to operate your Aircraft Radio Station is subject to all applicable laws, treaties and regulations and is subject to the right of control of the Government of the United States. This authority is valid for 90 days from the date the FCC Form 404 is mailed.

YOU MUST POST THIS TEMPORARY OPERATING AUTHORITY ON BOARD YOUR AIRCRAFT

NOTICE TO INDIVIDUALS REQUIRED BY PRIVACY ACT OF 1974 AND THE PAPERWORK REDUCTION ACT OF 1980
Sections 301, 303 and 308 of the Communications Act of 1934, as amended, (licensing powers) authorize the FCC to request the information on this application. The purpose of the information is to determine your eligibility for a license. The information will be used by FCC staff to evaluate the application, to determine station location, process information for enforcement and rulemaking proceedings and to maintain a current inventory of licensees. No license can be granted unless all information requested is provided. Your response is required to obtain this authorization.

FCC 404-A
October 1984

DETACH HERE—DO NOT MAIL THIS PART

Fig. 7-6. FCC 404, Temporary Operating Authority.

are limited coverage policies available that provide for losses to the airplane while on the ground, but not while in the air. You can save money here; however, discussion of coverages available is best left between you and the insurance agent you are doing business with. Your lending institution will require hull insurance for their protection.

A check of any of the various aviation publications will produce telephone numbers for several aviation underwriters. The larger insurance companies have "800" toll-free telephone numbers. Call them; it's free! Call all of them, as services, coverage, and rates do differ.

Don't buy a policy that has complicated exclusions or other specific rules involving maximum preset values for replacement parts or payment of losses. Purchase a policy that you can read and understand, one that is written in "lay English."

Something else to consider is your personal health and life insurance coverage. Be sure you are covered while flying a private airplane. Some policies do not, and in the event of injury or death, there might be no payoff.

Safekeeping of an Airplane

There is no way to make your airplane theftproof; however, it can be made less attractive to the thief. "Less attractive" means more difficult to steal.

The thief doesn't want to spend large amounts of time in stealing an airplane. He wants to get in and go. If you can delay him, you may discourage him.

There are several methods of delaying the thief; all involve locks of one type or another.

1. Store the airplane in a locked hangar.
2. Use cut-resistance chain and locks for the tiedowns.
3. Install a throttle lock. A throttle lock which is an excellent device for discouraging the would-be thief, is available from:

Spiser Aircraft Co., Inc.
Municipal Airport
Clay Center
KS 67432
Phone: (913)632-3217

Unfortunately, there is now another type of criminal loose in

America. This type will attempt to steal your property, and if unable to do so, will destroy it. His reasoning: If he can't have it, neither will you.

This criminal element is primarily found in urban areas breaking into Mercedes, BMW, and Volvo automobiles, but this disease has spread to some close-in airports during the past months.

How to Report a Stolen Airplane

What would you do if you drove out to the airport and your airplane had been stolen, or the plane has been broken into and some of your avionics were missing?

Naturally, you would notify your local police. They will come to the airport—maybe—and make a report of the theft, and possibly even process the crime scene by fingerprinting. The latter will be accomplished only if there is a "chance for prints."

There is no chance for prints if it has rained since the break-in, or if the scene has been contaminated by you or others by touching the airplane.

Don't expect the local (or even state) police to do very much about your loss. The reports will be filed and entries will be made into NCIC (National Crime Information Center) computer including registration numbers, serial numbers, etc. This will give a chance of recovery in the event that another police department on the other side of the country comes into contact with the stolen items.

Notify the FAA, as they will issue a nationwide stolen aircraft alert. If the registration numbers are not changed, and a controller is sharp, you have a chance of recovery.

Notify the IATB (International Aviation Theft Bureau) at phone: (301)695-2022 or Telex: 89-3445. The IATB is a part of the AOPA operation.

Notify your insurance company of the loss, and be ready to supply them with copies of all police reports, purchase receipts, etc.

140

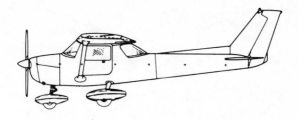

Chapter 8

Care and Maintenance of the 150/152

Once you own an airplane, you have to take care of it. Basically, there are four areas of care the owner/pilot needs to be concerned with. These are proper handling, effective storage, cleaning, and preventive maintenance. All four areas provide the owner with methods of becoming intimately acquainted with his airplane. Additionally, by properly caring for the airplane, one's investment will be protected, flying safety greatly increased, and a considerable amount of money saved.

GROUND HANDLING

Proper handling of an airplane while on the ground (moving by hand) is extremely important. If care is not taken, major structural damage can be done to the airplane that could cost thousands of dollars to repair.

Towing

A tow bar properly attached to the nose gear should be used for pulling, pushing, steering, and maneuvering the aircraft while on the ground (Figs. 8-1, 8-2). When towing the aircraft, never turn the nosewheel more than 30 degrees either side of center or the nose gear will be damaged.

If no tow bar is available, apply downward pressure at the horizontal stabilizer front spar adjacent to the fuselage to raise the

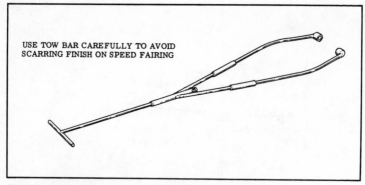

USE TOW BAR CAREFULLY TO AVOID
SCARRING FINISH ON SPEED FAIRING

Fig. 8-1. Old-style tow bar. (courtesy Cessna Aircraft Company)

nosewheel off the ground. Once the nosewheel is clear of the ground, the aircraft can be maneuvered by pivoting it about the main wheels. This is not the recommended procedure, but can be used in a pinch. The best method is to use a tow bar.

Should more pushing/pulling power be needed when moving the aircraft with the tow bar, use *only* the wing struts and landing gear legs as push points. *Don't* push on the wing edges, control surfaces, cabin doors, etc.

Never use the propeller as a push point! The engine could fire from only a slight movement, causing severe injury or death. If you are macho about that, then think about propeller blade failure caused by bending. Blade failure means complete separation caused by metal fatigue developed from stress caused by bending. I see airplanes pushed and pulled by their propellers all the time, as will you, but *don't do it.*

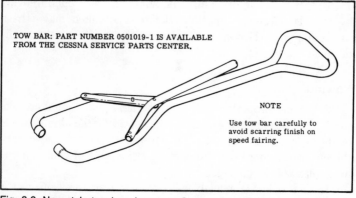

TOW BAR: PART NUMBER 0501019-1 IS AVAILABLE
FROM THE CESSNA SERVICE PARTS CENTER.

NOTE

Use tow bar carefully to
avoid scarring finish on
speed fairing.

Fig. 8-2. New-style tow bar. (courtesy Cessna Aircraft Company)

142

Parking

Parking procedures will depend principally on the local conditions of your airport, and the weather.

Under normal conditions, most pilots will park their airplanes, for short periods of time, merely by applying the parking brake and locking the controls. Further caution would call for wheel chocks. This procedure is adequate for short periods of time such as fueling, pit stops, and other short layovers when the airplane will not be out of sight. This only applies if there is no wind blowing.

If the airplane is going to be left unattended for more than a few minutes, then tie it down (Fig. 8-3).

When tying down the aircraft in the open, face it into the wind if possible. Lock the control surfaces with the internal control lock, and set the brakes. If no standard Cessna control lock is available, tie the controls down with the seat belt. Do not set the parking brakes during cold weather or when the brakes are overheated. Then accomplish the following:

1. Attach ropes, cables, or chains to the wing tiedown fittings. These fittings are located at the upper end of each wing strut. Secure the opposite ends to ground anchors.

2. Secure a tiedown rope (not a chain or cable) to the exposed portion of the engine mount and secure the opposite end to a ground anchor.

3. Fasten the middle of a rope to the tail tiedown ring, pull each end of the rope away at a 45-degree angle, and secure to ground anchors at each side of the tail.

4. Install surface control locks between the wingtip and aileron, and over the fin and rudder.

Tie the airplane down whether the wind is blowing or not. If you neglect to secure your airplane, and leave it unattended, you could return to find your plane has been damaged, or caused damage to other airplanes, by unexpected winds.

These unexpected winds often visit in the form of dust devils in the summertime. A dust devil is a miniature twister, and is quite capable of picking up a lightplane such as the 150 and slam-dunking it back down.

AIRPLANE STORAGE

There is much more to storing an airplane than mere hangar-

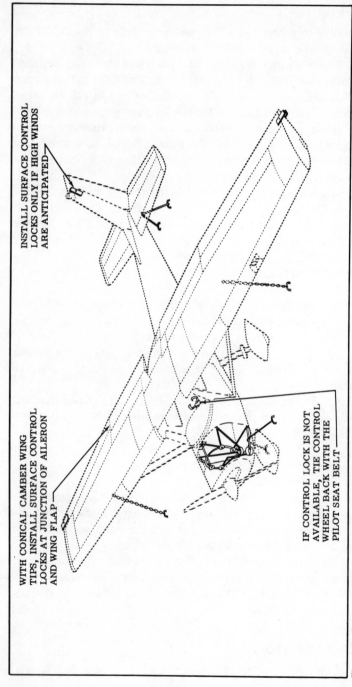

INSTALL SURFACE CONTROL LOCKS ONLY IF HIGH WINDS ARE ANTICIPATED

WITH CONICAL CAMBER WING TIPS, INSTALL SURFACE CONTROL LOCKS AT JUNCTION OF AILERON AND WING FLAP

IF CONTROL LOCK IS NOT AVAILABLE, TIE CONTROL WHEEL BACK WITH THE PILOT SEAT BELT

Fig. 8-3. Recommended tiedown. (courtesy Cessna Aircraft Company)

144

ing or parking. Unfortunately a large number of owner/pilots pay little attention to the proper storage of their airplanes during periods of non-use.

What really concerns me is the large number of airplanes parked at airports that never see any care. Some airplanes are parked in October and not moved (or even visited) until May. Most people wouldn't do that with their cars, yet there sit all those airplanes!

This unattended, uncared-for, sitting routine causes airplanes to die. Resurrection is expensive; proper care is cheap.

There are three categories of storage that will concern the airplane owner. These categories are time-based, with the planned length of storage time determining the category:

- □ Flyable Storage: The airplane is flown daily, or at least every few days.
- □ Temporary Storage: The storage of the airplane for up to three months.
- □ Indefinite Storage: "Mothballing" for an undetermined period of time. (I feel that if this is necessary, it is time to consider disposing of the airplane.)

Flyable Storage

Flyable storage is really the daily care of the airplane. Daily usage, or nearly daily usage, is the best form of storage for an airplane. Your body stays in best shape when you exercise regularly, and so does an airplane. Regular use is of prime importance for the engine.

In addition to regular usage, routine care—including exterior and interior cleaning and surface protection—must be taken.

At the end of each flight, service aircraft per normal Cessna instructions. This includes refueling, tiedown, etc.

If you do not fly the aircraft at least weekly:

Pull the propeller through every seven days by hand-rotating without running the engine. Rotate the engine six revolutions and stop the propeller 45 to 90 degrees from the original position.

Note—If your engine has less than 50 hours of operating time, pull the propeller through every five days. The reason for this is engines with few operating hours on them have not attained the varnish residue coating on the inside of the cylinders. Therefore, they are more susceptible to oxidation (rust) than a higher time engine.

CAUTION
For maximum safety, accomplish propeller rotation as follows:

- ☐ Check that the magneto switches are in the OFF position.
- ☐ Move the throttle to the CLOSED position.
- ☐ Set the mixture control to IDLE CUTOFF.
- ☐ Set the parking brake and block the aircraft's wheels.
- ☐ Leave the aircraft tiedowns installed.
- ☐ Open the cabin door.
- ☐ *Do not* stand within the arc of the propeller blades while turning the propeller.

Fly the airplane at least once every two weeks. This biweekly flight should last a minimum of 30 minutes, allowing the engine to reach, but not exceed, normal oil and cylinder operating temperatures.

If the biweekly cannot be accomplished on schedule due to weather, maintenance, etc., pull the propeller through daily and fly as soon as possible.

If the aircraft still cannot be flown, it should be placed in Temporary or Indefinite Storage. Ground running *is not* an acceptable substitute for flying.

For future reference, the propeller pull-through and flight time may be recorded in the engine log, or informally on a notepad.

Temporary Storage

Temporary storage of the aircraft is storage for a limited period, such as over the winter months. It should not be done for a period of more than three months.

Cessna aircraft are constructed of corrosion-resistant Alclad aluminum alloy, which will last indefinitely under normal conditions. However, these alloys are subject to corrosion if not properly cared for. The first indication of corrosion on unpainted surfaces is the forming of white deposits or spots. These spots may resemble a scattering of salt crystals in appearance. On painted surfaces, the paint becomes discolored or blistered. *Storage in a dry hangar is essential* to good preservation and such storage should be procured if possible.

To prepare an airplane for temporary storage:

Service the aircraft as you would at the end of a flight, including filling the fuel tanks with the correct grade of fuel.

146

Clean and wax the entire aircraft, inside and out.

Remove any grease or oil residue from the tires and coat them with a tire preservative.

Cover the nosewheel to protect it from oil dripping from the engine.

Block up the fuselage to remove the weight from the tires.

Note: Tires will take a set, causing them to become out-of-round, if an aircraft is left unmoved for extended periods.

Remove the top spark plug and spray preservative oil (MIL-L-46002, Grade 1) through the upper spark plug hole of each cylinder with the piston approximately in bottom dead center position. Rotate the crankshaft after each pair of opposite cylinders are sprayed. Stop the crankshaft with no piston at top dead center. A pressure pot or pump-up type garden pressure sprayer may be used for applying the preservative oil. However, the spray head must have ports around the circumference to allow complete coverage of the cylinder walls. To thoroughly cover all surfaces of the cylinder interior, move the nozzle or spray gun from the top to the bottom of the cylinder. After application has been made to each cylinder, respray inside each cylinder without rotating the engine. Re-install the spark plugs, torquing as required. Apply the preservative to the engine interior by spraying approximately two ounces through the oil filler tube.

Seal all engine openings exposed to the atmosphere using suitable plugs, or moisture resistant tape, and attach red streamers at each point.

Affix a tag to the propeller in a conspicuous place with the following notation on the tag:

DO NOT TURN PROPELLER
ENGINE PRESERVED
PRESERVATION DATE (ddmmyy)

Note: If the aircraft is not returned to flyable status at the expiration of the Temporary Storage, it must be placed into Indefinite Storage.

Returning the aircraft to service is easily accomplished by the following procedure:

Remove all seals, tape, paper and streamers from openings. The reason for the streamers is to identify seal locations.

Remove the bottom spark plugs from the cylinders, and hand-turn the propeller several revolutions. This will clear excess preservative oil from the cylinders. Re-install the spark plugs, torquing as needed.

Do a very complete walk-around inspection (preflight).

Start the engine as you normally would.

A test flight is recommended.

Indefinite Storage

Indefinite Storage is mothballing. The aircraft is placed into a state of storage where it can remain until such time as use is again planned. This could be for months, or even years.

In addition to preparing the airplane as you would for Temporary Storage:

Lubricate all movable airframe parts.

Cover all openings to the airframe to keep vermin, insects, and birds out.

Remove the battery and store it in a cool dry place, servicing it periodically.

Place covers over the windshield and rear windows.

Inspect the airframe for signs of corrosion at least monthly. Clean and wax as necessary.

Drain the engine oil and refill with MIL-C-6529 Type II.

The aircraft must then be flown for 30 minutes, allowing normal oil and cylinder temperatures to be attained. Allow the engine to cool to ambient temperature.

Using MIL-C-6529 Type II, follow the procedures for preservative application to the cylinders of the engine given under Temporary Storage. Do no re-install the top spark plugs. *Note:* MIL-C-6529 Type II can be formulated by thoroughly mixing one part compound MIL-C-6529 Type I (Esso Rust-Ban 628, Cosmoline No. 1223 or equivalent) with three parts new lubricating oil of the grade recommended for service (all at room temperature). Single grade oil is recommended.

Apply preservative to the engine interior by spraying MIL-L-46002, Grade 1 oil (approximately two ounces) through the oil filler tube.

Install dehydrator plugs in each of the top spark plug holes, making sure that each plug is blue in color when installed. Protect and support the spark plug leads.

If the carburetor is removed from the engine, place a bag of desiccant in the throat of the carburetor air adapter.

Seal the adapter with moisture resistant paper and tape on a cover plate.

Place a bag of desiccant in the exhaust pipes and seal the openings with moisture-resistant tape.

Seal the cold air inlet to the heater muff with moisture-resistant tape to exclude moisture and foreign objects.

Seal the engine breather by inserting a dehydrator plug in the breather hose and clamping in place.

Attach a red streamer to each place on the engine where bags of desiccant are placed. Attach red streamers to each sealed area with tape.

Attach a tag to the propeller in a conspicuous place with the following notation on the tag:

DO NOT TURN PROPELLER
ENGINE PRESERVED
PRESERVATION DATE (ddmmyy)

Aircraft in indefinite storage should be inspected every two weeks to check the dehydrator plugs for a change in color. Reapply preservative oil to the inside of any cylinder that displays a plug with changed color, and replace the dehydrator plug. If the color on more than two of the cylinders has changed, all desiccant material on the engine should be replaced.

Every six months the cylinder bores should be resprayed with corrosion preventive mixture—more frequently if a bore inspection indicates corrosion has started earlier than six months. Before spraying, make a bore inspection of at least one cylinder. If the cylinder shows the start of rust on the cylinder walls, the entire engine must be represerved. Also, remove at least one rocker box cover from each engine and inspect the valve mechanism. Replace all desiccant and dehydrator plugs.

To return the aircraft to normal service, accomplish the following:

Remove the aircraft from the blocks and check the tires for proper inflation.

Check the nose strut for proper inflation.

Remove all airframe covers and plugs, and inspect the interior of the airframe for debris and foreign matter.

Thoroughly search for vermin damage.

Check the battery and re-install.

Remove the cylinder dehydrator plugs from each engine cylinder.

Remove all paper, tape, desiccant bags, and streamers used

to preserve the engine.

Drain the corrosion preventive mixture from the crankcase and reservice with the recommended lubricating oil.

If the carburetor has been preserved with oil, drain it and flush with avgas, then re-install.

Remove the bottom spark plugs and rotate the propeller to clear excess preservative oil from the cylinders.

Re-install the spark plugs and rotate the propeller by hand through compression strokes of all the cylinders to check for possible liquid lock. *Note:* The ignition harness is to be disconnected from all spark plugs during this procedure.

Start the engine in a normal manner, allowing normal oil pressure to be attained and any remaining cylinder preservative oil to be burned off. Then shut the engine down.

Clean the interior and exterior of the aircraft.

Give the aircraft a thorough visual inspection and cleaning.

Test-fly the aircraft.

CLEANING THE AIRPLANE

Airplane ownership is a source of pride. To display this pride, you should own a clean airplane. but pride alone is not the real reason for keeping the appearance of an airplane in top shape. A clean airplane retains its economic value, normally indicates the owner cares for his airplane, and forces close inspection of the aircraft during cleaning.

Exterior Care

Complete washing with automotive-type cleaners will produce good results, and the materials used will be much cheaper than so called "aircraft cleaners." Automotive protective coatings, formerly called "wax," will protect painted and unpainted surfaces. The new "space age" silicone preparations are very easy to apply, won't whiten rubber components, and will protect your airplane's finish for many months. Just remember, there are a lot of surfaces on an airplane. . . many square feet. So use the best products available, unless you like to make a career of airplane polishing.

For those of you interested in polishing a bare metal airplane, there is the Cyclo Wonder Tool, a dual orbital polishing machine. I can say from personal experience that this machine is well worth the investment if you wish to keep a shiny unpainted bird in tip-top condition. It is also useful in stripping before painting, and will polish hard waxes. For further information contact:

Cyclo Manufacturing Co.
3841 Eudora Way
P.O. Box 2038
Denver, CO 80201

The following is a sampling of some of the available products for cleaning and preserving your aircraft's exterior. Most should be familiar to the automobile owner.

Gunk: Used for degreasing the engine area and front strut. It dissolves grease and can be washed off with water. When using Gunk inside the engine compartment, you must cover the magnetos and alternator with plastic bags to keep the cleaner and rinsewater out. Gunk is also good for cleaning the belly of the airplane if it is oil-stained.

Rubbing compound: Used to clean away stains caused by engine exhaust. Rubbing compounds are available in several strengths (abrasiveness); use the mildest. Avoid being overzealous in the application of rubbing compound, as you could remove paint by overdoing it.

Novus Polish #2: For windshield maintenance. Novus Polish #2 is mildly abrasive, and will polish out scratches and pitmarks that collect on Plexiglass. In effect, it is a very mild polishing compound.

Bugaway: A windshield cleaning solvent developed especially for aircraft use. This spray solution dissolves insect splatters and bird droppings instantly. Just spray it on, wait 10 seconds, then wipe clean with a soft cloth. Bugaway will not harm aluminum or painted surfaces.

Bugaway and Novus Polish #2 are available from:

Connecticut Aviation Products, Inc.
P.O. Box 12
East Glastonbury
CT 06025

Interior Care

The interior of the airplane is seen by all, including the pilot and his passengers. It is probably the most judged area of the airplane. It can be a major problem to keep clean. As in exterior care, I recommend cleaning by use of standard automobile cleaning methods, using automobile cleaning products. All of these cleaning products are available at your local auto supply store, or you may have them on hand for cleaning your automobiles.

In addition to the more normal cleaning items used, here is a short list of grocery store-available products that can be used in keeping the interior of your airplane clean and shining:

Pledge: Use on most hard surfaces including the windshield, vinyl surfaces (seats, dash panel, and doors).

409: Heavy-duty cleaner for the hard-to-remove stuff. Keep it away from the windshield, instruments, and painted surfaces.

Windex: Is an excellent product for small cleanup jobs. However, *never use it on the windshield or other windows!* Windex contains ammonia, and its use on such surfaces will cause a characteristic clouding and spoil the clear qualities. In time, you will have to replace the window.

Armor-All: Good as a final coat on the dash panel, kick panels, seats, etc. It makes vinyl look and smell new.

Scotch Guard: A spray-on product for seats, carpets, and other cloth areas. It will allow quick mop-up of small spills, and it prevents most liquids from soaking into upholstery.

WD-40: A general spray lubricant used to stop squeaks and ease movement. It's good on cables, controls, seat runners, door hinges, and latches. *Keep it off the windows.*

Heat and Sunlight Protection

The interior temperature of a parked aircraft can reach as much as 185 degrees. This is extremely destructive.

This heat buildup will not only damage avionics, but will cause problems with instrument panels, upholstery, and a mirad of other "plastic things."

A quick look around at the local airport will show four methods of heat protection:

- ☐ None at all.
- ☐ A chart or towel laying on the panel.
- ☐ An interior reflective cover.
- ☐ An exterior protective cover.

The first method is noticed most often on older, already sad-looking airplanes. There is certainly no ownership pride here, and the situation will only get worse.

Some owners of older planes recognize the need for protection from the sun's rays, so they lay a towel or chart over the top of the instrument panel. This is merely an exercise in futility, and prevents no heat buildup at all. The only use for such a measure would be when parking for a short period of time, such as refueling.

Inside covers protect the interior of the aircraft by reflecting the sun's rays away with their metallic-type reflective surfaces. The "heat shields," as they are called, attach to the interior of the aircraft by means of Velcro fasteners. Interior reflective heat shields are available from many sources and are advertised in all the aviation periodicals.

Exterior airplane covers provide similar protection for the interior of the aircraft, yet give additional exterior protection by covering the windshield, refueling caps, and fresh air vents. Exterior covers are also advertised in aviation magazines.

PREVENTIVE MAINTENANCE

The owner/pilot can do even more than cleaning and polishing his airplane. The FARs (Federal Aviation Regulations) specify that preventive maintenance may be performed by pilots/owners of airplanes not utilized in commercial service.

Preventive maintenance is defined as "simple or minor preservation operations and the replacement of small standard parts not involving complex assembly operations." Preventive maintenance is not a replacement for a licensed mechanic, as there are complex and sensitive workings in an aircraft that require expertise (and an FAA license). The reader is advised that when a question comes up about maintenance, and he is unsure, *consult a competent licensed mechanic.*

The FAA says:

In case your FBO is concerned about your attempts at saving money and tries to stop your efforts, be aware that the FAA is on your side. Here's a partial reprint of Advisory Circular AC no. 150/5190-2A, dated 4 Apr 72: "d. Restrictions on Self-Service. Any unreasonable restriction imposed on the owners and operators of aircraft regarding the servicing of their own aircraft and equipment may be considered as a violation of agency policy. The owner of an aircraft should be permitted to fuel, wash, repair, paint, and otherwise take care of his own aircraft, provided there is no attempt to perform such services for others. Restrictions which have the effect of diverting activity of this type to a commercial enterprise amount to an exclusive right contrary to law."

With these words the FAA has allowed the owner of an aircraft to save his hard-earned dollars—and to become very familiar with his airplane, the latter, no doubt, contributing to safety.

The FARs lists 28 preventive maintenance items in Appendix A of part 43.13. This means that only those operations listed in the FAR are considered preventive maintenance. The items applicable to the Model 150/152 airplanes are included here. Procedure instructions follow.

Preventive Maintenance Items

1. Removal, installation and repair of landing gear tires.
2. (Does not apply to 150/152 aircraft.)
3. Servicing landing gear struts by adding oil, air, or both.
4. Servicing landing gear wheel bearings, such as cleaning and greasing.
5. Replacing defective safety wiring or cotter pins.
6. Lubrication not requiring disassembly other than removal of nonstructural items such as cover plates, cowlings, and fairings.
7. (Does not apply to 150/152 aircraft.)
8. Replenishing hydraulic fluid in the hydraulic reservoir.
9. Refinishing decorative coatings of the fuselage, wing, and tail-group surfaces (excluding balanced control surfaces), fairings, cowlings, landing gear, cabin, or cockpit interior when removal or disassembly of any primary structure or operating system is not required.
10. Applying preservative or protective material to components when no disassembly of any primary structure or operating system is involved and when such coating is not prohibited or is not contrary to good practices.
11. Repairing upholstery and decorative furnishings of the cabin or cockpit when it does not require disassembly of any primary structure or operating system or affect the primary structure of the aircraft.
12. Making small, simple repairs to fairings, nonstructural cover plates, cowlings and small patches, and reinforcements not changing the contour so as to interfere with the proper airflow.
13. Replacing side windows where that work does not interfere with the structure or any operating system, such as controls and electrical equipment.

14. Replacing safety belts.

15. Replacing seats or seat parts with replacement parts approved for the aircraft, not involving disassembly of any primary structure or operating system.

16. Troubleshooting and repairing broken landing light wiring circuits.

17. Replacing bulbs, reflectors, and lenses of position and landing lights.

18. Replacing wheel and skis where no weight and balance computation is required.

19. Replacing any cowling not requiring removal of the propeller or disconnection of flight controls.

20. Replacing or cleaning spark plugs and setting of spark plug gap clearance.

21. Replacing any hose connection except hydraulic connections.

22. Replacing prefabricated fuel lines.

23. Cleaning fuel and oil strainers.

24. Replacing batteries and checking fluid level and specific gravity.

25. (Does not apply to 150/152 aircraft.)

26. (Does not apply to 150/152 aircraft.)

27. Replacement or adjustment of nonstructural standard fasteners incidental to operations.

28. (Does not apply to 150/152 aircraft.)

PROCEDURE INSTRUCTIONS

The following instructions and notes will assist you in performing preventive maintenance.

Tires

Maintain the tire pressure as specified in your aircraft owner's manual. When checking tire pressure, examine the tires for wear, cuts, bruises, and slipping. Damage to tires is very common when operating from unpaved runways. Remove oil and grease from the tires with soap and water. Petroleum products can rot rubber tires, rendering them unsafe.

Note: Recommended tire pressures should be maintained, especially in cold weather, as any drop in temperature of the air inside a tire causes a corresponding drop in air pressure.

Main Wheel Removal

a. Jack up one main wheel of the aircraft at a time. Place the jack at the universal jack point; do not use the brake casting as a jacking point. When using the universal jack point, flexibility of the gear strut will cause the main wheel to slide inboard as the wheel is raised, tilting the jack. The jack must be lowered for a second operation. Jacking both main wheels simultaneously with universal jack points is not recommended (Fig. 8-4).

b. Remove the speed fairing (if installed) (Fig. 8-5).

c. Remove the hub cap, cotter pin, and axle nut.

d. Remove the bolts and washers attaching back plate to brake cylinder and remove back plate.

e. Pull the wheel from the axle (Figs. 8-6, 8-7).

Wheel Disassembly

a. Remove the valve core and deflate the tire. Break the tire beads loose from the wheel rims.

WARNING

Injury can result from attempting to separate wheel halves with the tire inflated. Avoid damaging wheel flanges when breaking tire beads loose.

b. Remove the through-bolts and separate the wheel halves, removing the tire, tube, and brake disc (Figs. 8-8, 8-9).

c. Remove the grease seal rings, felts, and bearing cones from the wheel halves.

Wheel Inspection and Repair

a. Clean all metal parts and the grease seal felts in solvent and dry thoroughly.

b. Inspect the wheel halves for cracks. Cracked wheel halves shall be discarded and new parts used. Sand out nicks, gouges, and corroded areas. Where the protective coating has been removed, the area should be cleaned thoroughly, primed with zinc chromate, and repainted with aluminum lacquer.

c. If excessively warped or scored, the brake disc should be replaced with a new part. Sand smooth small nicks and scratches.

d. Carefully inspect the bearing cones and cups for damage and discoloration. After cleaning, pack the cones with clean air-

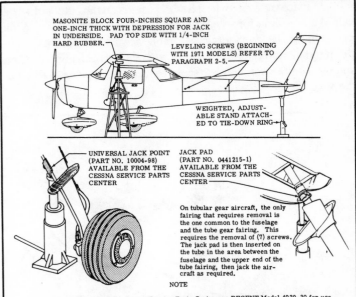

MASONITE BLOCK FOUR-INCHES SQUARE AND ONE-INCH THICK WITH DEPRESSION FOR JACK IN UNDERSIDE. PAD TOP SIDE WITH 1/4-INCH HARD RUBBER.

LEVELING SCREWS (BEGINNING WITH 1971 MODELS) REFER TO PARAGRAPH 2-5.

WEIGHTED, ADJUSTABLE STAND ATTACHED TO TIE-DOWN RING

UNIVERSAL JACK POINT (PART NO. 10004-98) AVAILABLE FROM THE CESSNA SERVICE PARTS CENTER

JACK PAD (PART NO. 0441215-1) AVAILABLE FROM THE CESSNA SERVICE PARTS CENTER

On tubular gear aircraft, the only fairing that requires removal is the one common to the fuselage and the tube gear fairing. This requires the removal of (7) screws. The jack pad is then inserted on the tube in the area between the fuselage and the upper end of the tube fairing, then jack the aircraft as required.

NOTE

Wing jacks available from the Cessna Service Parts Center are REGENT Model 4939-30 for use with the SE-576 wing stands. Combination jacks are the REGENT Model 4939-70 for use without wing stands. The 4939-70 jack (70-inch) may be converted to the 4939-30 jack (30-inch) by removing the leg extensions and replacing lower braces with shorter ones. The base of the adjustable tail stand (SE-767) is to be filled with concrete for additional weight as a safety factor. The SE-576 wing stand will also accommodate the SANCOR Model 00226-150 jack. Other equivalent jacks, tail stands, and adapter stands may be used.

1. Lower aircraft tail so that wing jack can be placed under front wing spar just outboard of wing strut.

2. Raise aircraft tail and attach tail stand to tie-down ring. BE SURE the tail stand weighs enough to keep the tail down under all conditions and is strong enough to support aircraft weight.

3. Raise jacks evenly until desired height is reached.

4. The universal jack point may be used to raise only one main wheel. Do not use brake casting as a jack point.

CAUTION

When using the universal jack point, flexibility of the gear strut will cause the main wheel to slide inboard as the wheel is raised, tilting the jack. The jack must be lowered for a second operation. Jacking both main wheels simultaneously with universal jack points is not recommended.

Fig. 8-4. Proper jacking instructions. (courtesy Cessna Aircraft Company)

craft wheel bearing grease before installing them in the wheel half.

Main Wheel Assembly

a. Insert the through-bolts through the brake disc and position it in the inner wheel half, using the bolts to guide the disc. Ascertain that the disc is bottomed in the wheel half.

b. Position the tire and tube with the tube inflation valve through the hole in the outboard wheel half.

c. Place the inner wheel half in position on the outboard wheel half. Apply a light force to bring the wheel halves together. While maintaining the light force, assemble a washer and nut on one through-bolt and tighten snugly. Assemble the remaining washers and nuts on the through-bolts and torque to the value marked on the wheel.

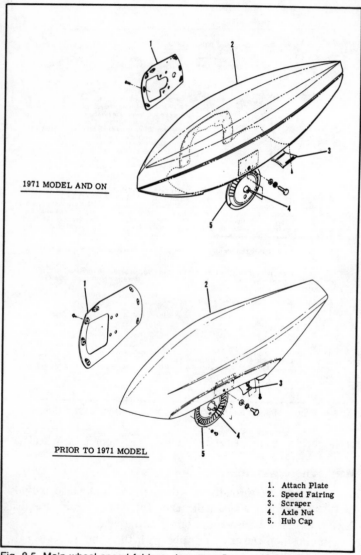

1971 MODEL AND ON

PRIOR TO 1971 MODEL

1. Attach Plate
2. Speed Fairing
3. Scraper
4. Axle Nut
5. Hub Cap

Fig. 8-5. Main wheel speed fairings. (courtesy Cessna Aircraft Company)

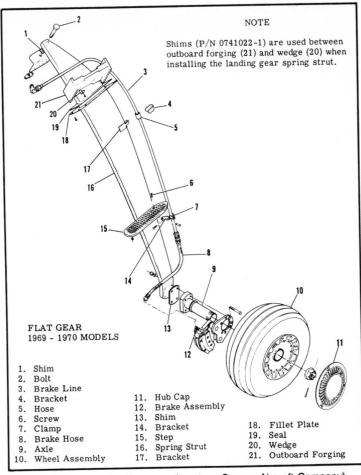

NOTE

Shims (P/N 0741022-1) are used between outboard forging (21) and wedge (20) when installing the landing gear spring strut.

FLAT GEAR
1969 - 1970 MODELS

1. Shim		
2. Bolt		
3. Brake Line		
4. Bracket	11. Hub Cap	
5. Hose	12. Brake Assembly	
6. Screw	13. Shim	
7. Clamp	14. Bracket	18. Fillet Plate
8. Brake Hose	15. Step	19. Seal
9. Axle	16. Spring Strut	20. Wedge
10. Wheel Assembly	17. Bracket	21. Outboard Forging

Fig. 8-6. Spring-type landing gear. (courtesy Cessna Aircraft Company)

CAUTION

Uneven or improper torque of the through-bolt nuts can cause failure of the bolts, with resultant wheel failure.

d. Clean and pack the bearing cones with new aircraft wheel bearing grease.

e. Assemble the bearing cones, grease seal felts, and rings into the wheel halves.

f. Inflate the tire to seat the tire beads, then adjust inflation to the correct pressure (see owner's manual).

Main Wheel Installation

a. Place the wheel assembly on the axle.

b. Install the axle nut and tighten until a slight bearing drag is obvious when the wheel is rotated. Back off the axle nut to the nearest castellation and install a cotter pin.

c. Place the brake back plate in position and secure it with bolts and washers.

d. Install the hub cap.

CAUTION

If you have speed fairings, be sure to check the scraper clearance before aircraft operation.

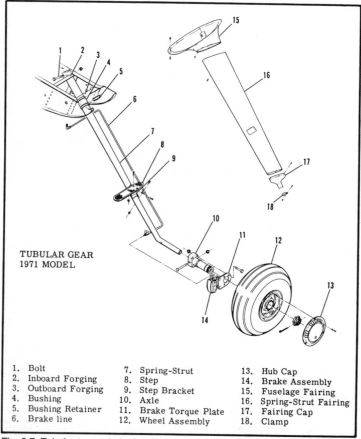

TUBULAR GEAR
1971 MODEL

1.	Bolt	7.	Spring-Strut	13.	Hub Cap
2.	Inboard Forging	8.	Step	14.	Brake Assembly
3.	Outboard Forging	9.	Step Bracket	15.	Fuselage Fairing
4.	Bushing	10.	Axle	16.	Spring-Strut Fairing
5.	Bushing Retainer	11.	Brake Torque Plate	17.	Fairing Cap
6.	Brake line	12.	Wheel Assembly	18.	Clamp

Fig. 8-7. Tubular-type tubular landing gear. (courtesy Cessna Aircraft Company)

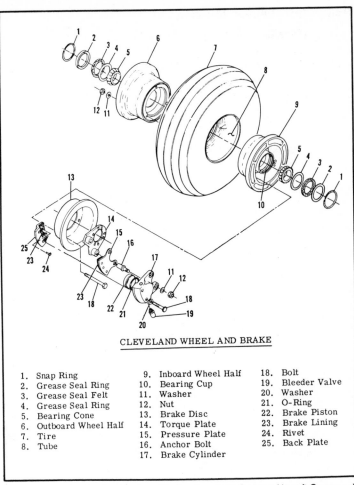

CLEVELAND WHEEL AND BRAKE

1. Snap Ring	9. Inboard Wheel Half	18. Bolt
2. Grease Seal Ring	10. Bearing Cup	19. Bleeder Valve
3. Grease Seal Felt	11. Washer	20. Washer
4. Grease Seal Ring	12. Nut	21. O-Ring
5. Bearing Cone	13. Brake Disc	22. Brake Piston
6. Outboard Wheel Half	14. Torque Plate	23. Brake Lining
7. Tire	15. Pressure Plate	24. Rivet
8. Tube	16. Anchor Bolt	25. Back Plate
	17. Brake Cylinder	

Fig. 8-8. Cleveland main wheel and brake. (courtesy Cessna Aircraft Company)

Nosewheel Removal

a. Weight to tie down the tail of the aircraft to raise the nosewheel off the ground.

b. Remove the nosewheel axle bolt (Figs. 8-10 through 8-12).

c. Pull the nosewheel assembly from the fork and remove the spacers and axle tube from the nose wheel. Loosen the scraper if necessary.

The wheel disassembly, inspection and repair, and assembly of the nosewheel follow similar procedures to those of the main wheels.

Nosewheel Re-installation

a. Place the nosewheel on the fork and install the axle tube and spacers.

b. Insert the axle bolt and tighten the axle bolt nut until a slight bearing drag is felt when the wheel is rotated. Back the nut off to the nearest castellation and install a cotter pin.

CAUTION

If you have speed fairings, be sure to check the scraper clearance before aircraft operation.

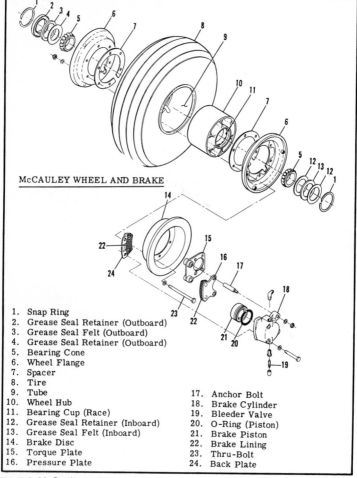

McCAULEY WHEEL AND BRAKE

1. Snap Ring
2. Grease Seal Retainer (Outboard)
3. Grease Seal Felt (Outboard)
4. Grease Seal Retainer (Outboard)
5. Bearing Cone
6. Wheel Flange
7. Spacer
8. Tire
9. Tube
10. Wheel Hub
11. Bearing Cup (Race)
12. Grease Seal Retainer (Inboard)
13. Grease Seal Felt (Inboard)
14. Brake Disc
15. Torque Plate
16. Pressure Plate
17. Anchor Bolt
18. Brake Cylinder
19. Bleeder Valve
20. O-Ring (Piston)
21. Brake Piston
22. Brake Lining
23. Thru-Bolt
24. Back Plate

Fig. 8-9. McCauley main wheel and brake. (courtesy Cessna Aircraft Company)

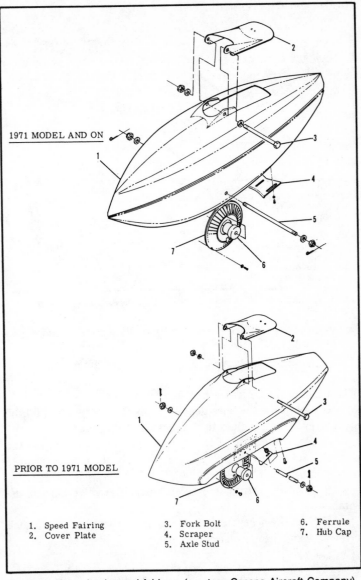

1971 MODEL AND ON

PRIOR TO 1971 MODEL

1. Speed Fairing	3. Fork Bolt	6. Ferrule
2. Cover Plate	4. Scraper	7. Hub Cap
	5. Axle Stud	

Fig. 8-10. Nosewheel speed fairings. (courtesy Cessna Aircraft Company)

Nose Gear Shock Strut

The nose gear shock strut requires periodic checking to ensure that the strut is filled with hydraulic fluid and is inflated to the correct air pressure (Fig. 8-13). Allowing the strut to collapse can re-

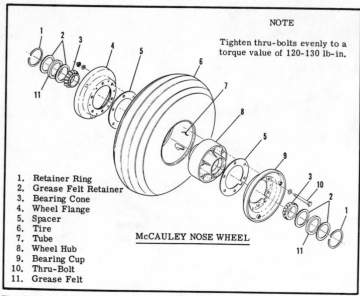

NOTE

Tighten thru-bolts evenly to a
torque value of 120-130 lb-in.

1. Retainer Ring
2. Grease Felt Retainer
3. Bearing Cone
4. Wheel Flange
5. Spacer
6. Tire
7. Tube
8. Wheel Hub
9. Bearing Cup
10. Thru-Bolt
11. Grease Felt

McCAULEY NOSE WHEEL

Fig. 8-11. McCauley nosewheel. (courtesy Cessna Aircraft Company)

sult in propeller contact with the ground. To service the nose gear
strut, proceed as follows:

a. Remove the valve cap and release the air pressure (Fig.
8-14).

b. Remove the valve housing.

c. Compress the nose gear to its shortest length and fill the
strut with hydraulic fluid to the bottom of the filler hole.

d. Raise the nose of the aircraft, extend and compress the
strut several times to expel any entrapped air, then lower the nose
of the aircraft and repeat step c.

e. With the strut compressed, install the valve housing assembly.

f. With the nosewheel off the ground, inflate the strut (check
owner's manual for exact pressure).

NOTE

Keep the nose gear shock strut clean of dust and grit, which
may harm the seals in the strut barrel.

Nose Gear Shimmy Dampener

The shimmy dampener should be serviced at least every 100

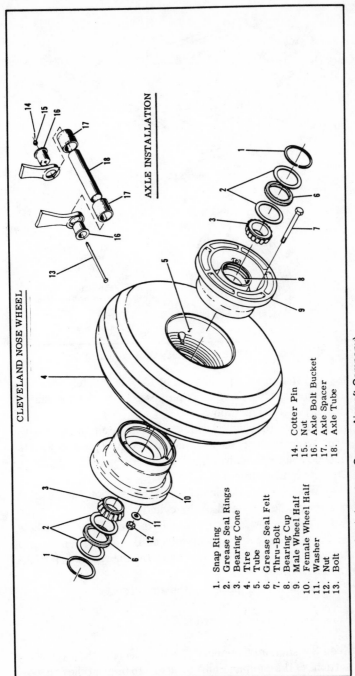

CLEVELAND NOSE WHEEL

AXLE INSTALLATION

1. Snap Ring
2. Grease Seal Rings
3. Bearing Cone
4. Tire
5. Tube
6. Grease Seal Felt
7. Thru-Bolt
8. Bearing Cup
9. Male Wheel Half
10. Female Wheel Half
11. Washer
12. Nut
13. Bolt
14. Cotter Pin
15. Nut
16. Axle Bolt Bucket
17. Axle Spacer
18. Axle Tube

Fig. 8-12. Cleveland nosewheel. (courtesy Cessna Aircraft Company)

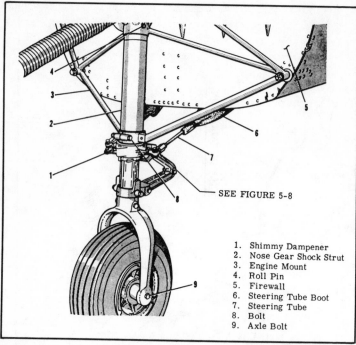

1. Shimmy Dampener
2. Nose Gear Shock Strut
3. Engine Mount
4. Roll Pin
5. Firewall
6. Steering Tube Boot
7. Steering Tube
8. Bolt
9. Axle Bolt

SEE FIGURE 5-8

Fig. 8-13. Nose gear installation. (courtesy Cessna Aircraft Company)

hours. The shimmy dampener must be filled completely with fluid, free of entrapped air, to serve its purpose. To service the shimmy dampener, proceed as follows:

a. Remove the shimmy dampener from the aircraft (Fig. 8-15).

b. While holding the dampener in a vertical position with the fitting end pointed downward, pull the fitting end of the dampener shaft to its limit of travel.

c. While holding the dampener in this position, fill the dampener through the open end of the cylinder.

d. Push the shaft upward slowly to seal off the filler hole.

e. Clean the dampener with solvent. Be sure to keep the shaft protruding through the filler hole until the dampener is installed on the aircraft.

f. Install the dampener on the aircraft.

NOTE

Keep the shimmy dampener clean—especially the exposed portions of the dampener piston shaft—to prevent the collec-

tion of dust and grit which could cut the seals in the dampener barrel. Keep the machined surfaces wiped free of dirt
and dust, using a clean, lint-free cloth saturated with hydraulic
fluid or kerosene. All surfaces should be wiped free of excess hydraulic fluid.

Airframe Lubrication

Lubrication requirements are shown in the associated figures
(Figs. 8-16 through 8-18).

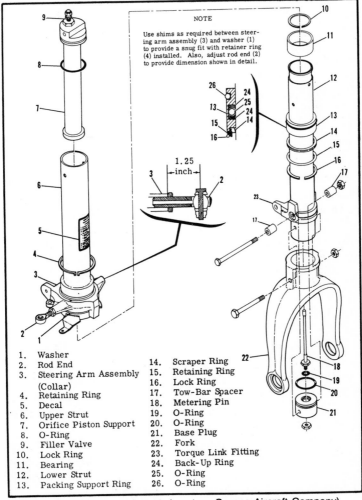

NOTE

Use shims as required between steering arm assembly (3) and washer (1)
to provide a snug fit with retainer ring
(4) installed. Also, adjust rod end (2)
to provide dimension shown in detail.

1.25
inch

1. Washer	14. Scraper Ring
2. Rod End	15. Retaining Ring
3. Steering Arm Assembly	16. Lock Ring
(Collar)	17. Tow-Bar Spacer
4. Retaining Ring	18. Metering Pin
5. Decal	19. O-Ring
6. Upper Strut	20. O-Ring
7. Orifice Piston Support	21. Base Plug
8. O-Ring	22. Fork
9. Filler Valve	23. Torque Link Fitting
10. Lock Ring	24. Back-Up Ring
11. Bearing	25. O-Ring
12. Lower Strut	26. O-Ring
13. Packing Support Ring	

Fig. 8-14. Nose gear shock strut. (courtesy Cessna Aircraft Company)

167

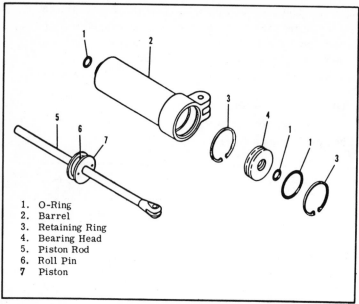

1. O-Ring
2. Barrel
3. Retaining Ring
4. Bearing Head
5. Piston Rod
6. Roll Pin
7 Piston

Fig. 8-15. Nose gear shimmy damper. (courtesy Cessna Aircraft Company)

Before adding grease to grease fittings, wipe all dirt from the fitting. Lubricate until grease appears around the parts being lubricated, then wipe excess grease away.

Wheel bearings should be cleaned and repacked at 500-hour intervals, unless heavy use or dirt strip operations occur. If the latter is the case, then service every 100 hours.

Lubricate the nose gear torque links every 50 hours of operation (more often under dusty conditions).

Engine Lubrication

Proper lubrication of the inside of the engine is essential (Figs. 8-19 through 8-21). No lubrication, no engine!

Engine lubrication will be determined by your particular aircraft's owner's manual. However, as a rule of thumb, never exceed 50 hours between oil changes. Oil is cheap, and I never heard of an engine that failed due to clean oil.

Oil changing for the airplane owner is no more complicated than for the family automobile. However, there is something you should do with the oil that is not normally done with auto oil. This is to obtain an engine oil analysis at each oil change.

Engine oil analysis will give indications of what is wearing—

and, over a period of time, how *quickly* it is wearing. Engine oil analysis services are available from several companies, many of which advertise in *Trade-A-Plane* and other aviation journals.

At oil change time you may decide to put an oil additive in the crankcase, along with the regular engine oil. The object of an additive is to reduce engine wear, resulting in longer engine life. One such additive is MICROLON, a Teflon product, approved by the FAA under FAR 33.49. MICROLON is a one-time additive. That means it is added to the oil only once in the life of the engine. After initial introduction to the crankcase oil, the product bonds itself to all surfaces within the engine, providing extremely good

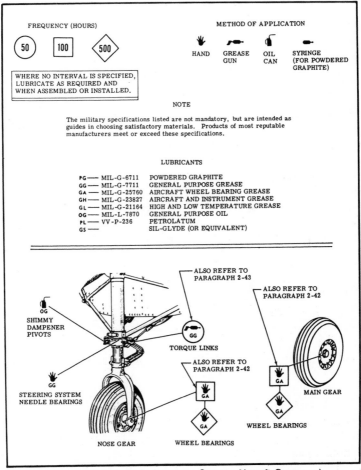

Fig. 8-16. Lubrication chart A. (courtesy Cessna Aircraft Company)

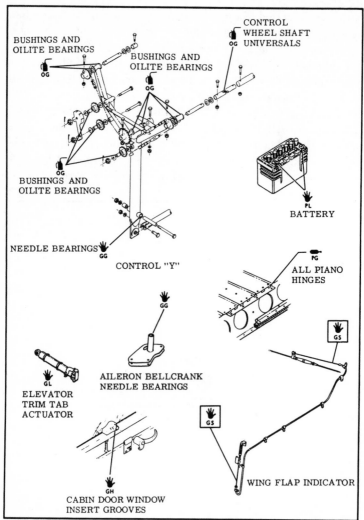

Fig. 8-17. Lubrication chart B. (courtesy Cessna Aircraft Company)

lubricating properties. MICROLON is available from:

Econo Systems
745 Penny Dr.
Pittsburgh, PA 15235

Spark Plugs

Spark plugs require constant attention for proper engine operation. If they fail to operate properly, the engine will fail to produce its rated power, run rough, or fail completely.

Before you attempt spark plug maintenance, see your mechanic. You will need his advice and instruction on the proper method of plug removal, cleaning, gapping, and installation (including proper torquing using a torque wrench) (Fig. 8-22).

Spark plugs can be examined for damage, color of residue, etc., that indicate what is happening inside your engine's combustion chamber. For a color chart depicting these important clues, write

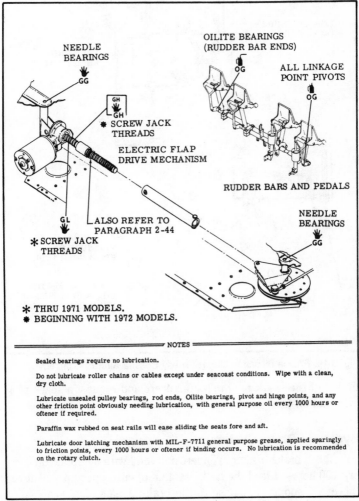

Fig. 8-18. Lubrication chart C. (courtesy Cessna Aircraft Company)

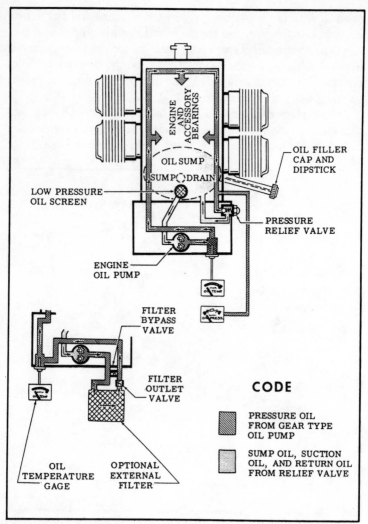

Fig. 8-19. Engine oil schematic. (courtesy Cessna Aircraft Company)

to any of the spark plug manufacturers and request a spark plug information kit.

Hydraulic Brake Systems

Check brake master cylinders and refill with hydraulic fluid every 100 hours. Bleed the brake system of entrapped air whenever there is a spongy response to the brake pedals.

Fairing Repair

The wheel fairings on Cessna 150s, wingtips, and metal/fiberglass on the cowling are all subject to cracking. Repairs to these surfaces are easy and effective.

For fiberglass:

a. Remove the fairing and drill a hole at the end of the crack to stop the crack from getting larger.

b. Dust the inside of the surface to be repaired with baking soda, then position a small piece of fiberglass cloth over the crack

PROBABLE CAUSE	ISOLATION PROCEDURE	REMEDY
NO OIL PRESSURE.		
No oil in sump.	Check with dipstick.	Fill sump with proper grade and quantity of oil.
Oil pressure line broken, disconnected, or pinched.	Inspect oil pressure line.	Replace or connect.
Oil pump defective.	Remove and inspect.	Examine engine. Metal particles from damaged pump may have entered engine oil passage.
Defective oil pressure gage.	Check with another gage. If second reading is normal, aircraft gage is defective.	Replace gage.
Oil congealed in gage line.	Disconnect line at engine and gage; flush with kerosene.	Pre-fill line with kerosene and install.
Pressure relief valve defective.	Remove and check for dirty or defective parts.	Clean and reinstall; replace defective parts.
LOW OIL PRESSURE.		
Low oil supply.	Check with dipstick.	Fill sump with proper grade and quantity of oil.
Low oil viscosity.		Drain sump. Refill with correct grade.
Plugged oil screen.	Inspect screen.	Remove and clean.
Dirt on oil pressure relief valve seat.	Remove and inspect.	Clean plunger and seat.
Oil pressure relief valve plunger sticking.	Remove and inspect.	Clean plunger.
Oil pump suction tube screen plugged.		Engine overhaul.
Oil pressure gage defective.	Test gage.	Replace or repair gage.
Internal oil leak.		Engine overhaul.
HIGH OIL PRESSURE.		
High oil viscosity.		Drain oil and refill sump with correct grade and quantity of oil.
Defective oil pressure gage.	Test gage.	Replace or repair gage.
HIGH OIL TEMPERATURE.		
Low oil supply.	Check with dipstick.	Fill sump with correct grade and quantity of oil.

Fig. 8-20. Oil pressure troubleshooting chart A. (courtesy Cessna Aircraft Company)

PROBABLE CAUSE	ISOLATION PROCEDURE	REMEDY
HIGH OIL TEMPERATURE (Cont).		
Dirty or diluted oil.	Check with dipstick.	Drain sump, and fill with fresh oil of proper grade.
Winter baffles installed.	Check for baffles installed.	Remove winter baffles.
Prolonged ground operation at high engine speed.		Avoid prolonged running on the ground.
Excessive rate of climb.		Avoid low airspeed.
Lean fuel-air mixture.		Avoid excessive lean mixture operation.
Defective oil temperature gage.	Test gage.	Replace or repair gage.
Defective oil temperature bulb.	Check for correct oil pressure, oil level, and cylinder head temperature. If they are correct, check oil temperature gage for being defective; if a similar reading is observed, bulb is defective.	Replace temperature bulb.

Fig. 8-21. Oil pressure troubleshooting chart B. (courtesy Cessna Aircraft Company)

Fig. 8-22. The improved one-piece cowling of the 152 makes for easy engine inspection and maintenance. (courtesy Cessna Aircraft Company)

and saturate the entire area with cyanoacrylate (Super Glue). Repeat step b.

c. From the outside, fill the crack with baking soda and harden with cyanoacrylate.

d. Sand smooth and repaint.

For metal:

a. Remove the fairing and drill a stop hole at the end of the crack to keep it from continuing further.

b. Cut a small piece of metal of the same type as the fairing being repaired. This should extend about one inch out from the crack in all directions.

c. Drill holes through the patch and fairing, then rivet same.

d. Touch up with paint as needed.

Paint Touch-Up

Touching-up small area on the wings or fuselage of an airplane is very easy, and really makes a marked improvement in the plane's appearance.

Many colors of touch-up paint are available in small spray cans from automobile parts houses. It is usually possible to select a close match in color to your airplane from these products.

For custom packaged touch-up paints in spray cans, contact:

Custom Aerosol Products, Inc.
P.O. Box 1014
Allen, TX 75002
Phone: (214) 727-6912

a. Thoroughly wash the area to be touched up. All preservatives such as wax and silicone products must be removed.

b. If there is any loose or flaking paint, it must be removed. Carefully use very fine sandpaper for this purpose. Do not sand the bare metal.

c. If bare metal is exposed, it must be primed with an aircraft-type zinc chromate primer.

d. Using sweeping spray strokes, apply at least two coats of touch-up paint.

COMPLETE REPAINTING

Although most owners would never attempt to paint their airplane, they should know just what makes a good painting job. The following information is general in nature, but applies to all current repainting methods.

Stripping the Aircraft

Aircraft paint removers are fast-acting water-washable products designed for use on aircraft aluminum surfaces.

While using remover, always wear rubber gloves and protect your eyes from splashes. If remover gets on your skin, flush with plenty of water. If any comes in contact with your eyes, flood repeatedly with water and call a physician. Have adequate ventilation.

Do not let remover come in contact with any fiberglass components of the aircraft such as wingtips, fairings, etc. Make sure that these parts are well-masked or removed from aircraft while stripping is in progress.

Apply the remover liberally by brush to the metal surface. When brushing, be sure to brush in only one direction. Keep surface wet with remover. If an area dries before the paint film softens or wrinkles, apply more remover. It is sometimes advisable to lay an inexpensive polyethylene drop cloth over the applied remover in order to hold the solvents longer, giving more time for penetration of the film. After the paint softens and wrinkles, use a pressure water hose to thoroughly flush off all residue.

In the case of an acrylic lacquer finish, the remover will only soften and will not wrinkle the film. A rubber squeegee or stiff bristle brush can be used to help remove this type of finish.

After all paint has been removed, flush the entire aircraft off with a pressure water hose. Let dry.

Using clean cotton rags, wipe all surfaces thoroughly with MEK (methyl ethyl ketone).

Corrosion Removal

After paint stripping, any traces of corrosion on the aluminum surface must be removed with aluminum wool or a Scotch Brite pad. Never use steel wool or a steel brush, as bits of steel will imbed in the aluminum, causing additional corrosion.

Metal Pretreatment

In the case of an aircraft that has been stripped of its previous coating, make sure that all traces of paint or paint remover residue have been removed. Give special attention to areas such as seams and around rivet heads.

Aircraft should be flushed with plenty of clean water to ensure removal of all contaminants. Let dry. Using clean cotton rags, wipe all surfaces thoroughly with MEK.

Apply a metal pretreatment liberally to all the aluminum surfaces of the aircraft. While keeping these surfaces thoroughly wet with the pretreatment, scrub briskly with a Scotch Brite pad. It is advisable to wear rubber gloves and to protect your eyes from splash during this procedure.

The pretreatment may be applied with clean rags or a brush. After the entire aircraft has been treated with this procedure, flush very thoroughly with plenty of clean water. Let dry.

The next step is to thoroughly wipe down the entire aluminum surface with MEK using clean cotton rags. This will ensure all contaminants are removed prior to application of primer.

Let dry and tack-rag all surfaces.

Priming the Cleaned Areas

The best aircraft primers available today are the two-part epoxy primers. They are specifically designed for aircraft and afford the best in corrosion protection. Epoxy primers give the best adhesion possible both to the substrata aluminum surface and to the finish top coat.

Mix the components of the epoxy primer per the manufacturer's instructions, then let stand for 15 to 20 minutes prior to starting application.

Pot life after mixture is limited and will vary from manufacturer to manufacturer.

Care must be taken that only enough primer be used to prime the surface evenly to about 0.0005 in., or one-half a mil film thickness. This means that the aluminum substrate should show through, with a light yellow coating of the primer coloring the metal.

Drying time of the primer will vary slightly due to differences in temperature and relative humidity at the time of application. As a general rule, primer should be ready for application of the finish coat within four to six hours.

After the primer is thoroughly dry, wipe the entire surface with clean, soft, cotton rags using a little pressure, as in polishing. Next, tack-rag the entire surface.

You are now ready for application of the top coat finishing system you have selected.

Conditions for Painting

For optimum results, temperature and humidity should be within the following limits:

- ☐ Relative Humidity: 20 to 60 percent.
- ☐ Temperature: Not less than 70 degrees F.

Departure from these limits could result in various application or finish problems.

Drying time of the finish coating will vary with temperature, humidity, amount of thinner used, and thickness of paint film.

Painting Safety Tips

- ☐ Ground the surface you are painting or sanding.
- ☐ Do not use an electric drill to mix dope or paint.
- ☐ Wear leather-soled shoes in the painting area.
- ☐ Wear cotton clothes while painting.
- ☐ Keep solvent-soaked rags in a fireproof safety container.
- ☐ Keep spray area and floor clean and free of dust buildup. Rinse with hose or wet-sweep.
- ☐ Have adequate ventilation. Do not allow mist or fumes to build up in a confined area.
- ☐ Do not smoke or have any type of open flame in the area.

Application of the Top Coat

Several types of top coat systems are discussed here, complete with application instructions.

Polyurethane Enamel

Polyurethane enamels are the finest aircraft finishes available today. They offer such important characteristics as superior gloss, excellent color retention, and resistance to abrasion, chemical damage, fuel staining, hydraulic fluid spills, and thermal shock.

These characteristics will remain with little or no maintenance over many years of active flying.

Mix the several parts of the polyurethane enamel per the manufacturer's instructions. Pot life after mixing is approximately six hours, but will vary with temperature and humidity.

Spray a relatively light tack coat on the first application. Let dry for at least 15 minutes.

The second coat is applied as a full wet cross-coat.

Care should be taken that too much paint is not being applied, resulting in "runs" or "sags."

Polyurethane enamel is a high solid material giving excellent hiding characteristics without excessive paint buildup.

An overnight dry is preferable before taping for trim color application unless forced drying is used. In such a case, one or two hours at 140 degrees F. is sufficient.

After masking, and before applying the trim color, lightly scuff the trim color surface using the #400 wet-or-dry sandpaper.

Tack-rag and apply the trim color. Remove masking tapes as soon as paint has started to set.

Acrylic Lacquer

Acrylic lacquers have been used by some of the largest aircraft and automobile manufacturers for many years. These are proven paints, with outstanding durability, good color, and excellent gloss retention characteristics.

Mix the paint and associated other elements per the manufacturer's instructions. Adjustments to this mixture might be necessary due to the spray equipment used or operator technique.

Spray a relatively light tack coat on the first application. Let dry for approximately 30 minutes. Follow this first coat with at least three full wet cross-coats, letting each dry for approximately 30 minutes between coats.

If the material is too heavy, orange peel or pinholes are likely to appear.

An overnight dry is preferable before taping for trim color application.

Remove the masking tape as soon as the trim paint has started to set.

Enamel

Enamels have been is use for many years, and can provide good service.

Mix the enamel as instructed by the manufacturer.

Spray on a light tack coat. Allow to dry for 15 to 20 minutes, then apply a full, wet cross-coat.

Allow to dry at least 48 hours before taping for trim colors.

After masking and before applying trim color, lightly scuff the trim color surface using #400 wet-or-dry sandpaper.

Tack-rag and apply trim color.

Remove masking tapes as soon as the paint has started to set.

Refinishing Fiberglass Components

When refinishing any fiberglass component of the aircraft such as wingtips, antenna, fairings, etc., it is extremely important that they are protected from paint remover or solvents.

The only safe method of removing paint from these components is to sand it off.

After the paint is removed by sanding, tack-rag the surface and apply a light coat of primer (automotive-type is acceptable).

When the primer is dry, briskly wipe the entire surface clean with soft, cotton rags. Next, tack-rag the surface and finish with the type of paint you are using on the airframe.

Headliner Removal and Installation

There is probably no more hair-tearing job for the do-it-yourself airplane fixer-upper than the removal and installation of a headliner. Follow these simple instructions taken from the Cessna Service Manual, and you can't miss (Fig. 8-23).

Removal

a. Remove the sun visors, all inside finish strips and plates, door post upper shields, front spare trim shield, dome light panel, and any other visible retainers securing the headliner.

b. Work the edges of the headliner free from the metal tabs that hold the fabric.

c. Starting at the front of the headliner, work the headliner down, removing the screws through the metal tabs which hold the wire bows to the cabin top. Pry loose the outer ends of the bows from the retainers above the doors. Detach each wire bow in succession.

Note: Always work from front to rear when removing the headliner;

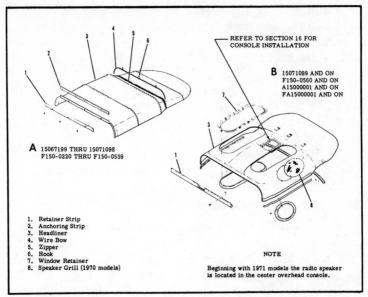

Fig. 8-23. Cabin headliner diagram. (courtesy Cessna Aircraft Company)

it is impossible to detach the wire bows when working from rear to front.

d. Remove the headliner assembly and bows from the airplane.

Note: Due to the difference in length and contour of the wire bows, each bow should be tagged to assure proper location in the headliner.

e. Remove the spun glass soundproofing panels (these are held in place by glue).

Installation

a. Before installing the headliner, check all items concealed by the headliner to see that they are mounted securely. Use wide cloth tape to secure loose wires to the fuselage, and to seal any openings in the wing roots. Straighten any tabs bent during the removal of the old headliner.

b. Apply cement to the skin areas where the soundproofing panels are not supported by wire bows, and press the panels into place.

c. Insert wire bows into the headliner seams, and secure the rearmost edges of the headliner after positioning the two bows at the rear of the headliner. Stretch the material along the edges to make sure it is properly centered, but do not stretch it tight enough to destroy the ceiling contours or distort the wire bows. Secure the edges of the headliner with sharp tabs, or, where necessary, rubber cement.

d. Work the headliner forward, installing each wire bow in place with the tabs. Wedge the ends of the wire bows into the retainer strips. Stretch the headliner just taut enough to avoid wrinkles and maintain a smooth contour.

e. When all bows are in place and fabric edges are secured, trim off any excess fabric and reinstall all items removed.

Seats and Seat Re-Covery

Re-covering the seats is generally easier (less hair pulled out) than installing a headliner. My only advice in seat re-covery is to work in a well-ventilated area, or the glue you'll be working with will have you flying without the airplane.

Due to the wide selection of materials and styles of seat covers available, I recommend you either contract the job with a professional aviation interior shop, or contact a supplier of complete interiors or slip covers (Fig. 8-24). The latter method is recommended

Fig. 8-24. Seat covers you can install yourself. (courtesy Cooper Aviation)

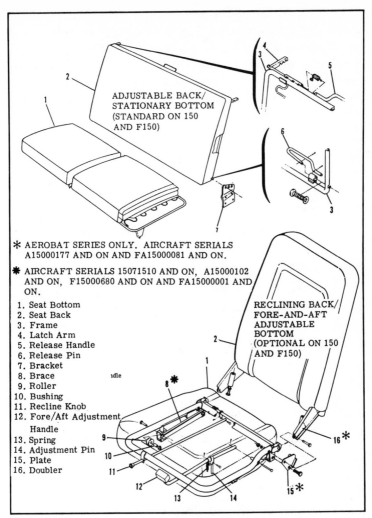

* AEROBAT SERIES ONLY. AIRCRAFT SERIALS
A15000177 AND ON AND FA15000081 AND ON.

* AIRCRAFT SERIALS 15071510 AND ON, A15000102
AND ON, F15000680 AND ON AND FA15000001 AND
ON.

1. Seat Bottom
2. Seat Back
3. Frame
4. Latch Arm
5. Release Handle
6. Release Pin
7. Bracket
8. Brace
9. Roller
10. Bushing
11. Recline Knob
12. Fore/Aft Adjustment
    Handle
13. Spring
14. Adjustment Pin
15. Plate
16. Doubler

ADJUSTABLE BACK/
STATIONARY BOTTOM
(STANDARD ON 150
AND F150)

RECLINING BACK/
FORE-AND-AFT
ADJUSTABLE
BOTTOM
(OPTIONAL ON 150
AND F150)

Fig. 8-25. Forward seats. (courtesy Cessna Aircraft Company)

if you are the hands-on type, and also want to save a dollar. One
such supplier is:

Cooper Aviation Supply Co.
2149 E. Pratt Blvd.
Elk Grove Village, IL 60007.

Also check *Trade-A-Plane* for listings of other suppliers.
Another alternative for seats and carpets is the aircraft wreck-

ing yards. They too advertise in *Trade-A-Plane*.

Individual seats are equipped with manually operated reclining seat backs. Rollers permit the seats to slide forward and back on seat rails. Pins, which engage various holes in the seat rails, lock the seats in selected positions. Stops limit ultimate travel.

Removal of a seat is accomplished by removing the stops and moving the seats forward and back on the rails to disengage them from the rails. Installation is in reverse order (Figs. 8-25, 8-26).

WARNING

It is *extremely* important that the pilot's seat stops be installed, since acceleration and deceleration could possibly permit the seat to become disengaged from the seat rails and create a hazardous situation, especially during takeoff and landing.

Safety Belts

Safety belts must be replaced when they are frayed, cut, or the

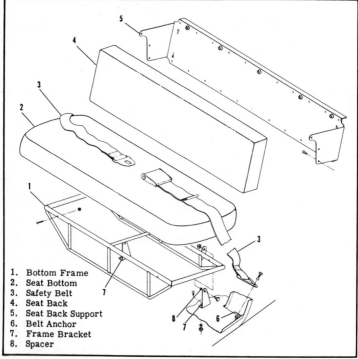

1. Bottom Frame
2. Seat Bottom
3. Safety Belt
4. Seat Back
5. Seat Back Support
6. Belt Anchor
7. Frame Bracket
8. Spacer

Fig. 8-26. Auxiliary seat. (courtesy Cessna Aircraft Company)

latches become defective. Attaching hardware should be replaced if faulty. Use only approved safety belts.

Side Window Replacement

A movable window, hinged at the top, is installed in doors. The window assembly may be replaced by pulling the hinge pins and disconnecting the window stop. To remove the frame from the plastic, it is necessary to drill out the blind rivets where the frame is spliced. When replacing a window in a frame, make sure that the sealing strip and an adequate coating of a sealing compound are used all around the edges of the plastic panel (Fig. 8-27).

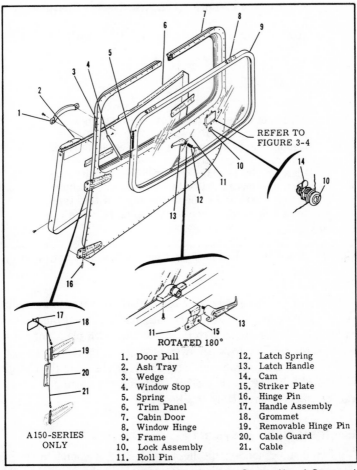

REFER TO
FIGURE 3-4

ROTATED 180°

A150-SERIES
ONLY

1. Door Pull	12. Latch Spring
2. Ash Tray	13. Latch Handle
3. Wedge	14. Cam
4. Window Stop	15. Striker Plate
5. Spring	16. Hinge Pin
6. Trim Panel	17. Handle Assembly
7. Cabin Door	18. Grommet
8. Window Hinge	19. Removable Hinge Pin
9. Frame	20. Cable Guard
10. Lock Assembly	21. Cable
11. Roll Pin	

Fig. 8-27. Cabin door and movable window. (courtesy Cessna Aircraft Company)

BATTERY HYDROMETER READINGS

READINGS	BATTERY CONDITION
1. 280 Specific Gravity	100% Charged
1. 250 Specific Gravity	75% Charged
1. 220 Specific Gravity	50% Charged
1. 190 Specific Gravity	25% Charged
1. 160 Specific Gravity..............	Practically Dead

NOTE

All readings shown are for an electrolyte temperature of 80° Fahrenheit. For higher temperatures the readings will be slightly lower. For cooler temperatures the readings will be slightly higher. Some hydrometers will have a built-in temperature compensation chart and a thermometer. If this type tester is used, disregard this chart.

Fig. 8-28. Battery Hydrometer readings. (courtesy Cessna Aircraft Company)

Battery

Battery servicing involves adding distilled water to maintain the electrolyte level with the horizontal baffle plate at the bottom of the filler holes. Be sure to flush the area with plenty of clean water after refilling to wash away any spilled battery acid.

The use of a hydrometer is required for checking the charge condition of the battery (Fig. 8-28). Charging and starting problems can be solved by referring to Fig. 8-29.

Electrical Lighting System

For troubleshooting the lighting system, a complete set of Cessna Service Manual diagrams and aids is shown (Figs. 8-30 through 8-33). Most troubleshooting can be accomplished with a VOM (volt-ohm meter).

Landing lights, navigation, strobe lights, and beacon lights will require replacement, unfortunately, on an all-too-often basis. They don't have the long lives of auto headlights and accessory bulbs (Figs. 8-34 through 8-37).

Fuel System

Understanding the Cessna Service Manual diagram of the fuel system will help you see where most problems will occur in the fuel system, and why you must be careful about water and debris in the system (Fig. 8-38).

Stainless Screw Kits

Have you noticed all those rusted screws on an airplane? It's easy to replace them with non-rusting stainless screws. Kits containing screws in the proper number and of the proper size are the recommended way to purchase supplies for this job.

PROBABLE CAUSE	ISOLATION PROCEDURE	REMEDY
BATTERY WILL NOT SUPPLY POWER TO BUS OR IS INCAPABLE OF CRANKING ENGINE.		
Battery discharged.	1. Measure voltage at "BAT" terminal of battery contactor with master switch and a suitable load such as a taxi light turned on. Normal battery will indicate 11.5 volts or more.	If voltage is low, proceed to step 2. If voltage is normal, proceed to step 3.
Battery faulty.	2. Check fluid level in cells and charge battery at 20 amps for approximately 30 minutes or until battery voltage rises to 15 volts. Check battery with a load type tester.	If tester indicates a good battery, the malfunction may be assumed to be a discharged battery. If the tester indicates a faulty battery, replace the battery.
Faulty contactor or wiring between contactor or master switch.	3. Measure voltage at master switch terminal (smallest) on contactor with master switch closed. Normal indication is zero volts.	If voltage reads zero, proceed to step 4. If a voltage reading is obtained, check wiring between contactor and master switch. Also check master switch.
Open coil on contactor.	4. Check continuity between "BAT" terminal and master switch terminal of contactor. Normal indication is 16 to 24 ohms (Master switch open).	If ohmmeter indicates an open coil, replace contactor. If ohmmeter indicates a good coil, proceed to step 5.
Faulty contactor contacts.	5. Check voltage on "BUS" side of contactor with master switch closed. Meter normally indicates battery voltage.	If voltage is zero or intermittant, replace contactor. If voltage is normal, proceed to step 6.
Faulty wiring between contactor and bus.	6. Inspect wiring between contactor and bus.	Repair or replace wiring.

Fig. 8-29. Troubleshooting the battery charging system. (courtesy Cessna Aircraft Company)

PROBABLE CAUSE	ISOLATION PROCEDURE	REMEDY
LANDING AND TAXI LIGHTS OUT.		
Short circuit in wiring.	1. Inspect fuse.	If fuse is open, proceed to step 2. If fuse is OK, proceed to step 3.
Defective wiring.	2. Test each circuit separately until short is located.	Repair or replace wiring.
Defective switch.	3. Check voltage at lights with master and landing and taxi light switches ON. Should read battery voltage.	Replace switch.
LANDING OR TAXI LIGHT OUT.		
Lamp burned out.	1. Test lamp with ohmmeter or new lamp.	Replace lamp.
Open circuit in wiring.	2. Test wiring for continuity.	Repair or replace wiring.
FLASHING BEACON DOES NOT LIGHT.		
Short circuit in wiring.	1. Inspect fuse.	If fuse is open, proceed to step 2. If fuse is OK, proceed to step 3.
Defective wiring.	2. Test circuit until short is located.	Repair or replace wiring.
Lamp burned out.	3. Test lamp with ohmmeter or a new lamp.	Replace lamp. If lamp is good, proceed to step 4.
Open circuit in wiring.	4. Test circuit from lamp to flasher for continuity.	If no continuity is present, repair or replace wiring. If continuity is present, proceed to step 5.
Defective switch.	5. Check voltage at flasher with master and beacon switch on. Should read battery voltage.	Replace switch. If voltage is present, proceed to step 6.
Defective flasher.	6. Install new flasher.	
FLASHING BEACON CONSTANTLY LIT.		
Defective flasher.	1. Install new flasher.	
ALL NAV LIGHTS OUT.		
Short circuit in wiring.	1. Inspect fuse.	If fuse is open, proceed to step 2. If fuse is OK, proceed to step 3.
Defective wiring.	2. Isolate and test each nav light circuit until short is located.	Repair or replace wiring.

Fig. 8-30. Troubleshooting the aircraft lighting system Chart A. (courtesy Cessna Aircraft Company)

The use of stainless screws on airplanes makes sense, as they don't rust and stain the surrounding area as do the stock screws.

Be very careful that you don't strip out the screw holes when removing/installing screws.

Trimcraft Aviation supplies packages kits of stainless screws (Fig. 8-39). Each kit contains everything you will need. Their kits are available from various suppliers that advertise in the airplane magazines and *Trade-A-Plane*. Direct supply is available from:

Trimcraft Aviation
P.O. Box 488
Genoa City, WI 53128
Phone: (414) 279-6896

LOGBOOK REQUIREMENTS

Entries must be made in the appropriate logbook whenever preventive maintenance is performed.

A logbook entry must include:

PROBABLE CAUSE	ISOLATION PROCEDURE	REMEDY
INSTRUMENT LIGHTS WILL NOT LIGHT (Cont).		
Defective wiring.	2. Test circuit until short is located.	Repair or replace wiring.
	3. Test for open circuit.	Repair or replace wiring. If no short or open circuit is found, proceed to step 4.
Defective rheostat.	4. Check voltage at instrument light with master switch on. Should read battery voltage with rheostat turned full clockwise and voltage should decrease as rheostat is turned counterclockwise.	If no voltage is present or voltage has a sudden drop before rheostat has been turned full counterclockwise, replace rheostat.
Lamp burned out.	5. Test lamp with ohmmeter or new lamp.	Replace lamp.
CONTROL WHEEL MAP LIGHT WILL NOT LIGHT THRU 1970 AIRCRAFT ONLY.		
Nav light switch turned off.	1. Nav light switch has to be ON before map light will light.	
Short circuit in wiring.	2. Check lamp fuse on terminal board located on back of stationary panel with ohmmeter.	If fuse is open, proceed to step 3. If fuse is OK, proceed to step 4.
Defective wiring.	3. Test circuit until short is located.	Repair or replace wiring.
	4. Test for open circuit.	Repair or replace wiring. If a short or open circuit is not found, proceed to step 5.
Defective map light assembly.	5. Check voltage at map light assembly with master and nav switches on.	If battery voltage is present, replace map light assembly.
	CAUTION	
	Failure to observe polarity shown on wiring diagram (page 20-19), will result in immediate failure of the transistor on the map light circuit board assembly.	
CONTROL WHEEL MAP LIGHT WILL NOT LIGHT 1971 AIRCRAFT & ON.		
Nav light switch turned off.	1. Nav light switch has to be ON before map light will light.	
Short circuit in wiring.	2. Check lamp fuse on terminal board located on back of stationary panel with ohmmeter.	If fuse is open, proceed to step 3. If fuse is OK, proceed to step 4.
Defective wiring.	3. Test circuit until short is located.	Repair or replace wiring.

Fig. 8-31. Troubleshooting the aircraft lighting system Chart B. (courtesy Cessna Aircraft Company)

PROBABLE CAUSE	ISOLATION PROCEDURE	REMEDY
ALL NAV LIGHTS OUT (Cont).		
Defective switch.	3. Check voltage at nav light with master and nav light switches on. Should read battery voltage.	Replace switch.
ONE NAV LIGHT OUT.		
Lamp burned out.	1. Inspect lamp.	Replace lamp.
Open circuit in wiring.	2. Test wiring for continuity.	Repair or replace wiring.
ONE ANTI-COLLISION STROBE LIGHT DOES NOT LIGHT.		
Flash tube burned out.	Test with new flash tube.	Replace flash tube.
Faulty wiring.	Test for continuity.	Repair or replace.
Faulty trigger head.	Test with new trigger head.	Replace trigger head.
BOTH ANTI-COLLISION STROBE LIGHTS WILL NOT LIGHT.		
Circuit breaker open.	Inspect.	Reset.
Faulty power supply.	Listen for whine in power supply to determine if power is operating.	
Faulty switch.	Test for continuity.	Repair or replace.
Faulty wiring.	Test for continuity.	Repair or replace.
DOME LIGHT TROUBLE.		
Short circuit in wiring.	1. Inspect fuse.	If fuse is open, proceed to step 2. If fuse is OK, proceed to step 3.
Defective wiring.	2. Test circuit until short is located.	Repair or replace wiring.
	3. Test for open circuit.	Repair or replace wiring. If no short or open circuit is found, proceed to step 4.
Lamp burned out.	4. Test lamp with ohmmeter or new lamp.	Replace lamp.
Defective switch.	5. Check for voltage at dome light with master and dome light switch on. Should read battery voltage.	Replace switch.
INSTRUMENT LIGHTS WILL NOT LIGHT.		
Short circuit in wiring.	1. Inspect fuse.	If fuse is open, proceed to step 2. If fuse is OK, proceed to step 3.

Fig. 8-32. Troubleshooting the aircraft lighting system Chart C. (courtesy Cessna Aircraft Company)

PROBABLE CAUSE	ISOLATION PROCEDURE	REMEDY
CONTROL WHEEL MAP LIGHT WILL NOT LIGHT 1971 AIRCRAFT & ON (Cont).		
	4. Test for open circuit.	Repair or replace wiring. If a short or open circuit is not found, proceed to step 5.
Defective map light assembly.	5. Check voltage at map light assembly with master and nav switches on.	If battery voltage is present, replace map light assembly.

Fig. 8-33. Troubleshooting the aircraft lighting system Chart D. (courtesy Cessna Aircraft Company)

□ Description of work done.
□ Date work is completed.
□ Name of the person doing the work.
□ Approval for return to service. (signature and certificate number) by the pilot approving the work.

The FARs require that all preventive maintenance work must be done in such a manner, and by use of materials of such quality,

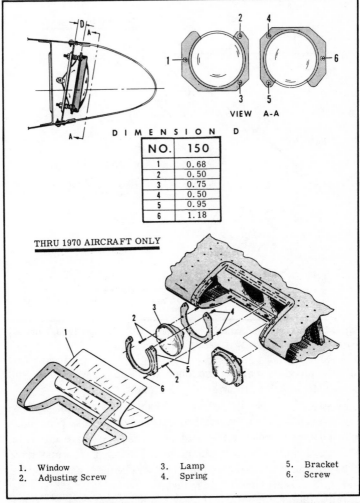

DIMENSION D

NO.	150
1	0.68
2	0.50
3	0.75
4	0.50
5	0.95
6	1.18

VIEW A-A

THRU 1970 AIRCRAFT ONLY

1. Window
2. Adjusting Screw
3. Lamp
4. Spring
5. Bracket
6. Screw

Fig. 8-34. Landing and taxi light installation, 1959 through 1970. (courtesy Cessna Aircraft Company)

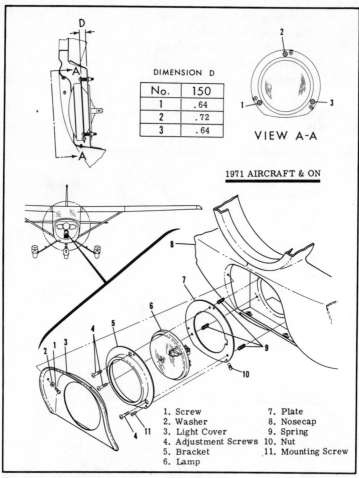

DIMENSION D

No.	150
1	.64
2	.72
3	.64

VIEW A-A

1971 AIRCRAFT & ON

1. Screw
2. Washer
3. Light Cover
4. Adjustment Screws
5. Bracket
6. Lamp
7. Plate
8. Nosecap
9. Spring
10. Nut
11. Mounting Screw

Fig. 8-35. Landing and taxi light installation, 1971 through 1983. (courtesy Cessna Aircraft Company)

that the airframe, engine, propeller, or assembly worked on will be at least equal to its original condition.

I strongly advise that before you undertake any of these allowable preventive maintenance procedures you discuss your plans with a licensed mechanic. The instructions/advice you receive from him may help you avoid making costly mistakes. You may have to pay the mechanic for his time, but it will be money well-spent—and, after all, his time is his money.

In addition to talking with your mechanic, get your own tools.

Don't borrow from your friend the mechanic, or he won't be your friend very long.

Properly performed preventive maintenance gives the pilot/owner a better understanding of his airplane, affords substantial maintenance savings, and gives a feeling of accomplishment.

For an in-depth study of preventive maintenance, see *Lightplane Owner's Maintenance Guide*, TAB #2244, by Cliff Dossey.

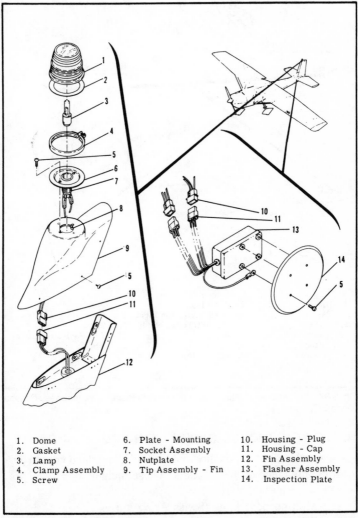

1. Dome	6. Plate - Mounting	10. Housing - Plug
2. Gasket	7. Socket Assembly	11. Housing - Cap
3. Lamp	8. Nutplate	12. Fin Assembly
4. Clamp Assembly	9. Tip Assembly - Fin	13. Flasher Assembly
5. Screw		14. Inspection Plate

Fig. 8-36. Flashing beacon light installation. (courtesy Cessna Aircraft Company)

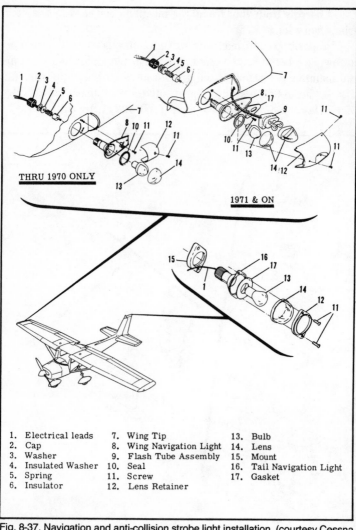

THRU 1970 ONLY

1971 & ON

1.	Electrical leads	7.	Wing Tip	13.	Bulb
2.	Cap	8.	Wing Navigation Light	14.	Lens
3.	Washer	9.	Flash Tube Assembly	15.	Mount
4.	Insulated Washer	10.	Seal	16.	Tail Navigation Light
5.	Spring	11.	Screw	17.	Gasket
6.	Insulator	12.	Lens Retainer		

Fig. 8-37. Navigation and anti-collision strobe light installation. (courtesy Cessna Aircraft Company)

TOOLS YOU SHOULD CARRY WITH YOU

A small quantity of quality tools should allow the owner to perform maintenance on his airplane. These include:

☐ Multipurpose knife (Swiss Army knife).
☐ 3/8″ ratchet drive with a flex head as an option.

- 2, 4, 6-inch 3/8" extensions.
- sockets from 3/8" to 3/4" in 1/16" increments.
- 6" crescent wrench.
- 10" monkey wrench.
- 6 or 12 point closed (box) wrenches from 3/8" to 3/4". In addition, I recommend a set of open end wrenches of the same dimensions.
- Pair of channel lock pliers (medium size).
- Phillips screwdriver set in the three common sizes.

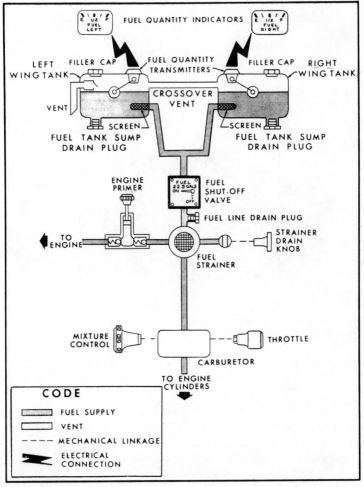

Fig. 8-38. Fuel system schematic. (courtesy Cessna Aircraft Company)

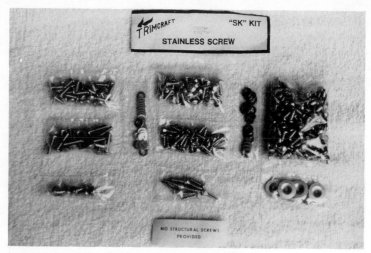

Fig. 8-39. Stainless screw kit. (courtesy Trimcraft)

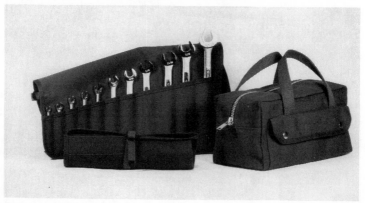

Fig. 8-40. Convenient tool kit. (courtesy Helsper Sewing Co., 80 Highbury Dr., Elgin, IL 60120 Phone: (312) 894-6127)

☐ Blade screwdriver set to include short (2″) to long (8″) sizes.
☐ Plastic electrical tape.
☐ Container of assorted nuts and bolts.
☐ Spare set of spark plugs.

A carrying bag or box will be very handy to keep your tools in order and protected (Fig. 8-40).

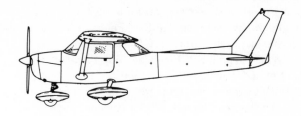

Chapter 9

STCs and Modifications

The STC (Supplemental Type Certificate) is required when a major change or modification is made to an airplane. These STC
changes can be as minor as approving a certain type of brake
change, or as complex as recontouring the flying surfaces of the
plane.

STCs

The following is a list of STCs for Cessna 150/152 airplanes.
When reading the list, the STC number appears first, followed by
the item/part modified by the STC, the airplane models the STC
applies to, and the name and address of the holder of the STC.

SA1-479: Aero control AP and heading lock GD (all 150); Her-
bert Baer, 90 Federal Street, Boston, MA 02109.

SA1-630: Dry vacuum pump and instrument vacuum system
113A5 (all 150); Airborne Mechanisms Division, Randolph
Manufacturing Company, 13229 Shaw Avenue, East Cleveland,
OH 44112.

SA4-965: Autopilot (all 150); Brittain Industries, Inc., P.O. Box
51370, Tulsa, OK 74151.

SA4-1342: Full flow lube oil filter 30409A with element 1A0235
(all 150); Winslow Aerofilter Corporation, 4069 Hollis Street,
Oakland, CA 94608.

SA4-1373: Brake locks AB-6531 and AB-6532 (all 150); Johns-Manville Corporation, 22 E. 40 Street, New York, NY 10001.

SA17WE: Conversion of aircraft for parachute jumping and aerial photography operations (all 150); Peterson Aviation, 3100 Airport Avenue, Santa Monica, CA 90406.

SA164WE: Fuel filter PFF-100 (all 150); Pioneer Aero Services, P.O. Box 227, Burbank, CA 91500.

SA534CE: Installation of Canairco 1214 WS supplementary light (all 150); Canairco Limited, 400 1st Avenue North, Minneapolis, MN 55401.

SA1433WE: Installation of Brittain Model CSA-1 Stability Augmentation Systems (all 150); Brittain Industries, P.O. Box 51370, Tulsa, OK 74151.

SA5733SW: Installation of long-range wing fuel tanks (all 150); Custom Aircraft Conversions, 222 West Turbo Drive, San Antonio, TX 78216.

SA1-124: Lube oil filter BP55-1 (all 150); Fram Corporation, 105 Pawtucket Avenue, Providence, RI 02916.

SA4-925: Magnetic flight director 2000 (all 150); Clarkson Company, Paul Spur, AZ.

SA220SO: Tow bar, release mechanism, and safety tow link (all 150); Gasser Banners, Inc., P.O. Box 3502, Metropolitan Airport, Nashville, TN 37217.

SA270SO: Water and ice detector in fuel gascolator and carburetor (all 150); Charles B. Shivers, Jr., 8928 Valleybrook Road, Birmingham, AL 35206.

SA316SO: Carburetor ice detector (all 150); Charles B. Shivers, Jr., 8928 Valleybrook Road, Birmingham, AL 35206.

SA971WE: Installation of Jasco 76540 (35A) alternator kit or Jasco 6555 (50A) alternator kit (all 150); Skytronics, Inc., 227 Oregan Street, El Segundo, CA 90245.

SA150NW: Installation of flap gap seals (150 thru M, A150 K-M); B&M Aviation, P.O. Box 1563, Bellingham, WA 98225.

SA172NW: Installation of drooped-type wingtips (150 through M, A150M); Robert C. Cansdale, 29511 9th Place S., Federal Way, WA 98002.

SA175GL: Installation of conventional landing gear (150 through M, A150K-M, 152, A152); Robert L. or Barbara Williams, Box 608, Udall, KS 67146.

SA221G1: Installation of wheel replacement type skis, Fluidyne all-metal (TSO approved) model A2000A main skis, Fluidyne Model AT2000A tail ski (150 thru M, A150K-M, 152); Robert

L. or Barbara Williams, Box 608, Udall, KS 67146.

SA223GL: Installation of the stall strips (150 through M, A150K-M, 152, A152); MacKenzie Aviation Company, 3847 Bassett Road, Rootstown, OH 44272.

SA268GL: Installation of wheel and ski adapters on Models 150F, G, H, J, K, L, M, 152 aircraft modified per STC SA175GL (150 through M, A150K-M, 152, A152); Robert L. or Barbara Williams, Box 608, Udall, KS 67146.

SA318GL: Installation of Bolen wheel extenders on Cessna models modified per STC SA175GL and/or SA268GL (150 through E); Robert L. or Barbara Williams, Box 608, Udall, KS 67146.

SA324GL: Installation of fuel tank caps (150 through M, A150K-M); John J. Francissen, 426 Pleasant Drive, Roseville, IL 60172.

SA326EA: Wet-to-dry vacuum pump conversion kit 300-3 (150 through H); Airborne Manufacturing Company, 711 Taylor Street, Elyria, OH 44035.

SA1398SO: Remove drain plug AN-806-6 from fuel line drain in belly of aircraft (150 through E); Middle Tennessee Acft. Components, P.O. Box 472, Smithville, TN 37166.

SA1422SO: Installation of Model CC-1 checkpoint computer (150 through M, A150M, 152, A152); Perception Systems, 4500 N. Dixie Hwy., #c-24, West Palm Beach, FL 33407.

SA1235SO: Replacement of the lower fuselage fuel drain cap (P/N AN929-6) with an adapter-type coupling, (belly drain P/N MT-101) and an exposed quick drain valve P/N CAV-160D (all 150/152); Larry L. Lofgren, P.O. Box 472, Smithville, TN 37166.

SA403CE: Install Fluidyne A2000A main skis and NA800 nose ski (150 through C); Fluidyne Engineering Corporation, 5900 Olson Memorial Highway, Minneapolis, MN 55422.

SA527CE: Installation of Hoskins Twilighter Mark I high-intensity light system (150 through G); Symbolic displays, Inc., 1762 McGaw Avenue, Irvine, CA 92705.

SA572CE: Installation of Lycoming 150 or 160-hp Model O-320 (150 through M, A150L-M normal category landplanes, 150G-K seaplanes); Barbara or Bob Williams, Box 431, 213 North Clark, Udall, KS 67146.

SA589WE: Installation of full-flow lube oil filters on aircraft for the benefit of the engine (all 150); Worldwide Aircraft Filter Corp., 1685 Abram Court, P.O. Box 175B, San Leandro, CA 94577.

SA615EA: Installation of Whelen anti-collision strobe light system, models H through D, HR or HS – 14 (14V) or – 28 (28V), as replacement for originally installed anti-collision lights (150 through M, A150K-M, 152, A152); Whelen Engineering Company, Inc., Winter Avenue, Deep River, CT 06417.

SA630WE: Installation of oil filter assemblies (150 through G); Nelson Filter, Division of Nelson Industries, Inc., P.O. Box 280, Stoughton, WI 53589.

SA633GL: Modify airplane to fly on unleaded automotive gasoline, 87 minimum antiknock index, per ATSM Spec. D-439, STC SE634GL; Approved unleaded automotive gasoline, 87 min. antiknock index (all 150); Experimental Aircraft Association, Wittman Airfield, Oshkosh, WI 54901.

SA672GL: Install Aero Ski Mfrg ski model M1500, M1800, or M2000 (150 through M, A150K, 152, A152); Aero Ski Manufacturing Co., Inc., P.O. Box 346, Park Rapids, MN 56470.

SA695CE: Install Frantz oil filter (150 through L, A150K); Schmidt Aero Service, Municipal Airport, Worthington, MN 56187.

SA750CE: Installation of Lycoming 150 and 160-hp Model O-320 engine and McCauley propeller 1C172/TM (150 through M, A150K-M) L; Robert L. and Barbara V. Williams, 117 East First, Udall, KS 67146.

SA844CE: Installation of electropneumatic stall warning system (most 150); Kaeton Engineering Company, 1000 West 55th Street South, Wichita, KS 67217.

SA890SW: Medairco Automatic Fuel Alert F-2 (all 150); Medairco, 3601 East Admiral Place, Tulsa, OK 74150.

SA909CEW: Install STOL kit (wing leading edge cuffs, drooped tips, stall fences, and aileron gap seals) (150 through M, 152 landplanes and 150G-K seaplanes); Horton Stol-Craft, Wellington Municipal Airport, Wellington, KS 67152.

SA944CE: STOL kit installation (150 through L): Bob or Barbara Williams, Box 608, Udall, KS 67146.

SA917EA: Installation of Grimes Manufacturing Co. aviation white anti-collision strobe light systems, two-light or three-light series 555 for wingtips and tail, P/N 30-0555 (150 through M, A150K-M); Grimes Manufacturing Company, 515 North Russell Street, Urbana, OH 43078.

SA1148NW: Installation of flap gap seals (150 through M, A150K-L, 152, A152); Tacoma Airways, Route 2, Box 2644, Spanway, WA 98287.

SA1261WE: Installation of control position indicator (CPI) system (150 through G); Sunstrand Data Control, Inc., Subsidiary Sunstrand Corporation, Overlake Industrial Park, Redmond, WA 98052.

SA1346CE: Chrome-plate brake disc installation (150 through K, A150K); Engineering Plating & Processing, Inc., 641 Southwest Blvd., Kansas City, KS 66103.

SA1418SO: Replacement of rotor vanes in Airborne 211CC and 212CW vacuum pumps (150 and 152); U.S. Air Source, Ltd., 3640 Atlanta Highway, Athens, GA 30604.

SA1455WE: Installation of Brittain Model CSA-1 Stability Augmentation System (all 150); Brittain Industries, P.O. Box 51370, Tulsa, OK 74151.

SA1473WE: Installation of Brittain Model B2C Flight Control System (all 150); Brittain Industries, P.O. Box 51370, Tulsa, OK 74151.

SA1512WE: Installation of exhaust gas temperature monitoring systems Model EGT-1 (all 150); K S Avionics, 18145 Judy Street, Castro Valley, CA 94546.

SA1663CE: Installation of strut/wing and strut/fuselage fairings, lightning hole covers, and aerodynamic putty (150 through M, 152, A152); Aircraft Development Company, 1326 North Westlink Boulevard, Wichita, KS 67212.

SA1944WE: Installation of Madras wingtips (150 through J); Madras Air Service, Route 2, Madras, OR 97741.

SA1977WE: Installation of recontoured wing and leading edge, stall fences, wingtips and positive aileron seals (150 through L); Robertson Aircraft Corporation, 839 W. Perimeter Road, Renton, WA 98055.

SA2053WE: An adjustable lateral trim capability through spring bungee control of aileron per Strato Engineering Company (150 through E); Consulting Aerospace Engineers, 1845 Empire, Burbank, CA 91504.

SA2850SW: Installation of leading edge cuffs, stall fences, aileron seals, wingtips (150 through M, A150K-M); Bob Williams C/B/A/ Bush Conversions, P.O. Box 431, Udall, KS 67146.

SA157NE: Installation of graphic engine monitor system, Model GEM-602 S/N 403 and subsequent (all 150); Insight Instrument Corporation, Box 194, Ellicott Station, Buffalo, NY 14205.

SA2105WE: Installation of Model EGT-3 exhaust gas temperature monitor (with rising temperature alarm) (all 150); K S Avionics, 18145 Judy Street, Castro Valley, CA 94546.

SA2119WE: Installation of recontoured wing and leading edge, stall fences, wingtips and positive aileron seals (150 through L); Robertson Aircraft Corporation, 839 W. Perimeter Road, Renton, WA 98055.

SA2219WE: Installation of Filtrator Company engine crankcase breather and vacuum pump air-oil separator (150 through L, A150L); Beryl D'Shannon Aviation Specialties, Inc., Route 1, Box 172D, Leesburg, FL 32748.

SA2790WE: Installation of angle of attack indicator (150 through L); Thompson Aircraft Company, 8219 Billy Mitchell Drive, Santee, CA 92071.

SA3112WE: Installation of flap slot closures (150 through M, A150L-M, 152, A152); Thermal Aircraft Company, 56 - 850 Thermal Street, Thermal, CA 92274.

SA3345WE: Recognition light installation on horizontal stabilizer (150 through M, A150K-M, 152, A152); Devore Aviation Corporation, Suite B, 6104 Kircher Street, N.E., Albuquerque, NM 87109.

SA4065SW: Metal chip detector in engine oil (150 through M, A150L, M, 152, A152); Aero Logistics International, P.O. Box 34395, Dallas, TX 75234.

SA4302WE: Installation of leading edge cuff on each wing (150 through M, A150M, 152, A152); Marshall E. Quackenbush, P.O. Box 2421, California City, CA 93505.

SA3037SWD: Automatic flight system AK457 consisting of Century I autopilot with optional omni tracker (150 through M); Mitchell Industries, Inc., P.O. Box 610, Municipal Airport, Mineral Wells, TX 76067.

SA2687WE: Installation of protective device on fuel tank vent line (150C-L); S. Harry Robertson, Research Engineers, 8002 E. Cypress Street, Scottsdale, AZ 85257.

SA607W: Installation of Mitchell automatic stabilizer model AK193 (150D-G): Century Flight Systems, Inc., F.M. 1195, P.O. Box 610, Mineral Wells, TX 76067.

SA808WA: Installation of Mitchell Model AK246 omni-tracker. Applicable to aircraft modified by the following STCs: SA603SW, SA606SW, SA607SW, SA621SW, SA624SW, SA637SW, SA66767SW, SA669SW, SA675SW, SA681SW, SA709SW, SA727SW, SA737SW, SA789SW, SA793SW, SA658SW, SA668SW (150D-G); EDO-AIRE Mitchell, P.O. Box 610, Municipal Airport, Mineral Wells, TX 76067.

SA1809WE: Installation of one 12-gallon auxiliary fuel tank in each outboard wing panel (150D-M, A150K-M, 152, A152); Flint

Aero, 8402 North Magnolia, Suite G, Santee, CA 92071.

SA2191WE: Installation of recontoured wing and leading edge, stall fences, wingtips and positive aileron seals (150 through L); Robertson Aircraft Corporation, 839 W. Perimeter Road, Renton, WA 98055.

SA2192WE: Installation of recontoured wing and leading edge, stall fences, wingtips and positive aileron seals (150 through L); Robertson Aircraft Corporation, 839 W. Perimeter Road, Renton, WA 98055.

SA3733WE: Installation of a special door (right-hand side only) to facilitate aerial photography (150D-L in utility category); Robert M. Craig, 131 Burwell Road, Highland, TX 77562.

SA1431WE: Installation of rudder trim system (150E-G); Robertson Aircraft Corporation, 839 W. Perimeter Road, Renton, WA 98055.

SA287GL: Installation of Lycoming O-320-D2M engine and McCauley Model 1C172/TM propeller using the existing installation hardware on an aircraft previously modified in accordance with STC SA572CE (150F); Max L. Shankin, 1769 Rooker Road, Mooresville, IN 46158.

SA1567SO: Installation of Appalachian Accessories brake rotor P/N 75-27 (150F-K, A150K); Appalachian Accessories, P.O. Box 1077, Tri-City Airport Station, Blountville, TN 37617.

SA2035WE: Installation of Aerial photographic camera kit serial No. 101 (150F-K); Federal Water Pollution Control Administration, Pacific Northwest Water Laboratory, 200 S.W. 35th Street, Corvallis, OR 97330.

SA2846SW: Conversion from tri-gear to conventional gear configuration and reconversion to tri-gear (150F-K); Custom Craft, Inc., 234 West Turbo Drive, San Antonio, TX 78216.

SA4278WE: Installation of quick-drain valve at low point of aircraft fuel system (150F-M, A150K-M, 152); Aircraft Metal Products Corp., 4206 Glencoe Avenue, Venice, CA 90291.

SA1615CE: Quick drain in fuel line at tee fitting forward of fuel selector valve (150F and subsequent, A150 and subsequent, 152, A152); Wells Aircraft, Inc., Municipal Airport, P.O. Box 858, Hutchinson, KS 67501.

SA1814NM: Installation of Lompoc Aero inner Plexiglas pane in swing-out window frames presently employing a single window (150G-M, A150K-M, 152, A152); Lompoc Aero Specialties, Lompoc Airport, Lompoc, CA 93436.

SA1395SW: Revise fuel and oil system for inverted flight

(A150K-L); M.H. Spinks, Sr., P.O. Box 11099, Fort Worth, TX 76110.

SA217RM: Installation of Lycoming O-360-A1A engine (180 hp), McCauley 1A170 propeller, revised engine mount and fuel system, dorsal fin, wing leading edge cuffs, wing fences, aileron gap closures and other changes (150L normal category); Nolan E. Stallcup, 2089 Florence, Aurora, CO 80010.

SA550GL: Installation of Mitchell automatic flight system Model AK457 consisting of Century I autopilot with optional omni tracker (152); Harold L. Riegle, 1213 Woodbridge, St. Clair Shores, MI 48080.

SA1000NW: Installation of Lycoming O-235-L2C (modified) (SE792NW) engine, McCauley 1A103/TCM 6958 propeller (152); Kennis G. Blackman, Building C-52-1, Plaine Field, WA 98204.

SA1219EA: Installation of a Sensenich Model 72CKS6-0-56 or -54 metal propeller and a S72CK spinner assembly (152); Sensenich Corporation, P.O. Box 1168, Lancaster, PA 17600.

SA2290NM: Installation of Elano P/N ELO99001-060 "b" (or later FAA app. revision) muffler in lieu of original Cessna muffler (152); Del-Air, 2121 South Wildcat Way, Porterville, CA 93257.

SA789GL: Installation of Lycoming O-235-L23 engine modified with STC SE70GL in combination with propellers, Sensenich 72CK-S6-0-54 or McCauley 1A103/TCM6958 (152, A152); Flying "C" Leasing, Ltd., 329 East 6th Street, Hinsdale, IL 60521.

SA1008NM: Installation of a Sensenich S72CKS6-0-52, -54 or -56 Propeller/spinner assembly on Lycoming O-235-L2C or O-235-L2C(M) engine (152, A152); Kennis G. Blackman, Building C-52-1, Paine Field, Everett, WA 98205.

SA4057WE: Installation of a muffler and exhaust heat exchanger (152, A152): Flight Research, Inc., Hangar 61, Mojave, CA 93501.

SA1384CE: Install Lycoming O-320-E2D engine and McCauley 1C172TM7458 Propeller (A152); Avcon Industries, 1006 W. 53rd Street N., Wichita, KS 67204.

POPULAR MODIFICATIONS

The following are some of the more popular conversions owners can make to their 150/152 airplanes:

STOL

STOL conversions are perhaps king of all the modifications available to the 150/152 owner. STOL is the military designation for Short Takeoff and Landing aircraft. STOL has been extended into general aviation markets, resulting in some rather spectacular—performance-wise—conversion aircraft. The typical STOL modification involves changes to the overall shape of the wing (usually in the form of a leading edge cuff), the addition of stall fences (to stop the stall from proceeding along the wing span-wise Fig. 9-1), gap seals, modified wingtips (Fig. 9-2), vortex generators to aid in directional control at low speed, and an increase in power (larger engine).

Here are the specifications Horton STOLcraft lists for a converted Cessna 150:

Gross weight:	1500 lbs
Takeoff Speed:	33 mph
Takeoff over 50' obst:	770 ft
Cruise Speed:	120 mph
Approach Speed:	36 mph
Landing over 50' obst:	540 ft

(These figures represent maximum performance)

Fig. 9-1. Stall fence installed as part of an STOL package.

Fig. 9-2. Wingtips sometimes used in STOL conversions, sometimes called "droop tips."

Compare these to the factory specifications in Chapter 3 of this book. For further information, contact:

Horton STOLcraft
Wellington Municipal Airport
Wellington, KS 67152
Phone: (800) 835-2051
    KS: (316) 326-2241

Sometimes an owner will make STOL modifications one part at a time, and often with STCs from several sources. Before proceeding with this method, check with your local GADO about the various STCs you are considering, as some are not compatible with others.

Power

Power increases are another popular modification made to the 150/152s, and are often done in conjunction with a STOL modification. These mods consist of engine replacement to increase the useful load and flight performance figures of the aircraft. The usual engine will be in the 150-horsepower range, although there are some

180-horsepower 150s around. The modifications can be extensive— and costly, although most are not much above the level of a good engine rebuild charge.

Custom Aircraft Conversions claims the following performance figures for their 150 and 180-hp conversions:

Speed		
Cruising (10,000 ft):	154	TAS
Stall:	47	mph
Takeoff Distance	250	ft
Rate of Climb:	1590	fpm
Service Ceiling:	21,500	ft
Gross Weight:	1760	lbs

Compare these figures to those found in Chapter 3 and you will quickly see why the "big iron" power-up conversions are popular.

For further information about these engine modifications, contact:

ACT
P.O. Box 119
Georgetown, CA 95634
Phone: (916) 333-2466

Wingtips

Wingtips are often changed to increase performance. Dr. Sighard Hoerner, Ph.D, designed a high-performance wingtip for the U.S. Navy, which provided information that led to the development of improved wingtips for small planes. A properly designed wingtip can provide an increase of 3 to 5 mph in cruise speed and a small increase in climb performance, but most important are the improved low-speed handling characteristics: 10 to 20 percent reduction in takeoff roll, 4 to 5 mph lower stall speed, and improved slow flight handling. Installation time can be as low as two to three hours. This is one of the most popular modifications for 150/152s. For more information, contact:

Ace Deemers
Madras Air Service
1914 NW Deemers Dr.
Madras, OR 97741

Met-Co-Aire
P.O. Box 2216
Fullerton, CA 92633
Phone: (714) 870-4610

Eddie P. Owens
2218 Ansbary Dr.
Houston, TX 77018
Phone: (713) 686-8890

Taildraggers

Taildragger conversion has become another popular modification among the owners of 150/152s. Basically, the nosewheel is removed, the main gear moved forward, and a tailwheel installed (Fig. 9-3). Performance benefits of 8 to 10 mph increase in cruise, shorter takeoff distances, and better rough-field handling are claimed. My own opinion is that if the need for a rough field machine is real, then a proper STOL and power-up modification should also be made in addition to the taildragger conversion. This will cost more money, but the results will be a very stable, safe, dependable, go-anywhere airplane.

Before you run out and have your tricycle-geared airplane modified, consider the difficulties you may encounter with your piloting skills. Taildraggers require considerably more precision when landing, and are far less forgiving of error than nosewheel airplanes.

A particularly nice taildragger conversion is the "Texas Taildragger" available from ACT. This is a well-planned kit that will take about 50 to 60 hours of mechanic time. It even allows return to tricycle configuration at a later date with only a few hours of labor. The tailwheel is hard rubber; however, a Scott or Maule tailwheel can be purchased as part of the STC.

ACT claims the following benefits from converting to a taildragger configuration:

- ☐ Speed increase of 9 mph.
- ☐ 65 fpm rate of climb increase.
- ☐ Better fuel economy.
- ☐ Increase of 10 lbs in useful load.
- ☐ More propeller-to-ground clearance.
- ☐ No nosewheel shimmy.
- ☐ More versatile aircraft.

Fig. 9-3. Taildragger conversion. (courtesy Custom Aircraft Conversions)

For further information, contact:

ACT
P.O. Box 119
Georgetown, CA 95634
Phone: (916) 333-2466

Gap Seals

Gap seals are extensions of the lower wing surface from the rear spar to the leading edge of the flap and/or aileron. Their use covers approximately six square feet of open space, allowing a smoother flow of air. In addition to the reduction of parasitic drag, the aircraft will cruise from 1 to 3 mph faster, and stall from 5 to 8 mph slower. Gap seals are often part of a STOL installation. Gap seals are available from:

B&M Aviation
2048 Airport Way
Bellingham, WA 98226
Phone: (206) 676-1750

(This version of gap seal is aluminum, and requires two to three hours of installation time.)

Fuel Tanks

Fuel tanks are sometimes added to increase operational range. Additionally, they are required if you have a large engine installed in your aircraft. Such modifications are available from:

ACT
P.O. Box 119
Georgetown, CA 95634
Phone: (916) 333-2466

Flint Aero
8665 Mission Gorge Rd.
Building D1
Santee, CA 92071
Phone: (619) 448-1551

Noise

Noise reduction has been a problem for all small airplane

Fig. 9-4. Sound-reducing windows. (courtesy Lompoc)

owners; however, one manufacturer produces an inner window. To reduce cabin noise, the inner windows are installed in the doors, and amount to "storm" windows. By increasing the window thickness, and including a dead air space, interior noise is reduced (Fig. 9-4). For further information, contact:

Lompoc Aero Specialties
Lompoc Airport
P.O. Box 998
Lompoc, CA 93438
Phone: (805) 736-1273

Doors

Door catches on older 150s are usually rusted and no longer function to hold the doors open. The installation of a Sky Catch will eliminate this problem. For further information, contact:

Sky Craft Quality Aviation Products
8933 Pawnee Rd.
Homerville, OH 44235
Phone: (216) 948-2778

Drain Valve

In production 150/152 airplanes there is no method of properly draining water from the lowest point of the fuel system, the very place where water will gather. The installation of a belly drain at this lowest point will facilitate proper contamination removal. The drain unit costs only a few dollars and can be installed in about 10 minutes. For further information, contact:

C-MODs
P.O. Box 506
Morrisville, NC 27560
Phone: (919) 544-5137

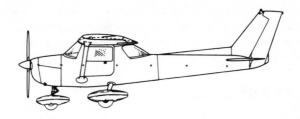

Chapter 10

Modern Avionics

The Cessna 150/152 airplanes can trace their heritage back to 1946. The same basic method of construction is still used, but inside, on the instrument panel, is where there is no similarity.

New airplanes have instrument panels that resemble those of spaceships more than the displays needed for simple flying. However, what appears complex is really straightforward in operation and is designed to make flying and navigation easier.

SPACE-AGE EQUIPMENT

The avionics of today are full of capabilities: digital displays, computerized functions, small size. They are about as similar to past equipment as a hand calculator is to a pad and pencil. Pricewise, the new equipment represents bargins as never before seen.

Fifteen years ago a good NAV/COMM cost about $1800. This gave you 200 NAV channels and 360 COMM channels. The radio was panel-mounted, and the VOR display, CDI, was mounted separately. Considering that as a rule of thumb most consumer purchases—rent, houses, automobiles, etc.—today cost three times what they did 15 years ago, that NAV/COMM would cost $5400 today.

Electronics have changed in the past years. Today the radio for $1800 (and, in many cases, a good deal less) will be a NAV/COMM that has the same 200 NAV channels, a necessary increase to 720 COMM channels, digital display, user-programmable memory channels, and a built-in CDI—all this in a smaller combined package than the radio alone of 15 years ago.

Don't let the price fool you. I've been watching the market moving towards the under-$1000 complete NAV/COMM. Modern avionics really are bargins.

AVIONICS DEFINITIONS

Everything about aviation is identified in abbreviations or buzz words, it seems. Avionics is no different:

COMM: A VHF transceiver for voice radio communications with FAA facilities, FBOs (UNICOM), and other airplanes.

NAV: A VHF navigation receiver for making use of VORs.

NAV/COMM: A combination of a NAV receiver and a COMM radio into one unit.

CDI: Course Deviation Indicator, a panel-mounted, or built into the radio, unit giving a visual output of the NAV radio.

LOC/GS: Localizer/Glideslope, a visual output, via CDI, of the glidepath.

XPNDR: Transponder (may or may not have altitude encoding).

ADF: Automatic Direction Finder.

DME: Distance Measuring Equipment.

RNAV: Random Area Navigation, a microprocessor-based system that allows considerable flexibility in course planning and flying by making use of the VOR system.

LORAN C: The latest in navigational technology. It is a system of very accurate radio/computer-based navigation completely separate from the VOR-based systems.

A-Panel: Audio panel; allows centralized control of all radio equipment.

ELT: Emergency Locator Transmitter (required by FARs for all but local flying).

MBR: Marker Beacon Receiver.

HT: Handheld Transceiver.

YOUR NEEDS

Most older Cessna two-seaters are poorly equipped in the realm trainers had only minimal equipment in the first place. The new of avionics, partly due to age, and partly due to the fact that many

owner is faced with making decisions about installing new avionics.

Between the current FAA requirements and aviation industry standards, minimums of avionics equipment have been set. As to what minimums will apply, examine your current and planned flying practices.

VFR Flying

In order to equip a plane for VFR flying, you must determine where the flying will be done. Are you planning to fly only from large airports, or only from small, uncontrolled fields? The equipment you install can limit you, particularly with the TCA and ARSA requirements.

At the barest minimum, VFR operation requires a NAV/COMM, transponder, and ELT. You could do with only the ELT, but there is just no sense to it if you plan to go anywhere except around the patch.

Although it wasn't too many years ago that most cross-country flying was done by pilotage (reading charts and looking out the windows for checkpoints) today's avaiator has become accustomed to the advantages of modern navigation systems.

To properly take advantage of the modern navigation system and the safety it can provide, I recommend that a VFR installation include a NAV/COMM (720 channel), transponder, ELT, and LORAN C. With this installation you can be comfortable and go pretty much wherever you want.

IFR Flying

Flying IFR requires considerably more equipment—naturally, at a much higher cash investment. For operational IFR, the following minimum of equipment is necessary:

- ☐ Dual NAV/COMM (720 channel)
- ☐ MBR
- ☐ LOC/GS
- ☐ Altitude reporting XPNDR
- ☐ ELT
- ☐ Clock

To make IFR flying livable, a few items of additional equipment need to be added:

☐ RNAV
☐ ADF
☐ LORAN C
☐ Audio Panel
☐ DME

UPDATING YOUR AIRPLANE

There are several methods of filling those vacant spots on the instrument panel. Some are more expensive than others. Some are more practical than others. The two do not necessarily equate.

New Equipment

New equipment, as stated earlier, is state-of-the-art, offering the newest innovations, best reliability, and—best of all—a warranty. An additional benefit of new equipment is the fact that the new solid-state electronics units are physically smaller and draw considerably less electric power than their tube-type predecessors. This is extremely important for the person wanting a "full panel" in a small plane.

New avionics can be purchased from your local avionics dealer, or from a discount house (mail order or by 800 telephone).

You can visit your local dealer, purchase all the equipment you want, and have it installed. Of course, this will be the most expensive route you can take when upgrading your avionics. However, in the long run, it can be the most practical. You'll have new equipment, expert installation, and sevice backup. You will also have a nearby dealer you can "discuss" problems with, should they arise.

Discount house prices will be considerably cheaper for the initial purchase; however, you may be left out in the cold if there is ever a need for warranty service. Some manufacturers will not honor warranty service requests unless the equipment was purchased from and installed by an authorized dealer. Check first before purchasing.

Perhaps this sounds unfair to you; however, it will keep the authorized dealers in business. If they stay in business, you can find them to repair your equipment.

Used Equipment

Used avionics can be purchased from dealers or individuals.

Trade-A-Plane is a good source of used equipment. However, a few words of caution about used avionics:

- ☐ Don't purchase anything with tubes in it.
- ☐ If it's over six years old, pass it up.
- ☐ If the manufacturer has gone the way, don't buy it; parts could be a real problem.
- ☐ If the radio is "working when removed" or "as is," let it stay where is!

Used equipment can be a wise investment, but it can also be very risky. Unless you happen to be an avionics technician, or have access to one, I recommend against the purchase of used avionics. The sole exception to this would be if you are very familiar with the source. Even then I would not recommend the purchase of used equipment for primary IFR service.

Reconditioned Equipment

Several companies advertise reconditioned avionics at bargain —or at least low—prices.

This equiment has been removed from service and completely checked out by an avionics shop. Parts that have failed, are near failure, or are likely to fail have been replaced.

However, you are still getting what you pay for. Reconditioned is not new, not even remanufactured! It is used. Everything in the unit has been used, but not everything will be replaced during reconditioning. You will have some new parts and some old parts.

Reconditioned equipment purchases make sense for the budget-minded owner. Reconditioned radios do offer a fair-priced buy and are usually warranteed by the seller. Few pieces of reconditioned equipment will exceed six or seven years of age.

LORAN

Long range navigation, called LORAN, is based upon low-frequency radio signals, rather than the vhf (very high frequency) signals normally associated with FAA nav-aids.

LORAN is operated by the United States Coast Guard, not the FAA, and was not really intended for general aviation usage. However, with the advent of computer-based LORAN C, LORAN has become the hottest new equipment on the avionics market.

The first general aviation LORAN units on the market were

reworked marine versions. In recent months new versions have entered the avionics market, which are designed solely for aviation. Most are not certified for IFR work; however, this does not mean they are incapable or inaccurate. This only means the manufacturer was unwilling to spend the many dollars necessary for certification. It is also an indicator of price. Certified models are available. The uncertified versions are generally available for under $2000, while the certified units will run better than $8000.

Without going into extensive theory about operation, the LORAN C unit can, by receiving several LORAN signals at one time and comparing them with preprogrammed known factors, determine its exact location with accuracy of a few feet! This will be displayed on the readout as latitude and longitude. Then, by use of "waypoints," the pilot can navigate. The waypoints are geographical locations entered into the LORAN unit by the pilot via the keyboard.

The waypoints can be geographical coordinates or standard three-letter designators (i.e., DCA—Washington National; SJT—San Angelo, TX). The unit will then compare the known signals to the geographical inputs and give constant trip progress information concerning course direction, time elapsed, estimated time enroute, distance traveled, distance to destination, etc.—all this in one box!

LORAN C offers distinct advantges over normal vhf navaids such as VORs. Due to the propagation properties of radio waves at the frequencies utilized by LORAN, there is no line-of-sight range limit. This means that, unlike VORs (usable only within a short range of less than 50 to 100 miles), LORAN is usable many hundreds of miles from the actual transmitting station. This can be very practical for typical lightplane operation.

A lot of lightplane flying is conducted at low (under 2000 ft.) altitude, and in remote areas. This can be a limiting factor when navigating by use of standard VORs. The use of low altitude means that the VOR may be of little or no use, as the VOR's vhf signals are line-of-sight. This is where LORAN shines. LORAN C is usable right down to the ground.

There are drawbacks as well. LORAN does not, at this time, cover the entire country. It does cover the coastal areas very well, but in some interior areas, mid-continent, coverage is spotty.

There are many makes of LORAN C units on the market. They vary primarily in the number and type of features found on the individual unit. Prices vary accordingly.

AVIONICS SUMMARY

My strongest recommendation for purchasing avionics is to save your money until you can buy new equipment. The new equipment offers more features each model year, the size goes down, the electrical appetite is reduced, and the reliability factor goes up. Additionally, due to inflation, current avionics are more of a bargain than were those of 15 years ago.

Don't trade in equipment that is currently working properly. You cannot replace it for what a dealer will give you. Keep it as your second system.

Recommended reading: *Upgrading Your Airplane's Avionics,* TAB #2301 by Timothy R.V. Foster, and *Flying With LORAN C,* TAB #2370, by Bill Givens.

CREATURE COMFORTS

After sitting for many hours in a 150 on a long trip, my ears hurt. Even after landing, my ears will buzz and hurt for several hours. This is a normal effect of flying a small airplane, and it is possible to damage your hearing with constant assaults of loud noise. The airplane cabin is just the right place for such injurious assaults to take place.

The FAA recently issued Advisory Circular AC 91-35, partially reprinted here for your information:

AC: 91-35
Subject: Noise, Hearing Damage, and Fatigue in General Aviation Pilots

1. Purpose. This circular will aquaint pilots with the hazards of regular exposure to cockpit noise. Especially pertinent are piston-engine, fixed-wing, and rotory-wing aircraft.

2. Background.

a. Modern general aviation aircraft provide comfort, convenience, and excellent performance. At the same time that the manufacturers have developed more powerful engines, they have given the occupants better noise protection and control, so that today's aircraft are more powerful, yet quieter than ever. Still, the levels of sound associated with powered flight are high enough for general aviation pilots to be concerned about participating in continuous operations without some sort of personal hearing protection.

b. Most long-time pilots have a mild loss of hearing. Many pilots report unusual amounts of fatigue after flights in particularly noisy aircraft. Many pilots have temporary losses of hearing sensitivity after flights; and many pilots have difficulty understanding transmissions from the ground, especially during critical periods under full power, such as takeoff.

3. Discussion

Like carbon monoxide, noise exposure has harmful effects that are cumulative—they add together to produce a greater effect on the listener both as sound intensity is increased, and as the length of time he listens is increased. A noise that could cause a mild hearing loss to a man who heard it once a week for a few minutes might make him quite deaf if he worked in it for eight hours.

As with everything, there is a "fix." In the case of airplanes, the pilot and his passenger can use a headphone intercom system.

Intercom systems come in all types and with varied capabilities. Some are an extension of the audio panel, primarily for the use of the pilot in his duties; others stand alone. "Stand alone" means they are not hooked to anything in the airplane, but rather are completely portable.

No matter what type you select, ear protection will be provided by the headphones, and actual voice communications carried on via the intercom.

The quality of the headphones used will control the amount of ear protection afforded. For proper ear protection you must use full ear cover headsets, not the lightweight stereo types so popular with the high school set. There are several manufacturers of adequate headsets, and you will see their ads in the magazines and *Trade-A-Plane*.

Don't make a selection based solely on an advertisement. Talk to other pilots, then go to an aviation supply store and try a few. Pay particular attention to the weight, as the weight will become a fatigue factor over long periods of flying. Also watch out for headphones that seem to grip too tightly; your head will feel like it is in a vise after only a few minutes in these. After you find the system you like, purchase it and *use it*.

Using headphones is also great for supplying the necessary background music for the aerial adventures of zooming through the mountains and valleys of the mighty clouds that create the geography of the skies.

A few pilots supply their passengers headsets without microphones. I don't advocate this. Flying is a fun thing, and no one should be shut out, but it is an interesting point.

OTHER MODERN DEVICES

In the present world of high technology we have become hung up on digital readouts. They are seen every day on the clock at the bank, wristwatches, TVs, etc. Airplanes are no different, and several small instruments are available with digital readouts.

Among the more commn are the digital outside air temperature gauge, the digital volt meter, and the digital chronometer.

PANEL ART

To some pilots the instrument panel is a functional device; to others it is a statement made by the owner. In either case, care must be taken when filling up the panel. Don't install instrumentation merely for the sake of filling holes. Plan it well, and make it functional and easy to use. Above all else, do it economically.

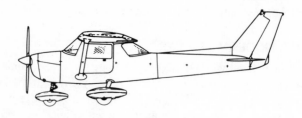

Chapter 11

Learn to Fly in

Your Own Airplane

Some years ago, Cessna Aircraft embarked on a campaign to encourage student pilots to purchase a new airplane and learn to fly in it. Although the prices of a new airplane have gone straight through the roof, this is not to say that a carefully selected used 150 might not be a wise first-time airplane investment for the student pilot.

The object of ownership we shall examine in this chapter will be limited to those individuals who wish to proceed with flying as a career and need to amass lots of practice time for a commercial license. This, I feel, is the only time there is financial justification for student ownership of an airplane. Notice I said "financial justification"—that equates to saving money.

OWNERSHIP

Ownership of an airplane is a source of great pride, to say nothing of the convenience of going at any time and returning at any time, with no restrictions (save for those of the pilot's license and the weather). The owner will never be tied to some FBO's schedule.

Now let's look at the real costs of ownership, those that are not included in the price of purchase! I shall assume that cash will be paid for the airplane, as discussion of aircraft financing would be too broad for consideration at this level. As we look at costs we will again discover new words and phrases to be reckoned with:

Fixed costs: The cost of ownership, before any flying is done. Included in fixed costs are hangar or tie-down fees, state or local property tax on the aircraft, insurance premiums, and the cost of the annual inspection (sometimes a vague/grey area).

Operating cost: The cost of fuel per hour (gas and oil), an engine reserve account (for the day when TBO arrives), and a general maintenance fund (to repair those usually small items that need a mechanic's or technician's attention), oil changes, periodic AD inspections, minor mechanical defects, avionics problems, etc.

Use cost: The total fixed and operating costs, divided by the number hours of operation. It is the use cost that is the all-important number that will show if ownership is practical.

Here is a worksheet to help you figure out all the costs involved with ownership. I use the term "all" very loosely, as nothing is fixed with airplane ownership, except that it will cost you money!

Fill in the blanks, and follow the instructions for computations.

Fixed Cost

12 months of storage	——
Annual state/local tax	——
Annual state license	——
Insurance premium (12 mos)	——
Annual inspection (est)	350.00
Total fixed cost	——

Operating Cost

Fuel @ gal × GPH =	——
Engine reserve per hour	——
General maintenance per hour	——
Total operating cost per hour	——

These computations will give solo cost only. Check your local FBO's for instruction in owner-flown airplanes. The rates may be higher than in the FBO's own airplanes. Be sure to consider this when figuring your projected hourly costs.

Examples

Let's examine a hypothetical case of ownership. A check with the local FBO for charges allows us to fill in the blanks for computation.

Fixed Cost

12 months of storage	$ 300.00
Annual state/local tax	60.00
Annual state license	9.00
Insurance premium (12 mos)	660.00
Annual inspection (est)	350.00
Total fixed cost	1379.00

Operating Cost

Fuel at $ 1.90/gal × 5 GPH =	$ 9.50
Engine reserve per hour	2.50
General maintenance per hour	3.00
Total operating cost	15.00 per hour

The above example is based upon $25 per month for outside tiedown, which is very modest. A one percent local tax is applied to the $6000 value of our hypothetical airplane, and a state license costs $9 per annum. The insurance cost is an estimate based on the value of the airplane and the pilot's lack of experience. The annual inspection is a grey area, as who is to know what expenses lurk within our airplane waiting to be discovered at inspection time? I do feel that for a typical 150 that has had good care, the estimate given will be adequate. The five GPH is an estimate of 150 fuel usage. An engine reserve of $2.50 per hour should be adequate to properly maintain an engine and assure its overhaul at TBO. The general maintenance rate of $3.00 per flying hour will allow a reserve to build up for unforseen mechanical difficulties (brakes, nosewheel, shimmy, flap actuator jack problems, radio failure, etc.) to be repaired. At the end of our computations, we have a fixed cost of $1379 per year, and an operating cost of $15 per hour.

Now let's take this further into our projected costs based upon the amount of planned flying. Use the following formula to determine the projected hourly costs of aircraft operation:

Annual hours to be flown from × $15 = _____
+
Annual fixed costs _____
Total _____
Total/Number of hours flown = _____ per hour

Let's apply our hypothetical costs to this formula. The first example will be for one flying hour per year.

1 hour to be flown × $15 = $ 15
+
Annual fixed costs 1379
Total 1395
Total/Number of hours flown = $ 1395 per hour

This is a worst case of flying only one hour for the year. It will serve to show that the more hours flown, the cheaper the hourly costs will be.

Now let's do the same problem for 50 hours of flying, which is often all an airplane sees:

50 hours to be flown × $15 = $ 750
+
Annual fixed costs 1379
Total 2129
Total/Number of hours flown = $ 42.58 per hour

And again for 100 hours:

100 hours to be flown × $15 = $ 1500
+
Annual fixed costs 1379
Total 2879
Total/Number of hours flown = $ 28.79 per hour

And a last time for 200 hours of operation:

200 hours to be flown × $15 = $ 3000
+
Annual fixed costs   1379
Total   4379
Total/Number of hours flown = $ 21.90 per hour

More Examples

This was a very economical example, so now let's do the same group of computations for what is more likely to be the cost in a metropolitan area.

Fixed Cost

12 months of storage	$ 1500.00
Annual state/local tax	288.00
Annual state license	25.00
Insurance premium (12 mos)	660.00
Annual inspection (est)	700.00
Total fixed cost	$ 3173.00

Operating Cost

Fuel at $ 2.20/gal × 5 GPH =	$ 11.00
Engine reserve per hour	2.50
General maintenance per hour	3.00
Total operating cost	16.50 per hour

The above example is based upon $125 per month for a T-hangar (very reasonable). A 4.8 percent local property tax is applied to the $6000 value of our hypothetical airplane, and a state license costs $25 per annum. The insurance cost is an estimate based on the value of the airplane and the pilot's lack of experience. The annual inspection is still a grey area, so I have upped the cost to include fixing some poorly maintained items from a previous owner. The cost of fuel per gallon is what I was quoted when I called the FBO at Dulles International Airport, and the 5 GPH is still an estimate of 150 fuel usage. The engine reserve and maintenance per flight hour remain the same. At the end of our computations, we have a fixed cost of $3173 per year, and an operating cost of $16.50 per hour.

Now let's apply this to the formulas again and see how we compare to the rather rosy picture I painted for our first example.

50 hours to be flown × $16.50 = $ 825
+
Annual fixed costs   3173
Total   3998
Total/Number of hours flown = $ 79.96 per hour

And again for 100 hours:

100 hours to be flown × $16.50 = $ 1650
+
Annual fixed costs   3173
Total   4823
Total/Number of hours flown = $ 48.23 per hour

And a last time for 200 hours of operation:

200 hours to be flown × $16.50 = $ 3300
+
Annual fixed costs   3173
Total   6473
Total/Number of hours flown = $ 32.37 per hour

Now go forth and compare these figures with straight rental of an airplane at your local FBO. Keep in mind that you can sometimes purchase blocks of time from an FBO for a reduced rate, often reduced by as much as 10 percent. Just out of interest, my local FBO charges $40.00 per hour for a 152.

AGAINST OWNERSHIP

At the first part of this chapter I mentioned the pride of ownership, and the convenience of being free of the FBO's control. This is all very true, but there is a price to be extracted for ownership.

All maintenance will be your responsibility; you won't have a squawk book to write pilot/renter complaints into and have the FBO repair same before you fly again. You will have to either fix them yourself or pay to have them fixed out of your own pocket.

Do you like the clean airplane the FBO rents you? If you own it, *you* will have to keep it clean. Know how big the airplane is? Just the top surfaces of the wings are better than 150 square feet, and that's a lot when you are washing and polishing—just think of the *total* surface to be cleaned and polished. I have not mentioned the windshields, upholstery, carpets, oil-stained belly, etc., etc.

If the real incentive for ownership is to log hours cheaply, you may find ownership a financial advantage—providing you purchase a good airplane that can be later sold at a similar price to that of purchase.

Should you desire an airplane to learn in, then later keep for your own use, you will not view the various maintenance and cleaning as loading yourself down with work. That will all be found under pride of ownership.

ADVICE

Seek out a Cessna Flight Training Center and get their advice. Cessna has made a science of pilot training. They have good answers to just about any question you could possibly ask.

Additionally, Cessna offers a flight training program that includes all the materials, ground schooling, and flight time as will be necessary for an individual to get a license—all this at a guaranteed price.

A LITTLE STORY

This talk about Cessna pilot training brings to mind a story related to me by a friend at the Cessna factory.

It seems that Cessna Aircraft ran an ad publicizing their guaranteed-price pilot training program that read: "Cessna will make you a pilot for $2990. Guaranteed." A short time after this ad was first run, Cessna received a letter from a small group of women from the Midwest. The letter read:

"Dear Cessna, In response to your ad in the latest Popular Mechanics Magazine, we would like to order a pilot. The following particulars should be built into your design: Male— quick learner, height six feet two inches to six feet five inches, weight 190 pounds, chest 46 inches, waist 34 inches, shoe size 11—optional: hairy chest, muscular build, dark blue eyes, and wavy brown hair.

"We see by your ad that this pilot is guaranteed, but we would prefer to take him on approval. We have several other people also interested in your pilot program. Could we get a discount on case lots?"

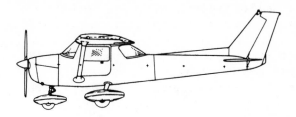

Chapter 12

Hangar Flying the Little Wonders

Go to any airport, sit around, talk and listen. This is hangar flying. There's more hangar flying done than any other type of flying. Although you sometimes have to filter out the rumors, tall tales, and the like, you can learn a lot from hangar flying, just by listening.

In these last pages of this book I have included some hangar flying to help you gain a complete understanding of the 150/152 airplanes.

Included are bits and pieces about type clubs, comments from owners, pilots, mechanics, lineboys, and even charts that compare the relative safety of the 150 to other light planes.

CLUBS

The single most useful productive action an owner/pilot can do is join a type club that supports his type (model) of airplane. For the 150/152, there is the Cessna 150/152 Club.

The Cessna 150/152 Club is the single organization that supports only these airplanes. This unique club offers a monthly newsletter, the *Cessna 150-152 News,* which includes:

☐ Maintenance and modification ideas.
☐ Exchange of technical information.
☐ Manufacturers' Service Letters.
☐ Service Difficulty Reports.

☐ Airworthiness Directives.
☐ Airworthiness Alerts.
☐ Mail box.
☐ Want ads.

Additionally, there is an annual fly-in, and help as close as a telephone—so much, for so little, at one source. Join and support the Cessna 150/152 Club. For more information, contact:

Cessna 150-152 Club
P.O. Box 15388
Durham, NC 27704
Phone: (919) 471-9492

WHAT THEY SAY

The following is a synopsis of what "they" say about the Cessna 150/152s. The term "they" means everyone from insurance carriers to line boys. There's lots of these planes around, so lots of things are said. Additionally, a large percentage of today's pilots learned to fly in them.

Insurance Carriers Say:

"Cessna 150/152 airplanes are good business for us. Whether the plane is used for instructional or purely recreational flying, we feel confident in insuring them."

"The 150 is a rugged plane, very easy to fly, yet has quirks that require the pilot to be proficient in his skills."

"Mechanically, the little Cessnas are easy to put back together if they are broken. Parts are never the problem they can be on some other makes and models."

Cost-wise, insurance is expensive, no matter how you put it, but coverage cost for a 150 is low, even for a low-time pilot.

Lineboys Say:

"Cessna 150s don't create much excitement 'round here, but they're cheap to fly. Can't say that about many other planes."

"Used to be the only 150s coming here had a grinning student pilot inside with a logbook needing a signature. Recently, though, I've begun to see some that are privately owned, not just students passing through. Some of 'em are fixed up real fancy."

"High wings are harder to fuel then low wings."

"Wish all Cessna had steps on the struts. They make refueling much easier, and eliminate the need for a stepladder."

"All the old Cessna drivers were sure happy to see 'red' (80/87 octane) fuel again."

" 'Mini-heavy iron,' I call them. That's the highly modified 150s I've been seeing lately. Saw one the other day with a 180-hp engine and a constant-speed prop. He left the ground in about a hundred feet. It had big 'tundra' wheels, even on the nose."

"Some of the 150 drivers are refueling out of their cars. Guess it saves money for the owners, and they claim the auto gas runs better in their planes."

"We sell mogas here, and the older 150s seem to run well on it; besides, it's cheaper than 100LL."

"150s mean students on cross-country flights."

Mechanics say:

"There's not much that can go wrong with a Cessna high-wing that creates any mystery. They were built tough."

"The new 150s with the key start can be a problem with the starter drive. Cessna should have left it simple with the pull handle; at least you could still start if the handle broke."

"The new Lycoming engine doesn't get on much better with 100LL fuel than the older Continentals. Guess that's the price of progress."

"These planes are simple enough for the typical owner to care for with little supervision."

"Any plane that can take the abuse a trainer gets and come back for more—that's thousands of hours or more—is okay by me."

"Have the quick drain installed in the belly. It'll keep the water and debris out of the carb."

"I wish all pilots—not just 150 and 152 drivers—would learn to properly lean. This simple procedure would add hundreds of hours to each engine, save lots of little pesky maintenance, and save fuel."

"Probably the biggest complaint I hear is nosewheel shimmy. It's easy to fix—in fact, sometimes for free. Just keep the nose light when taking off and landing. You don't have to be doing 70 mph before you take it into the air."

The following is based on an article that appeared in the *Cessna 150-152 News* (courtesy of the AVCO Lycoming Flyer) about sticking valves:

"An aircraft had been purchased recently and the owner flew it to altitude in the vicinity of his home airport to satisfy himself of the aircraft's capability to fly over mountainous terrain during a planned vacation trip. Content that the aircraft and engine were capable of meeting his requirements, the vacation trip was undertaken. All went smoothly on the first 300-mile leg of the trip, which ended with a planned overnight stop.

"When the engine was started the next day, it was very, very rough, but smoothed out and ran normally after a short time. With the engine running smoothly, the vacation trip continued to its destination. The aircraft was then tied down and not operated until it was time for the return trip . . . a period of about a week.

"As the engine was started for the return trip, it again gave indications that a valve was momentarily sticking . . . it ran very rough for several seconds, but then smoothed out. With the engine running smoothly again, the return trip was started. After one to two hours of flight at altitude, over mountainous terrain, the engine ran very rough again for a short period of time, and then smoothed out. The pilot decided to land at the nearest airport.

"Examination of the engine revealed a considerable amount of oil leakage. The cause . . . a valve which had stuck solidly and caused the pushrod to bend. This bending ruptured the pushrod shroud tube and allowed oil to escape. This is a classic example of the damage which sticking valves can cause.

"The lesson to be learned is quite simple: Do not neglect the warning signs. Perhaps the experience related here will allow others to recognize a rough-running engine at startup as a possible indication of sticking valves. The next step is to take immediate action to prevent damage.

"Although there may be occasional exceptions, it is almost always an exhaust valve which sticks. To prevent further valve sticking and to reduce the possibility of damage, all exhaust valve guides should be cleaned of any carbon, varnish, or other contamination buildup. This is accomplished by reaming the guides to their original size as specified by the manufacturer."

NTSB Says:

The following tables of comparative accident data is a compilation of a study made by the NTSB (National Transportation Safety Board). All figures are based upon the adjusted rate of 100,000 hrs of flying time.

It's interesting to note where the various makes/models are placed on these charts. Placement is shown by worst at the top, best at the bottom.

If you are unsure of what some of the mentioned makes/models are, I suggest you consult *The Illustrated Buyer's Guide to Used Airplanes* (TAB book No. 2372).

Fatal Accident Rate Comparison by Manufacturer

Make	Mean Fatal Accident Rate
Bellanca	4.84
Grumman	4.13
Beech	2.54
Mooney	2.50
Piper	2.48
Cessna	1.65*

Engine Failure

Aircraft	Rate
Globe GC-1	12.36
Stinson 108	10.65
Ercoupe	9.50
Grumman AA-1	8.71
Navion	7.84
Piper J-3	7.61
Luscombe 8	7.58
Cessna 120/140	6.73
Piper PA-12	6.54
Bellanca 14-19	5.98
Piper PA-22	5.67
Cessna 195	4.69
Piper PA-32	4.39
Cessna 210/205	4.25
Aeronca 7	4.23
Aeronca 11	4.10
Taylorcraft BC	3.81
Piper PA-24	3.61
Beech 23	3.58
Cessna 175	3.48
Mooney M-20	3.42
Piper PA-18	3.37

Aircraft	Rate
Cessna 177	3.33
Cessna 206	3.30
Cessna 180	3.24
Cessna 170	2.88
Cessna 185	2.73
Cessna 150	2.48*
Piper PA-28	2.37
Beech 33, 35, 36	2.22
Grumman AA-5	2.20
Cessna 182	2.08
Cessna 172	1.41

In-Flight Airframe Failure

Aircraft	Rate
Bellanca 14-19	1.49
Globe GC-1	1.03
Ercoupe	0.97
Cessna 195	0.94
Navion	0.90
Aeronca 11	0.59
Beech 33, 35, 36	0.58
Luscombe 8	0.54
Piper PA-24	0.42
Cessna 170	0.36
Cessna 210/205	0.34
Cessna 180	0.31
Piper PA-22	0.30
Aeronca 7	0.27
Beech 23	0.27
Cessna 120/140	0.27
Piper PA-32	0.24
Taylorcraft BC	0.24
Piper J-3	0.23
Mooney M-20	0.18
Piper PA-28	0.16
Cessna 177	0.16
Cessna 182	0.12
Cessna 206	0.11
Grumman AA-1	0.09
Cessna 172	0.03
Cessna 150	0.02*

Stall

Aircraft	Rate
Aeronca 7	22.47
Aeronca 11	8.21
Taylorcraft BC	6.44
Piper J-3	5.88
Luscombe 8	5.78
Piper PA-18	5.49
Globe GC-1	5.15
Cessna 170	4.38
Grumman AA-1	4.23
Piper PA-12	3.27
Cessna 120/140	2.51
Stinson 108	2.09
Navion	1.81
Piper PA-22	1.78
Cessna 177	1.77
Grumman AA-5	1.76
Cessna 185	1.47
Cessna 150	1.42*
Beech 23	1.41
Ercoupe	1.29
Cessna 180	1.08
Piper PA-24	0.98
Beech 33, 35, 36	0.94
Cessna 175	0.83
Piper PA-28	0.80
Mooney M-20	0.80
Cessna 172	0.77
Cessna 210/205	0.71
Bellanca 14-19	0.60
Piper PA-32	0.57
Cessna 206	0.54
Cessna 195	0.47
Cessna 182	0.36

Hard Landing

Aircraft	Rate
Beech 23	3.50
Grumman AA-1	3.02
Ercoupe	2.90
Cessna 177	2.60

Aircraft	Rate
Globe GC-1	2.58
Luscombe 8	2.35
Cessna 182	2.17
Cessna 170	1.89
Beech 33, 35, 36	1.45
Cessna 150	1.37*
Cessna 120/140	1.35
Cessna 206	1.30
Piper PA-24	1.29
Aeronca 7	1.20
Piper J-3	1.04
Grumman AA-5	1.03
Cessna 175	1.00
Cessna 180	0.93
Cessna 210/205	0.82
Piper PA-28	0.81
Cessna 172	0.71
Piper PA-22	0.69
Taylorcraft BC	0.48
Cessna 195	0.47
Piper PA-18	0.43
Piper PA-32	0.42
Cessna 185	0.42
Navion	0.36
Mooney M-20	0.31
Piper PA-12	0.23
Stinson 108	0.19

Ground Loop

Aircraft	Rate
Cessna 195	22.06
Stinson 108	13.50
Luscombe 8	13.00
Cessna 170	9.91
Cessna 120/140	8.99
Aeronca 11	7.86
Aeronca 7	7.48
Cessna 180	6.49
Cessna 185	4.72
Piper PA-12	4.67
Piper PA-18	3.90
Taylorcraft BC	3.58

Aircraft	Rate
Globe GC-1	3.09
Grumman AA-1	2.85
Piper PA-22	2.76
Ercoupe	2.74
Beech 23	2.33
Bellanca 14-19	2.10
Piper J-3	2.07
Cessna 206	1.73
Cessna 177	1.61
Grumman AA-5	1.47
Piper PA-32	1.42
Cessna 150	1.37*
Piper PA-28	1.36
Piper PA-24	1.29
Cessna 210/205	1.08
Cessna 182	1.06
Cessna 172	1.00
Mooney M-20	0.65
Beech 33,35,36	0.55
Navion	0.36
Cessna 175	0.17

Undershoot

Aircraft	Rate
Ercoupe	2.41
Luscombe 8	1.62
Piper PA-12	1.40
Globe GC-1	1.03
Cessna 175	0.99
Grumman AA-1	0.95
Taylorcraft BC	0.95
Piper PA-22	0.83
Piper PA-32	0.70
Bellanca 14-19	0.60
Aeronca 11	0.59
Piper PA-28	0.59
Aeronca 7	0.59
Piper PA-24	0.57
Piper J-3	0.57
Stinson 108	0.57
Cessna 120/140	0.53
Cessna 195	0.47

Aircraft	Rate
Grumman AA-5	0.44
Piper PA-18	0.43
Beech 23	0.43
Cessna 185	0.41
Mooney M-20	0.37
Cessna 170	0.36
Navion	0.36
Cessna 150	0.35*
Cessna 210/205	0.33
Cessna 206	0.32
Cessna 172	0.26
Cessna 182	0.24
Beech 33,35,36	0.21
Cessna 180	0.15
Cessna 177	0.10

Overshoot

Aircraft	Rate
Grumman AA-5	2.35
Cessna 195	2.34
Beech 23	1.95
Piper PA-24	1.61
Piper PA-22	1.33
Cessna 175	1.33
Stinson 108	1.33
Cessna 182	1.21
Aeronca 11	1.17
Luscombe 8	1.08
Piper PA-32	1.03
Globe GC-1	1.03
Mooney M-20	1.01
Cessna 172	1.00
Cessna 170	0.99
Grumman AA-1	0.95
Piper PA-12	0.93
Cessna 210/205	0.89
Cessna 177	0.88
Piper PA-18	0.81
Cessna 206	0.81
Piper PA-28	0.80
Cessna 120/140	0.71
Ercoupe	0.64

Aircraft	Rate
Bellanca 14-19	0.60
Cessna 180	0.56
Navion	0.54
Aeronca 7	0.48
Cessna 150	0.35*
Piper J-3	0.34
Cessna 185	0.31
Beech 33,35,36	0.23

Owners Say:

"My old 150 was real good on maintenance; it didn't need much. Wish I had it back!"

"My last annual cost $275, and that's in the high-cost Washington, D.C. area. I'm real happy with that."

"The 12-volt batteries for the 150s are a lot cheaper than the 24-volt jobs needed for the 152."

"The 152 uses more gas than the 150 I used to have, and I still have a lead fouling problem. I can't say that I am overjoyed with the 152, not for what it cost me compared to how I benefitted."

"The 150 is today's Model 'A' of the airplane world."

"The only real problem I've had is nosewheel shimmy. Just keep the nosewheel light on rollout."

"I wish the wingtips were made of something more durable than the junk plastic Cessna uses. Nothing seems to patch them except replacement."

"The guy who put the key start in the 150s had a brother-in-law who manufactures starter parts, and I'm supporting him!"

"Either is a cheap plane to fly, about the cheapest around, unless you have an old Cub. But that'll cost you more to buy than a 150, and a lot more to maintain. You wash and polish aluminum; you replace fabric!"

"I like the straight-tail 150s, with pull starters and manual flaps. They don't cost as much to maintain."

"The mogas STCs are good; now we can do legally what we've been doing for many years. We never had a fuel tank here for airplanes, just for the tractor and mowing machine. I've often wondered if the fellow that delivered the gas ever wondered about all the gallons of fuel we used in the tractor.

Pilots Say:

"The 150's not the greatest on takeoff in the summer, but it gets there, even with two big guys aboard."

"The nosewheel shimmies."

"I jazzed mine up with a new interior and a set of sheepskin seat covers."

"I have the large wheels and heavy nose gear on mine, and will land anywhere that a taildragger will. I've been doing it for years, and have never bent anything. Just keep the weight off the nosewheel."

"The noise level is too high, so I bought sound-reducing (headache-reducing) headphones."

"I just had a 150-hp engine installed—wow! The next step is a Horton STOL conversion."

"I have the auto fuel STC. Now when I need gas I taxi across the road to the corner gas station and fill it up. Of course, I never did this before (wink)!"

"They can really give you a rough ride on a bumpy day."

"I used to take out the right seat and load up with watermelons, 300 or 400 pounds of them, then fly off from between the rows of melon plants. It's not hard to do if you're young and stupid!"

"The cabin is a little narrow for two big people."

"If you're doing a lot of dirt strip work, get a set of improved wingtips like Deemers. They will allow you to touch down a little slower. Also, get protective material installed on the leading edge of the prop to protect it from little stones."

"Most of the time I fly by myself, so this is a very economical (cheap) plane to fly and maintain. Not fast, but it gets there."

"The visibility in a busy traffic pattern is poor, but that's the same for all high-wingers."

"Love the big flaps. They can really save a poor approach."

"I have a '64 model with manual flaps, and plan to keep it. I don't like the electric flaps; there's too much that can break on them."

"I like the manual flaps, I have instant positive control of them, unlike the slow electric jobs."

"I was going to build a homebuilt, but having a 150 is cheaper. Besides, if I ever want to sell it, I can. Try that with your homebuilt!"

"I want to put a STOL kit and larger engine on mine, then I can tackle the off-airport places here on the farm."

"The 150 keeps you sharp in windy conditions. It's light, and blows around."

"You have to pay attention to your speed on approaches, or you'll learn about stalls very quickly."

"If you make your approach too fast, you'll pass right over the best part of the runway, still in the air!"

"The 150 is a two-finger airplane. You can fly it with the lightest of touches. Perhaps 'spritely' would be more appropriate a phrase. It's not at all like the heavy-feeling Piper PA-28s. I feel there is a real connection between the pilot and the airplane. You order, and the plane responds! There is no pushing around the 150. Guess I just can't say enough good about how it handles."

The last comment made is about as close to defining the true handling characteristics of a 150 as I have ever heard. I have to agree, the 150 is a two-finger airplane. However, this lightness can be a detriment in windy conditions.

Sales People Say:

"I like to sell 150s to novices, as they can finish their learning in the plane, get their hours, and then get their investment back."

"I've sold several to older couples who no longer have a need for a larger, more expensive plane."

"Sometimes you will find a real bargain, if you are willing to overlook some minor appearance problems."

"A 150 makes a good investment; if you take care of it, it will take care of you. You'll get most every penny back out of it that you put in . . . maybe even a profit!"

"Recently, I sold a 150 with a STOL kit on it to a couple who retired to the back of nowheres. they sold their $65,000 plush flier, and went for the rough-and-ready."

Appendix A

Advertising Abbreviations

AD	Airworthiness Directive
ADF	Automatic Direction Finder
AF	airframe
AF&E	airframe and engine
AI	aircraft inspector
ALT	altimeter
ANN	annual inspection
ANNUAL	annual inspection
AP	autopilot
ASI	airspeed indicator
A&E	airframe and engine
A/P	auto pilot
BAT	battery
B&W	black and white
CAT	carburetor air temperature
CHT	cylinder head temperature
COMM	communications radio
CS	constant speed propeller
C/S	constant speed propeller
C/W	complied with

DBL	double
DG	directional gyro
DME	Distance Measuring Equipment
FAC	factory
FBO	fixed base operator
FGP	full gyro panel
FWF	firewall forward
GAL	gallons
GPH	gallons per hour
GS	glideslope
HD	heavy-duty
HP	horsepower
HSI	horizontal situation indicator
HVY	heavy
IFR	Instrument Flight Rules
ILS	Instrument Landing System
INS	Instrument Navigation System
INSP	inspection
INST	instrument
KTS	knots
L	left
LDG	landing
LE	left engine
LED	light emiting diode
LH	left hand
LIC	license
LOC	localizer
LTS	lights
L&R	left and right
MB	marker beacon
MBR	marker beacon
MP	manifold pressure
MPH	miles per hour
MOD	modification

NAV	navigation
NAV/COM	navigation/communication radio
NDH	no damage history
OAT	outside air temperature
OX	oxygen
02	oxygen
PMA	parts manufacture approval
PROP	propeller
PSI	pounds per square inch
R	right
RC	rate of climb
REMAN	remanufactured
REPALT	reporting altimeter
RH	right hand
RMFD	remanufactured
RMFG	remanufactured
RNAV	Random Area Navigation
ROC	rate of climb
SAFOH	since airframe overhaul
SCMOH	since (chrome/complete) major overhaul
SEL	single engine land
SFACNEW	since factory new
SFN	since factory new
SFNE	since factory new engine
SFREM	since factory remanufacture
SFREMAN	since factory remanufacture
SFRMFG	since factory remanufacture
SMOH	since major overhaul
SNEW	since new
SPOH	since propeller overhaul
STC	supplemental type certificate
STOH	since top overhaul
STOL	short takeoff and landing
TAS	true airspeed
TBO	time between overhaul
TLX	telex
TNSP	transponder

TNSPNDR	transponder
TSN	time since new
TSO	Technical Service Order
TT	total time
TTAF	total time airframe
TTA&E	total time airframe and engine
TTE	total time engine
TTSN	total time since new
TXP	transponder
T&B	turn and bank
VAC	vacuum
VFR	Visual Flight Rules
VHF	Very High Frequency
VOR	Visual Omni Range
XC	cross-country
XMTR	transmitter
XPDR	transponder
XPNDR	transponder
3LMB	three light marker beacon

Appendix B

Telephone Area Codes

201	NJ north
202	Washington, DC
203	CT
205	AL
206	WA west
207	ME
208	ID
209	CA Fresno
212	NY City
213	CA Los Angeles
214	TX Dallas
215	PA east
216	OH northeast
217	IL central
218	MN north
219	IN north
301	MD
302	DE
303	CO
304	WV
305	FL southeast
307	WY
308	NE west

309	IL Peoria area
312	IL northeast
313	MI east
314	MO east
315	NY north central
316	KS south
317	IN central
318	LA west
319	IA east
401	RI
402	NE east
404	GA north
405	OK west
406	MT
408	CA San Jose area
409	TX southeast
412	PA southwest
413	MA west
414	WI east
415	CA San Francisco
417	MO southwest
419	OH northwest
501	AR
502	KY west
503	OR
504	LA east
505	NM
507	MN south
509	WA east
512	TX south central
513	OH southwest
515	IA central
516	NY Long Island
517	MI central
518	NY northeast
601	MS
602	AZ
603	NH
605	SD
606	KY east
607	NY south central

608	WI southwest
609	NJ south
612	MN central
614	OH southeast
615	TN east
616	MI west
617	MA east
618	IL south
619	CA southeast
701	ND
702	NV
703	VA north & west
704	NC west
707	CA Santa Rosa area
712	IA west
713	TX Houston
714	CA southwest
715	WI north
716	NY west
717	PA central
718	NY southeast & NYC
801	UT
802	VT
803	SC
804	VA southeast
805	CA west central
806	TX northwest
808	HA
812	IN south
813	FL southwest
814	PA northwest & central
815	IL north central
816	MO northwest
817	TX north central
818	CA southwest
901	TN west
904	FL north
906	MI northwest
907	AK
912	GA south
913	KS north

914	NY southeast
915	TX southwest
916	CA northwest
918	OK northeast
919	NC east

Appendix C

Inspections

These are the general inspection requirements, as taken from the Cessna 150 Service Manual:

To avoid repetition throughout the inspection, general points to be checked are given below. In the inspection, only the items to be checked are listed; details as to how to check, or what to check for, are excluded. The inspection covers several different models. Some items may apply only to specific models, and some items are optional equipment that may or may not be found on a particular airplane. Check the FAA Airworthiness Directives and Cessna Service Letters for compliance at the time specified by them. Federal Aviation Regulations require that all civil aircraft have a periodic (annual) inspection as prescribed by the Administrator, and performed by a person designated by the Administrator. The Cessna Aircraft Company recommends a 100-hour periodic inspection for the airplane.

Check as Applicable:

Movable Parts for: Lubrication, servicing, security of attachment, binding, excessive wear, safetying, proper operation, proper adjustment, correct travel, cracked fittings, security of hinges, defective bearings, cleanliness, corrosion, deformation, sealing, and tensions.

Fluid Lines and Hoses for: Leaks, cracks, dents, kinks, chafing, proper radius, security, corrosion, deterioration, obstructions, and foreign matter.

Metal Parts for : Security of attachment, cracks, metal distortion, broken spotwelds, corrosion, condition of paint, and any other apparent damage.

Wiring for: Security, chafing, burning, defective insulation, loose or broken terminals, heat deterioration, and corroded terminals.

Bolts in Critical Areas for: Correct torque in accordance with proper torque values, when installed or when visual inspection indicates the need for a torque check.

Filters, Screens, and Fluids for: Cleanliness, contamination and/or replacement at specified intervals.

AIRPLANE FILE:

Miscellaneous data, information, and licenses are a part of the airplane file. Check that the following documents are up-to-date and in accordance with current Federal Aviation Regulations. Most of the items listed are required by the United States Federal Aviation Regulations. Since the regulations of other nations may require other documents and data, owners of exported aircraft should check with their own aviation officials to determine their individual requirements.

To be displayed in the airplane at all times:

    ☐ Aircraft Airworthiness Certificate
    ☐ Aircraft Registration Certificate
    ☐ Aircraft Radio License

To be carried in the airplane at all times:

    ☐ Weight and Balance and associated papers
    ☐ Aircraft Equipment List

To be made available upon request:

    ☐ Aircraft Logbook and Engine Logbook

ENGINE RUN-UP

Before beginning the step-by-step inspection, start, runup, and shut down the engine in accordance with instructions in the Owner's Manual. During the run-up, observe the following, making note of any discrepancies or abnormalities:

- ☐ Engine temperatures or pressures.
- ☐ Static rpm.
- ☐ Magneto drop.
- ☐ Engine response to changes in power.
- ☐ Any unusual engine noises.
- ☐ Fuel selector valve; operate the engine on each position long enough to make sure the valve functions properly.
- ☐ Idling speed and mixture; proper idle cutoff.
- ☐ Alternator.
- ☐ Suction gauge.

After the inspection has been completed, an engine run-up should again be performed to ascertain that any discrepancies or abnormalities have been corrected.

PERIODIC INSPECTIONS

Continental Engine: If the engine is equipped with an external oil filter, change the engine oil and filter element at 50-hour intervals. If the engine is *not* equipped with an external oil filter, change the engine oil and clean the oil screen *every 25 hours.*

Lycoming Engine: If the engine is *not* equipped with an external oil filter, change the engine oil and clean the oil screens at 50-hour intervals. If the engine is equipped with an external oil filter, the engine oil change intervals may be extended to 100 hour intervals, providing the external filter element is changed at 50-hour intervals.

The 50-hour inspection includes a visual check of the engine, propeller, and aircraft exterior for any apparent damage or defects; an engine oil change as required above; and accomplishment of lubrication and servicing requirements. Remove the propeller spinner and engine cowling, and replace after the inspection has been completed.

The 100-hour (or annual) inspection includes everything in the 50-hour inspection, and oil change as required above. Also loosen or remove the fuselage, wing, empennage, and upholstery inspection doors, plates, and fairings only as necessary to perform a thorough, searching inspection of the aircraft. Replace after the inspection has been completed.

Note: In the charts below, numbers appearing in the time column indicate the time between inspections/servicing.

Propeller   *Time*

1. Spinner and spinner bulkhead................ 50
2. Blades..................................... 50
3. Hub....................................... 50
4. Bolts and/or nuts......................... 50

Engine Compartment

Check for evidence of oil and fuel leaks, then clean the entire engine and compartment, if needed, prior to inspection.

                                                                Time

1. Engine oil, screen, filler cap, dipstick, drain plug, and filter.................................... 50
2. Oil Cooler................................. 50
3. Induction air filter........................ 50
4. Induction airbox, air valves, doors, and controls.. 50
5. Cold and hot air hoses..................... 50
6. Engine baffles............................ 50
7. Cylinders, rocker box covers, and push rod housings.................................. 50
8. Crankcase, oil sump, accessory section, and front crankshaft seal.......................... 50
9. All lines and hoses........................ 50
10. Intake and exhaust systems................. 50
11. Ignition harness.......................... 50
12. Spark plugs and compression............... 100
13. Crankcase and vacuum system breather lines.... 50
14. Electrical wiring.......................... 50
15. Vacuum pump, oil separator, and relief valve.... 50
16. Vacuum relief valve filter................... 100
17. Engine controls and linkage................. 50
18. Engine shock mounts, engine mount structure, and ground straps........................ 50
19. Cabin heater valves, doors, and controls........ 50
20. Starter, solenoid, and electrical connections...... 50
21. Starter brushes, brush leads, and commutator.... 200
22. Alternator and electrical connections........... 50
23. Alternator brushes, brush leads, and commutator or slip ring................................ 500
24. Voltage regulator mounting and electrical leads... 50
25. Magnetos (externally) and electrical connections.. 50

26. Slick magneto timing........................ 100
27. Carburetor................................. 50
28. Firewall 100
29. Engine cowling............................ 50
30. Carburetor drain plug for security............. 50

Fuel System

Time

1. Fuel strainer, drain valve, and control.......... 50
2. Fuel strainer screen and bowl................. 100
3. Fuel tanks, fuel lines, drains, filler caps, and
   placards................................. 100
4. Drain fuel and check tank interior, attachment,
   and outlet screens......................... 1000
5. Fuel vents and vent valves................... 100
6. Fuel selector valve and placards.............. 100
7. Engine primer............................. 100

Landing Gear

Time

1. Brake fluid, lines and hoses, linings, disc, brake
   assemblies, and master cylinders.............. 100
2. Main gear wheels, wheel bearings, step and
   spring strut, tires, and fairings................ 100
3. Main and nose gear wheel bearing lubrication... 500
4. Torque link lubrication...................... 50
5. Nose gear strut servicing.................... 100
6. Nose gear shimmy damper service............ 100
7. Nose gear wheels, wheel bearings, strut, steering
   system, shimmy damper, tire, fairing, and torque
   links.................................... 100
8. Parking brake system...................... 100

Airframe

Time

1. Aircraft exterior........................... 50
2. Aircraft structure.......................... 100
3. Windows, windshield, and doors.............. 50
4. Seats, stops, seat rails, upholstery, structure, and
   seat mounting............................ 50
5. Safety belts and attaching brackets............ 50
6. Control U bearings, sprockets, pulleys, cables,

254

chains, and turnbuckles. 100
7. Control lock, control wheel, and control U
   mechanism 100
8. Instruments and markings. 100
9. Gyros, central air filter. 100
10. Magnetic compass compensation. 1000
11. Instrument wiring and plumbing. 100
12. Instrument panel, shock mounts, ground straps,
    cover, and decals and labeling. 100
13. Defrosting, heating, and ventilating systems, and
    controls 100
14. Cabin upholstery, trim, sun visors, and ashtrays. . 100
15. Area beneath floor, lines, hoses, wires, and control
    cables 100
16. Lights, switches, circuit breakers, fuses, and spare
    fuses 50
17. Exterior lights. 50
18. Pitot and static system. 100
19. Stall warning sensing unit, pitot warning heater. . . 100
20. Radio and radio controls. 100
21. Radio antennas. 100
22. Battery, battery box, and battery cables. 100
23. Battery electrolyte level. 50

Control Systems

In addition to the items listed below, always check for correct
direction of movement, correct travel, and correct cable tension.

Time

1. Cables, terminals, pulleys, pulley brackets, cable
   guards, turnbuckles, and fairleads. 100
2. Chains, terminals, sprockets, and chain guards. . . 100
3. Trim control wheel, indicators, and actuator. 100
4. Travel stops. 100
5. All decals and labeling. 100
6. Flap control switch (or lever), flap rollers and
   tracks, flap transmitter and linkage, and flap position indicator flap electric motor and transmission. 100
7. Elevator trim. 100
8. Rudder pedal assemblies and linkage. 100
9. Skin and structure of control surface and trim tabs 100
10. Balance weight attachment. 100

Appendix D

Cessna 150/152
Current Price Guide

The following is a guide to prices for used Cessna 150/152 airplanes. The prices are based upon average* asking/selling prices for 1987.

Year	Model	Asking
1959	150	$5000
1960	150	5000
1961	150	5400
1962	150	5800
1963	150	6000
1964	150	6200
1965	150	6300
1966	150	6500
1967	150	6600
1968	150	6700
1969	150	6800
1970	150	6900
1971	150	7000
1972	150	7200
1973	150	7400
1974	150	7600
1975	150	7800
1976	150	8300
1977	150	8700
1978	152	9500

Year	Model	Asking
1979	152	10100
1980	152	12000
1981	152	16000
1982	152	20000
1983	152	26500
1984	152	n/a

Add $250 for the Aerobat A150 Model.
Add $1000 for the Aerobat A152 Model.
*Average equipment (avionics-wise) and with middle time on the engine. Middle time on the engine is defined as the middle one-third of the TBO (i.e., on an 1800-hour engine, this would be 600 to 1200 hours SMOH).

Index

Edited by Steven H. Mesner

Other Bestsellers From TAB

☐ **GOOD TAKEOFFS AND GOOD LANDINGS—Joe Christy**

This book is a reference that thoroughly examines takeoffs and landings, and the critical transitions accompanying each, for single-engine aircraft. The author stresses that every pilot must continuously evaluate ever-changing factors of wind, air pressure, precipitation, traffic, temperature, visibility, runway length, and braking conditions. *Good Takeoffs and Good Landings* belongs on every pilot's required reading list. 192 pp., 70 illus.

Paper $14.95 $21.95
Book No. 2487

☐ **ABCs OF SAFE FLYING—2nd Edition—David Frazier**

Attitude, basics, and communication are the ABCs David Frazier talks about in this revised and updated second edition of a book that answers all the obvious questions, and reminds you of others that you might forget to ask. This new edition includes additional advanced flight maneuvers, and a clear explanation of the Federal Airspace System. 192 pp., 69 illus.

Paper $12.95   Hard $19.95
Book No. 2430

☐ **MOUNTAIN FLYING—Doug Geeting and Steve Woerner**

Every licensed, active pilot can expect to encounter mountains at some point in their flying career. Minimize the risks of mountain flying with proper training and practice, and this book. Providing an excellent resource on the subject, the authors examine mountain flying from the aspects of the pilot, the airplane, weather and topography, mechanical performance capabilities, and techniques. Covered in detail are sources of weather, pressure systems, temperature, clouds, icing, turbulence, air circulation, and effects of peaks, ridges, passes. 208 pages, Illustrated.

Paper $16.95   Hard $24.95
Book No. 2426

☐ **DOWN THE RUNWAY: THE MAKING OF A PILOT—by Samuel Hawkins**

"I could not put it down . . . [Hawkins] knows what he's writing about and tells it straight and well. It flows. It reads . . . enjoyable . . ."
—**Arthur H. Sanfelici**
Editor, *AOPA Newsletter*

This book is about aviation people, but anyone who appreciates talented storytelling will enjoy it. The story of a Texas farm boy learning to fly in a homebuilt airplane during the '30s is interspersed with humorous and tragic tales of later flying experiences and of fascinating people encountered during the 50 years of his pilot career. Don't miss it! 156 pages.

Paper $10.95   Book No. 2425

Other Bestsellers From TAB